Toolkit Texts
Selected by Anne Goudvis and Stephanie Harvey

Short Nonfiction for American History
The American Revolution and Constitution

1770   1775   1780   1785   1790

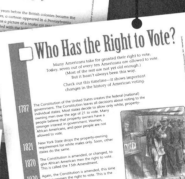

Heinemann
DEDICATED TO TEACHERS™

DEDICATED TO TEACHERS™

Heinemann
361 Hanover Street
Portsmouth, NH 03801–3912
www.heinemann.com

Offices and agents throughout the world

© 2015 by Anne Goudvis and Stephanie Harvey

All rights reserved. No part of this book may be reproduced in any form or by any electronic or mechanical means, including information storage and retrieval systems, without permission in writing from the publisher, except by a reviewer, who may quote brief passages in a review; and with the exception of reproducibles (identified by the *Toolkit Texts: Short Nonfiction for American History: American Revolution and Constitution* copyright line), which may be photocopied for classroom use.

> *The authors have dedicated a great deal of time and effort to writing the content of this book, and their written expression is protected by copyright law. We respectfully ask that you do not adapt, reuse, or copy anything on third-party (whether for-profit or not-for-profit) lesson-sharing websites. As always, we're happy to answer any questions you may have.*
> **—Heinemann Publishers**

"Dedicated to Teachers" is a trademark of Greenwood Publishing Group, Inc.

All Carus Publishing Company material is copyright by Carus Publishing Company, a division of ePals Media and/or various authors and illustrators. Any commercial use or distribution of material without permission is strictly prohibited. Please visit www.cobblestonepub.com/guides_permission.html for permissions and www.cobblestonepub.com/index.html for subscriptions.

Title page image (George Washington Crossing the Delaware River): © HIP/Comstock/Getty Images.

Post-it® Brand is a registered trademark of the 3M Company.

Library of Congress Cataloging-in-Publication Data
Goudvis, Anne.
  Toolkit texts: short nonfiction for American history: the American Revolution and Constitution/ selected by Anne Goudvis and Stephanie Harvey.
    pages cm—(Comprehension toolkit series)
   ISBN 0-325-04882-7—ISBN 978-0-325-04882-6 1. United States—History—Revolution, 1775–1783—Study and teaching (Middle school) 2. United States. Constitution—Study and teaching (Middle school) 3. Constitutional history—United States—Study and teaching (Middle school) I. Harvey, Stephanie. II. Title. III. Title: American Revolution and Constitution.
   E208.H377 2014
     973.3071—dc23   2014042668

Editor: Heather Anderson
Production editor: Stephanie J. Levy
Typesetter: Eclipse Publishing Services
Cover Design: Suzanne Heiser
Manufacturing: Steve Bernier

Printed in the United States of America on acid-free paper
21 20 19 18 17   EBM   2 3 4 5

Acknowledgments

The *Comprehension Toolkit* series is all about collaboration. None of this would be possible without the commitment, diligence, and hard work of our Heinemann team. Most of all, we are extremely grateful to our fabulous editor, Heather Anderson. Stephanie Levy, Tina Miller, Anita Gildea, Charles McQuillen, David Stirling, and Steven Bernier put forth the energy, creative thinking, and hard work that has brought this resource to life. A special thanks to Mark Corsey and Ruth Linstromberg for their talented design work for this series. We thank the entire Heinemann team for their enthusiasm and ongoing support of our work.

—Steph and Anne

Contents

Introduction xiii
Bibliography xxiv
Works Cited xxvi

Lessons for Close Reading in History

1 Read and Annotate:
   Stop, think, and react using a variety of strategies to understand L-1

2 Annotate Images:
   Expand understanding and learning from visuals L-3

3 Build Background to Understand a Primary Source:
   Read and paraphrase secondary sources to create a context for a topic . . . L-6

4 Read and Analyze a Primary Source:
   Focus on what you know and ask questions to clarify and explain L-9

5 Compare Perspectives:
   Explore the different life experiences of historical figures L-12

6 Read Critically:
   Consider point of view and bias L-15

7 Organize Historical Thinking:
   Create a question web L-18

8 Read with a Question in Mind:
   Focus on central ideas L-21

9 Surface Common Themes:
   Infer the big ideas across several texts L-24

10 Synthesize Information to Argue a Point:
   Use claim, evidence, and reasoning L-27

   Unrecognized Revolutionaries L-31

Articles

Overview: The American Revolution and the Constitution 1
By the 1700s, America was making the transition from a colony of Great Britain to a country in its own right. The colonists started to fight back against King George III and the British laws and taxes imposed on them. Events would spark the Revolutionary War, and after a long and difficult road, the United States of America would be created.

LEADING UP TO THE REVOLUTION

The Revolution's Frontier Front 5
The American Revolution wasn't just fought in the villages and cities of the east coast colonies. The fight for independence also extended to the west, and the raw frontier.

War in the West 6
The struggle over who would control the rich lands of the west created conflict between the British, French, Americans, and Native Americans.

Contest for an Empire: 1754 to 1763 10
The French and Indian wars were a battle between France and Britain over American territory. It was a conflict over who would control lucrative hunting and fishing territories, and ultimately a huge new empire.

Breaking Up Is Hard to Do 12
The first Americans were British citizens, but soon the struggle between governing and being governed would create tension between America and England. It soon became clear that a break with England was looming.

The Wigmaker's Boy and the Boston Massacre 16
A wigmaker's apprentice and his friends—and an unpaid bill—helped spark the Boston Massacre. Read about this from the apprentice's perspective and learn about Crispus Attucks, the first person shot in the incident.

■ PRIMARY SOURCE: JOHN TUDOR'S DIARY, 1770
John Tudor, a patriot in Boston, describes in his own words what he witnessed at the Boston Massacre. 19

■ PRIMARY SOURCE: CAPTAIN THOMAS PRESTON'S LETTER TO A FRIEND, 1770
In this letter, British officer Captain Thomas Preston tells a friend about the Boston Massacre from the British point of view. 20

■ HISTORICAL IMAGES: BOSTON MASSACRE 21–22

Tea Troubles: The Boston Tea Party 23
The British required the colonists to pay a special tax on tea. In protest, a group of patriots decide to dump some of that British tea into Boston Harbor, resulting in the world's biggest "tea party."

Just Say No! The Daughters of Liberty 26
Women could not vote or join the army during the revolution, but they found other ways to support the cause of independence from Britain.

Interview with Author Louise Borden:
Sleds on Boston Common 29
Meet historical fiction author, Louise Borden, and learn about her extensive historical research and poetic writing style.

FIGHTING THE REVOLUTION

Major Events of the American Revolution............................ 33
Conflict between the British and the American patriots would soon become war, and both sides would have to learn how to fight each other as events quickly unfolded.

Intelligence, Counterintelligence, and Gunpowder 34
How did stores of gunpowder, a network of colonial spies, and surprise attacks help spark the war?

Watchful Eyes in Boston... 37
The city of Boston was a dangerous place as both patriots and British prepared for war. And both sides used the eyes and ears of spies to learn about each other.

The Famous Ride of Paul Revere 38
While Revere's famous ride is one of the best-known legends of the American Revolution, what really happened on that April night? Learn about Revere, as well as Dawes and Prescott, two riders who played an important role, too.

- PRIMARY SOURCE: PAUL REVERE'S LETTER TO DR. JEREMY BELKNAP, 1798
  Read about Revere's famous ride in his own words. 42

Militias and Minutemen 43
The American patriots were not just untrained farmers who confronted the British. Many were members of militias or elite Minutemen, who were well-prepared to fight.

- PRIMARY SOURCE: THOMAS THORP'S JOURNAL, 1775
  Thomas Thorp was one of the Minutemen on the Lexington Green, and he wrote an account of the battle in his journal. 46

- HISTORICAL IMAGE: LEMUEL HAYNES 47

- HISTORICAL IMAGE: DEBORAH CHAMPION'S CLOAK 48

- PRIMARY SOURCE: DEBORAH CHAMPION'S LETTER TO A FRIEND, 1775
  Deborah Champion made a dramatic ride to Boston in 1775 with hidden messages for General Washington. 49

- PRIMARY SOURCE: PATRICK HENRY'S SPEECH TO THE VIRGINIA ASSEMBLY, 1775
  In this famous speech, Patrick Henry spoke the famous words "Give me liberty or give me death!" which would become a rallying cry for the American Revolution. 50

- PRIMARY SOURCE: EXCERPT FROM THE DECLARATION OF INDEPENDENCE
  Read the famous opening words of a document that changed American history. 51

Following the Army 53
A reenactor tells what life was like for a woman who became a camp follower during the Revolution.

Playing the Bad Guy 55
In the world of Revolutionary War reenactments, "living historians" portray soldiers on both sides of the conflict. Some choose to portray patriots fighting for America's freedom, while others choose to play members of the British regiment.

Daniel Granger, Boy Soldier 59
Daniel Granger was only 13 when he joined in the Revolution, first as a soldier and then as a drummer.

- HISTORICAL IMAGE: BATTLE OF BUNKER'S HILL 62

- HISTORICAL IMAGE: AFRICAN AMERICAN SOLDIERS 63

- HISTORICAL IMAGE: SALEM POOR 64

- PRIMARY SOURCE: COLONEL JOHN FITZGERALD'S DIARY, 1776
  In his diary, Colonel John Fitzgerald describes what it was like to cross the frozen Delaware River with George Washington. 65

- HISTORICAL IMAGE: WASHINGTON CROSSING THE DELAWARE 67

Loyalists in the American Revolution. 68
Not all Americans supported independence from Britain. Loyalists believed in the right of Britain to rule the colonies.

- PRIMARY SOURCE: STOCKBRIDGE INDIAN SPEECH
  In 1775, a member of the Stockbridge tribe of Native Americans gave a speech to the Massachusetts Congress, seeking protection and offering support. 72

- HISTORICAL IMAGES: NATIVE AMERICAN WARRIORS 74–75

Secret Help from Spain. 76
During the American Revolution, Spain secretly sent money to help support the patriots' cause . . . and protest its own interests.

The French Alliance. 79
In 1777, the French Marquis de Lafayette met George Washington. He and his country would provide valuable help to America in its fight against Great Britain.

World Turned Upside Down 83
After six years of war, the American forces were ragged, starving, and unpaid. How could they possibly defeat the British forces?

Partisans Spring into Action 86
A band of partisan fighters in North and South Carolina helped keep the British army unbalanced through a series of daring raids and attacks.

Washington Makes His Move 90
British general Cornwallis and his troops were firmly settled in Yorktown, Virginia. But there were signs that General Washington was ready to make his move and perhaps bring the war to an end.

Dictionary of American Portraits, Dover, 1987

James Armistead: Master Spy 93
Born a slave, James Armistead was one of the Revolution's more successful spies, and a double agent who passed valuable British information to the French and Americans.

Your Life as a Farmer 99
What happened to farmers when they returned home to Western Massachusetts after fighting in the Revolutionary War?

- PRIMARY SOURCE: YANKEE DOODLE
  What is the classic American song "Yankee Doodle" really about?. 102

- HISTORICAL IMAGE: THE FLUTIST 103

- HISTORICAL IMAGE: FRAUNCES TAVERN. 104

A Difficult Decade. 105
Americans had just won a war of independence from Britain. But the decade that followed the Revolution was anything but easy.

viii   Contents

WHOSE REVOLUTION?

Eliza Lucas Pinkney: A New Crop for a New Country 109
America needed new crops to feed itself and for international trade. And Eliza Lucas Pinckney was just the woman to develop them.

- PRIMARY SOURCE: A LETTER BY ELIZA LUCAS, 1740
  At only 16, Eliza's letter describes how she manages three plantations and experiments on a new crop. 111

The Wild Colt: Abigail Adams 112
As a girl, she preferred books and farming to being ladylike, and she would grow up to be America's second First Lady, and one who never stopped speaking her mind.

- HISTORICAL IMAGE: ABIGAIL ADAMS 115

- PRIMARY SOURCE: ABIGAIL ADAMS' LETTER TO JOHN ADAMS, JUNE 18, 1775
  Abigail describes the events of the Battle of Bunker Hill to her husband. 116

- PRIMARY SOURCE: ABIGAIL ADAMS' LETTER TO JOHN ADAMS, MARCH 31, 1776
  Abigail pleads with her husband, when making laws for the new country, to "remember the Ladies!" 118

Elizabeth Burgin: "Indefatigable" 119
Not much is known about Elizabeth Burgin, but she helped save the lives of more than 200 American prisoners of war.

George Washington and Slavery 122
He was the father of our country, but it took George Washington a lifetime to free all the slaves that he owned.

George Washington: Did You Know? 125
Learn little known facts about George Washington, the leader of the Continental Army during the American Revolution and the first president of the United States.

Oney Judge: Washington's Runaway Slave 127
She was a slave in Washington's household, but with the help of free black friends, she escaped from the President's house and lived the rest of her life as a fugitive.

Olaudah Equiano: Sailing from Slavery to Freedom 129
Olaudah Equiano was sold into slavery at the age of eleven and sailed around the world. He would become one of America's best-known abolitionists.

- PRIMARY SOURCE: OLAUDAH EQUIANO'S ACCOUNT
  Olaudah Equiano writes of his kidnapping in Africa at the age of eleven. 130

- HISTORICAL IMAGES: OLAUDAH EQUIANO 131–132

Petitioning for Freedom 133
Even before the Revolution, enslaved African Americans were petitioning for their freedom, just as the patriots were petitioning Britain for their independence.

New York City's African Burial Ground 137
A park in New York City marks the site of the last resting place of over four hundred African Americans from the colonial era.

A Closer Look at the Big Five 139
Between 1500 and 1700, the Cherokees, Creeks, Choctaws, Chickasaws, and Seminoles were the "big five" of the southeast Native American tribes.

> ▰ PRIMARY SOURCE: DELAWARE TRIBE SPEECH
> The Delaware and twelve other tribes created a plan of the U.S. government to use in creating boundaries between their land and white settlements. 143

DESIGNING THE CONSTITUTION

Library of Congress

Road to a Constitution 145
This timeline shows the steps along the way to America's Constitution.

Three Men, Three Plans 146
The fifty-five delegates responsible for creating a new constitution did not all agree on how the new central government should be structured. They would have to consider three men and three different plans.

A Product of Argument and Compromise 150
The men who wrote the United States Constitution had different goals, and sometimes they disagreed. It took argument and compromise to create a plan for a new kind of government.

A Quiet Room 155
In May of 1776, in a quiet room in Philadelphia, Thomas Jefferson penned the words that would become The Declaration of Independence.

A Bitter Debate 159
One of the biggest battles surrounding the writing of The Declaration of Independence was a controversial section about slavery.

"A Republic, If You Can Keep It" 161
When Benjamin Franklin was asked what form the new American government should take, he replied, "A republic—if you can keep it."

The Five Freedoms 165
The opening words of the Bill of Rights are known as the Five Freedoms. What are these freedoms, and are they still important to us?

A Chat with Thomas Jefferson 168
Chat with Thomas Jefferson . . . or someone who acts just like him.

> ▰ PRIMARY SOURCE: THE BILL OF RIGHTS
> Read the text of the First Amendment and the Five Freedoms it describes. . . . 171

> ▰ HISTORICAL IMAGE: DECLARATION OF INDEPENDENCE 173

> ▰ HISTORICAL IMAGE: WRITING THE DECLARATION OF INDEPENDENCE 174

> ▰ HISTORICAL IMAGE: THOMAS JEFFERSON PORTRAIT 175

> ▰ PRIMARY SOURCE: BENJAMIN BANNEKER'S LETTER TO THOMAS JEFFERSON
> Benjamin Banneker, a free African American scientist, wrote a letter to Thomas Jefferson on behalf of racial equality. 176

Founding Father 178
Benjamin Franklin is one of the Founding Fathers of the United States, and he dreamed of uniting all the separate colonies into one country.

A LASTING LEGACY

Making Changes 183
The Founding Fathers did not want to make it easy to change the Constitution. But they did create a way to amend it if it became necessary.

Celebrating Citizenship! 184
Being an American citizen means being guaranteed certain rights, but it also brings with it certain responsibilities.

Land of Opportunity and Obstacles 187
Meet Sofiya, a professional actress from New York. She shares the story of her family's immigration and hopes to start a new life in the United States in a recent interview.

> PRIMARY SOURCE: EXCERPT FROM THE CIVICS (HISTORY AND GOVERNMENT) QUESTIONS FOR THE NATURALIZATION TEST
> Could you pass this test to become an American citizen? 191

Who Has the Right to Vote? 194
Follow the timeline to see important changes concerning who has the right to vote in America.

America's Boldest Experiment 196
The first sixteen words of the First Amendment are responsible for the greatest experiment in freedom of religion that the world has ever seen.

Freedom of the Press: How Far Does It Go? .. 199
One of the Five Freedoms is freedom of the press. That freedom includes expressing both popular and unpopular opinions, but it does not protect all types of speech.

Brown v. Board of Education. 201
It is one of the most famous cases ever to come before the U.S. Supreme Court, and it changed the lives of children everywhere.

Tinker v. Des Moines 203
Do students have the right to free speech and free expression when they're in school? This was a question that faced the Supreme Court in 1969.

The **DIGITAL COMPANION RESOURCE** includes:
- all of the articles in full color,
- primary source documents,
- a full-color bank of additional historical images not included in the book, and
- "Teaching for Historical Literacy," by Anne Goudvis and Stephanie Harvey (Educational Leadership, March 2012).

For instructions on how to access the Digital Companion Resource, turn to page xxi.

Introduction

Reading, writing, viewing, listening, talking, doing, and investigating are the hallmarks of active literacy. Throughout the school day and across the curriculum, kids are actively inferring, questioning, discussing, debating, inquiring, and generating new ideas. An active literacy classroom fairly bursts with enthusiastic, engaged learning.

The same goes for our history and social studies classrooms: They, too, must be thinking- and learning-intensive (President and Fellows of Harvard College 2007). To build intrigue, knowledge, and understanding in history, students read and learn about the events, mysteries, questions, controversies, issues, discoveries, and drama that are the real stuff of history.

Disciplinary Literacy

When students acquire knowledge in a discipline such as history and think about what they are learning, new insights and understandings emerge and kids generate new knowledge. Fundamental to this understanding is the idea that there's a difference between information and knowledge. Kids have to construct their own knowledge: only they can turn information into knowledge by thinking about it. But we educators must provide the environment, resources, and instruction so kids become curious, active learners.

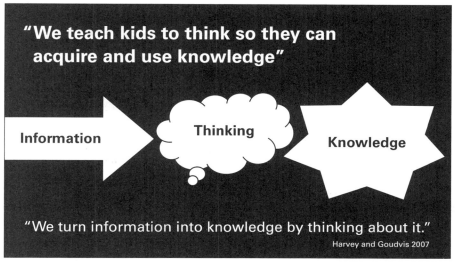

From Anne Goudvis, Stephanie Harvey, Brad Buhrow, and Anne Upczak-Garcia, 2012. *Scaffolding the Comprehension Toolkit for English Language Learners*. Portsmouth, NH: Heinemann.

But too often students experience history as a passive slog through the textbook, with a "coverage" curriculum that's a mile wide and an inch deep. Instead, students should be reading and actively responding to a wide range of historical sources; viewing and analyzing images; reading historical fiction, first-person accounts, letters, and all manner of sources; and engaging in simulations so they can understand and empathize with the experiences of people who lived "long ago and far away."

In this approach to disciplinary literacy, students use reading and thinking strategies as tools to acquire knowledge in history, science, and other subject areas. P. David Pearson and colleagues (Pearson, Moje, and Greenleaf 2010) suggest that:

> Without systematic attention to reading and writing in subjects like science and history, students will leave schools with an impoverished sense of what it means to use the tools of literacy for learning or even to reason within various disciplines (460).

Reading and thinking about historical sources and introducing students to ways of thinking in the discipline of history teaches them that there are many ways to understand the people, events, issues, and ideas of the past. But we also want students to understand the power and potential of their own thinking and learning so that they learn to think for themselves and connect history to their own lives.

CONTENT MATTERS

Cervetti, Jaynes, and Hiebert (2009) suggest that reading for understanding is the foundation for students acquiring and using knowledge. In the figure below, Cervetti et al. explain the reciprocal relationship between knowledge and comprehension—how background knowledge supports comprehension and in turn, through comprehension/reading for understanding, we "build new knowledge" (83).

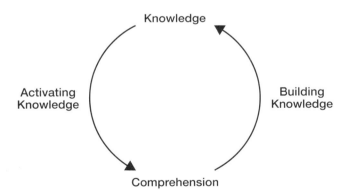

Research (Anderson and Pearson 1984) has long supported the strong relationship between background knowledge and school learning: Students' prior knowledge about content supports their new learning. From our perspective, history, more than many subjects, demands that students have a context for their learning, that they understand the essential ideas that emerge within a larger time span, and that they can discern the big picture.

But activating background knowledge is just the beginning. Researchers emphasize the knowledge-building side of this figure, which underscores the idea that when we comprehend, we add to and enhance our store of knowledge. "Knowledge, from this perspective, does not refer to a litany of facts, but rather to the discipline-based conceptual understandings … (which) engage students in becoming experts on the world around them" (Cervetti, Jaynes, and Hiebert 2009).

This is a reciprocal process that occurs as students build their knowledge in many content areas and disciplines. P. David Pearson sums it up well with his quip: "Today's new knowledge is tomorrow's background knowledge." The more students know, the more they will learn, and even more important, the more they will want to learn!

Historical Literacy

Our approach is to embed reading and thinking strategies in our social studies and history instruction, so that comprehension and thinking strategies become tools for learning and understanding content. Teaching historical literacy means we merge thoughtful, foundational literacy practices with challenging, engaging resources to immerse kids in historical ways of thinking.

What might this look like?

Students:

- read and reason through many different kinds of sources about the past, connecting to the experiences, dilemmas, discoveries, and reflections of people from other times and places
- ask their own authentic questions, just like historians do
- learn to read critically—to understand different purposes and perspectives, asking, "Who wrote this? Why did they write it? What are the authors' biases, points of view, and purposes?"
- try out ways of thinking about history—inferring, analyzing, and interpreting facts and evidence to surface themes and important ideas.

We believe these practices, above all, promote engagement with the discipline and motivate kids to want to find out more. When kids actively read, think, debate, discuss, and investigate, they have the best shot at becoming enthusiastic students of history. Not incidentally, zeroing in on content literacy in this way will go a long way in helping students meet district and state standards, including the Common Core State Standards (CCSS), which focus on 21st-century skills and learning across disciplines. The instructional practices advocated in this resource are supported by research that emphasizes a content-rich, standards-based approach:

A multisource, multigenre curriculum. We envision the active literacy classroom awash in engaging historical resources of all kinds: maps, timelines, artifacts, songs, poems, journals, letters, feature articles, biographies, and so on. Allington and Johnston (2002) found that students evidenced higher achievement when their classroom focused on a multisource, multigenre, multiperspective curriculum rather than a one-size-fits-all coverage approach. This research fits the bill.

Standards-based. The CCSS, as well as many state standards, highlight the importance of reading in the disciplines and reading for deeper meaning. Comprehension and thinking strategies are foundational for many of these standards. We don't "teach the standards," of course; we design instruction that supports students to read, reason, and respond so that they meet the appropriate standards. This resource includes ways in which comprehension and thinking strategies further the active use of knowledge and greater understanding in history and social studies.

Social studies strands. This resource provides a range of reading in the different social studies strands: history, culture, economics, government, and geography. A chart correlating the articles to the social studies strands appears on pages xix and xx.

History is the study of people, events, and achievements in the past. Learning about history helps students understand how people and societies behave. It also allows students to make connections between themselves and others who lived long ago. In addition, history helps students to understand the process of change and better prepare themselves for changes they will encounter in their lives.

Culture is the customs, traditions, habits, and values of a group of people. Learning about culture helps students to better understand and relate to others. By examining their own cultural traditions, students can understand the values of their society. By examining the cultural institutions of other groups, students can gain an appreciation of people who live differently from themselves and also see similarities they might not have otherwise realized.

Economics is the study of production, distribution, and consumption of goods and services. When students learn about economics, they learn how individuals, groups, and governments all make choices to satisfy their needs and wants. Understanding economics helps students to make better financial decisions in their own lives and also helps them to make sense of the economic world we live in.

Government is a system for making laws and keeping order in a city, state, or country. By learning about government, students are preparing themselves to be good citizens and take part in their political system. Not only does understanding government help students understand the modern-day world and its events, it also gives them the power to change that world through public actions.

Geography is the study of the Earth's surface and features and of the ways in which those features affect people around the world. Understanding geography helps students understand the physical world in which they live. It helps them see how different parts of their environment are connected and how all of those parts impact their lives and the lives of others.

Text Matters
SHORT TEXTS FOR LEARNING ABOUT THE AMERICAN REVOLUTION AND THE CONSTITUTION

Kids need engaging texts and resources they can sink their teeth into. Just as with previously published *Toolkit Text* collections of articles, these articles on the American Revolution and the Constitution offer rich, engaging content that paints a vivid "big picture" of this time period. In this resource, we have included families of articles on a common topic or theme, with the understanding that the more widely kids read on a common topic, the more they learn and understand. The CCSS and other state standards expect that children will read a variety of texts on a common topic and synthesize the ideas and information across those texts.

Included here are informational articles in a number of genres: first-person accounts, plays, historical fiction, and feature articles. Images, portraits, and paintings, and all kinds of features, such as maps, charts, and timelines, provide visual interest and additional information in the articles. Primary sources, including historical speeches, images, and documents, can be found for each topic. We have also included a short bibliography of books, magazines, documentaries, and websites for investigation. We encourage you to add as many other texts and images on a topic as you can find, to bring history to life and encourage important research skills and practices.

WHY THESE SELECTIONS?

We considered the following criteria in selecting the articles, primary sources, and images:

Interest/content Kids love to learn about the quirky, the unusual, the unexpected, and the surprises that are essential to the study of history! Here we highlight those important but often lesser-known or unrecognized perspectives and voices from the past, for example, young people, women, Native Americans, and others. These are compelling voices, and we anticipate that these articles will ignite kids' interest as they explore historical ideas and issues.

Visual literacy Visual literacy is an essential 21st-century skill, so included here are primary sources, such as historical images, paintings, and maps. Other information-filled features in the articles include diagrams, timelines, charts, and photographs, all of which encourage interpretation, analysis, and comparison across texts and images. Images also provide another entry point for students to access historical texts. You may consider projecting the color versions of the historical images or articles rich with art for students to view closely as one way to generate a conversation about students' background knowledge. We also use images to introduce a particular theme or concept and model interpretation and analysis. Historical images with explanations are located throughout the book; additional historical images can be accessed on the Digital Companion Resource or through further research online.

Writing quality and accuracy When we think back to history class, we remember writing that was dull and voiceless—too often full of the generalizations and information overload common to textbook writing. To get kids excited about history and motivated to dig deeper and learn more, we searched for articles that had vibrant language and active voice. Variety makes a difference, so we include a rich assortment of nonfiction texts and visual features, as well as a bibliography of additional well-written, authentic resources.

Our knowledge of historical times and people is ever-changing as historians learn more and unearth additional artifacts and sources. Each article has been carefully vetted for accuracy by content experts and historical researchers.

Reading level/complexity Differentiation is key. Included in the collection are articles at a variety of reading levels to provide options for student practice. For example, there are shorter, more accessible articles and longer, more in-depth ones on the same or similar topics. All articles have carefully chosen images designed to enhance the content. This allows for differentiation according to students' reading proficiency levels as well as their interest levels.

We have also carefully selected primary source documents that will give students an authentic view of and unique insights into this time period. Arcane or unusual vocabulary and unfamiliar sentence structures can present significant reading challenges. We recommend building background knowledge and historical context (see Lesson 3) before digging into these authentic documents with your students. We offer strategies for approaching the close reading of primary source documents with your students in Lesson 4.

Assigning a grade level to a particular text is arbitrary, especially with content-rich selections, particularly in nonfiction with all of its supportive features. We suggest you look carefully at all the articles and choose from them based on your kids' interests and tastes as well as their reading levels.

CORRELATION CHART TO SOCIAL STUDIES STRANDS

Read across the chart to determine which social studies strands are covered in each article.

Article	History	Culture	Economics	Geography	Government
Overview: The American Revolution and the Constitution	yes	yes	yes	yes	yes
Leading up to the Revolution					
The Revolution's Frontier Front				yes	
War in the West	yes	yes	yes	yes	
Contest for an Empire: 1754 to 1763	yes		yes	yes	
Breaking Up Is Hard to Do	yes	yes	yes		yes
The Wigmaker's Boy and the Boston Massacre	yes				
Tea Troubles: Boston Tea Party	yes		yes		yes
Just Say No! The Daughters of Liberty	yes	yes	yes		yes
Interview with Author Louise Borden: *Sleds on Boston Common*	yes	yes		yes	
Fighting the Revolution					
Major Events of the American Revolution	yes			yes	
Intelligence, Counterintelligence, and Gunpowder	yes				yes
Watchful Eyes in Boston	yes	yes			
The Famous Ride of Paul Revere	yes			yes	
Militias and Minutemen	yes	yes			yes
Following the Army		yes			
Playing the Bad Guy		yes			
Daniel Granger, Boy Soldier	yes	yes			
Loyalists in the American Revolution	yes	yes	yes		yes
Secret Help from Spain	yes		yes	yes	yes
The French Alliance	yes		yes		yes
The World Turned Upside Down	yes	yes			yes
Partisans Spring into Action	yes	yes		yes	yes
Washington Makes His Move	yes			yes	yes
James Armistead: Master Spy	yes	yes			yes
Your Life as a Farmer		yes		yes	
A Difficult Decade	yes		yes		yes
Whose Revolution?					
Eliza Lucas Pinkney: A New Crop for a New Country	yes	yes	yes		
The Wild Colt: Abigail Adams	yes	yes			yes
Elizabeth Burgin: "Indefatigable"	yes	yes			yes

chart continues on page xx

CORRELATION CHART TO SOCIAL STUDIES STRANDS (continued from on page xix)

Article	History	Culture	Economics	Geography	Government
Whose Revolution? *(continued)*					
George Washington and Slavery	yes	yes	yes		yes
Oney Judge: Washington's Runaway Slave	yes	yes			
Olaudah Equiano: Sailing from Slavery to Freedom	yes	yes		yes	
Petitioning for Freedom	yes	yes			yes
New York City's African Burial Ground	yes	yes			
A Closer Look at the Big Five	yes	yes		yes	yes
Designing the Constitution					
Road to a Constitution	yes				yes
Three Men, Three Plans	yes				yes
A Product of Argument and Compromise	yes				yes
A Quiet Room	yes	yes			yes
A Bitter Debate	yes				yes
"A Republic, If You Can Keep It"	yes	yes			yes
The Five Freedoms					yes
A Chat with Thomas Jefferson	yes				
Founding Father	yes	yes			yes
A Lasting Legacy					
Making Changes					yes
Celebrating Citizenship!		yes			yes
Land of Opportunity and Obstacles		yes			yes
Who Has the Right to Vote?	yes	yes	yes		yes
America's Boldest Experiment	yes	yes			yes
Freedom of the Press: How Far Does It Go?	yes	yes			yes
Brown v. Board of Education	yes	yes			yes
Tinker v. Des Moines	yes	yes			yes

HOW TO ACCESS THE DIGITAL COMPANION RESOURCE

The Digital Companion Resource provides all of the reproducible texts, plus primary source documents, and a bank of more than sixty additional historical images in a full-color digital format that is ideal for projecting and group analysis. We've also included the professional journal article, "Teaching for Historical Literacy."

To access the Digital Companion Resource:

1. Go to www.heinemann.com.
2. Click on "login" to open or create your account. Enter your email address and password or click "register" to set up an account.
3. Enter keycode TTSNFARC and click register.
4. You will receive a link to download *The American Revolution and Constitution* Digital Companion.

You can print and project articles and images from the Digital Companion. Please note, however, that they are for personal and classroom use only, and by downloading, you are agreeing not to share the content.

These buttons are available at the top of each article for your convenience:

will print the current article.

will jump to the next article.

will jump to the image bank when there are correlating images.

For best results, use Adobe Reader for Windows PC or Mac. Adobe Reader is also available as an app for iPad and Android tablets. However, the Print function will not work on tablets.

HOW MIGHT I USE THIS RESOURCE?

In the first column we summarize foundational comprehension strategies that foster student engagement and understanding across content areas, but particularly in content literacy. As students build their own repertoire of reading and thinking strategies, these become tools they use 24/7. The second column describes how students use these strategies to acquire knowledge and deepen their understanding of history.

Comprehension strategies for content literacy	Students use these in history when they:
Monitor understanding.	Stop, think, and react during reading.
	Learn new information and leave tracks of thinking by annotating the text.
	Respond to and discuss the text by asking questions, connecting to prior knowledge and experiences, drawing inferences, and considering the big ideas.
Activate and build background knowledge.	Connect the new to the known; use background knowledge to inform reading.
	Recognize misconceptions and be prepared to revise thinking in light of new evidence.
	Consider text and visual features.
	Pay attention to text structures and different genres.
Ask and answer questions.	Ask and answer questions to:
	Acquire information.
	Investigate and do research.
	Interpret and analyze information and ideas.
	Read with a critical eye and a skeptical stance.
	Explore lingering and essential questions.
Draw inferences and conclusions.	Infer ideas, themes, and issues based on text evidence.
	Analyze and interpret different perspectives and points of view.
Determine importance.	Sort and sift important information from interesting but less important details.
	Construct main ideas from supporting details.
	Evaluate the information and ideas in a text.
	Distinguish between what the reader thinks versus what the author wants the reader to understand.
Summarize and synthesize.	Analyze, compare, and contrast information across sources to build content knowledge and understanding.
	Evaluate claims and supporting evidence.
	Generate new knowledge and insights.

Adapted from Anne Goudvis and Stephanie Harvey, 2012. "Teaching for Historical Literacy." *Educational Leadership* March 2012: 52–57.

TEN CONTENT LITERACY LESSONS FOR CLOSE READING IN HISTORY

"The most obvious way to enhance students' world knowledge is to provide knowledge-enriching experiences in school; yet literacy programs have long missed the opportunity to use reading, writing, and speaking as tools for developing knowledge" (Cervetti et al. 2009).

This is especially true for history. We believe strongly that kids should be reading, writing, thinking, and doing in history. But far too often, conventional history instruction has focused on memorizing facts and dates without learning about the time period, the people themselves, and the challenges they faced. Students too often experience social studies and history as a passive slog through the textbook. This dumbed-down approach to history is a sure way to put students to sleep and guarantee they never come to understand the discipline, much less engage in it.

In this resource, we have designed ten lessons that merge effective, foundational content-literacy practices with thoughtful approaches to reading historical articles, viewing images, and reasoning through documents. These lessons encourage thoughtful reading and discussion that go far beyond answering the questions at the end of the chapter. By teaching these ten lessons, teachers will guide students to use reading and thinking strategies as tools to acquire and actively use knowledge in history.

Lesson	Title	Page
1	Read and Annotate: Stop, think, and react using a variety of strategies to understand	L-1
2	Annotate Images: Expand understanding and learning from visuals	L-3
3	Build Background to Understand a Primary Source: Read and paraphrase secondary sources to create a context for a topic	L-6
4	Read and Analyze a Primary Source: Focus on what you know and ask questions to clarify and explain	L-9
5	Compare Perspectives: Explore the different life experiences of historical figures	L-12
6	Read Critically: Consider point of view and bias	L-15
7	Organize Historical Thinking: Create a question web	L-18
8	Read with a Question in Mind: Focus on central ideas	L-21
9	Surface Common Themes: Infer the big ideas across several texts	L-24
10	Synthesize Information to Argue a Point: Use claim, evidence, and reasoning	L-27

Bibliography

Our passion for historic reading goes way beyond this book. Here is a list of terrific, engaging books and resources to keep history alive in your classroom.

BOOKS ABOUT THE AMERICAN REVOLUTION AND CONSTITUTION

Allen, Thomas. *George Washington, Spymaster: How the Americans Outspied the British and Won the Revolutionary War.* Washington, DC: National Geographic, 2004.

Ammon, Richard. *Valley Forge.* New York: Holiday House, 2004.

Anderson, Laurie Halse. *Chains.* New York: Atheneum, 2010.

——— *Forge.* New York: Atheneum, 2012.

——— *Independent Dames: What You Never Knew About the Women and Girls of the American Revolution.* New York: Simon and Schuster, 2008.

Borden, Louise. *Sleds on Boston Common.* New York: Simon and Schuster, 2000.

Brown, Don. *Let It Begin Here! The Day the American Revolution Began.* New York: Roaring Book Press, 2008.

Burgan, Michael. *The Split History of the American Revolution.* Mankato, MN: Compass Point, 2013.

Castrovilla, Selene. *Revolutionary Friends: General George Washington and the Marquis de Lafayette.* Honesdale, PA: Highlights, 2013.

Finkelman, Paul. *The Constitution.* Washington, DC: National Geographic, 2006.

Fleming, Candace. *Ben Franklin's Almanac: Being a True Account of the Good Gentleman's Life.* New York: Atheneum, 2003.

Fleming, Thomas. *Everybody's Revolution.* New York: Scholastic Nonfiction, 2006.

Furbee, Mary Rodd. *Outrageous Women of Colonial American.* New York: Wiley and Sons, 2001.

Griffin, Judith. *Phoebe the Spy.* New York: Penguin, 1977.

Hakim, Joy. *A History of US: From Colonies to Country.* 3rd ed. New York: Oxford University Press, 2007.

Harness, Cheryl. *The Remarkable Benjamin Franklin.* Washington, DC: National Geographic, 2005.

Hoose, Phillip M. *We Were There, Too! Young People in U.S. History.* New York: Farrar Straus Giroux, 2001.

Kalman, Maira. *Thomas Jefferson: Life, Libery and the Pursuit of Everything.* New York: Penguin, 2014.

Kirkpatrick, Katherine. *Redcoats and Petticoats.* New York: Holiday House, 1999.

Malaspina, Ann. *Phillis Sings Out Freedom: The Story of George Washington and Phillis Wheatley.* Chicago: Whitman and Co., 2010.

Murphy, Jim. *The Crossing: How George Washington Saved the American Revolution.* New York: Scholastic, 2010

Nelson, Kadir. *Heart and Soul: The Story of America and African Americans.* New York: HarperCollins, 2011.

Pinkney, Andrea D. *Dear Benjamin Banneker.* Orlando, FL: Harcourt Brace, 1994.

Schanzer, Rosalyn. *George vs. George: The American Revolution As Seen from Both Sides.* New York: National Geographic Children's Books, 2007.

Tarrant-Reid, Linda. *Discovering Black America.* New York: Abrams Books for Young Readers, 2012.

Weatherly, Myra. *Benjamin Banneker: American Scientific Pioneer.* Minneapolis, MN: Compass Point Books, 2006.

Woelfle, Gretchen. *Mumbet's Declaration of Independence.* Minneapolis, MN: Carolrhoda Books, 2014.

Yero, Judith. *The Bill of Rights.* Washington, DC: National Geographic, 2006.

DOCUMENTARIES

Liberty! The American Revolution. PBS, 2004. DVD

MAGAZINES

Cobblestone, an American history magazine for grades 5–9

Dig, an archaeology and history magazine for grades 5–9

Kids Discover, a social studies and scientific magazine for grades 3–7

Junior Scholastic, a current events and social studies magazine for grades 5–8

The New York Times Upfront, a current events and social studies magazine (both national and international news) for middle and high school students

Scholastic News, a curriculum-connected current events news weekly online for grades 1–6

US Studies Weekly, a U.S. history newspaper for students in grades K–9

WEBSITES

Library of Congress: http://www.loc.gov

National Archives: http://www.archives.gov/

National Constitution Center: http://constitutioncenter.org/

Smithsonian Museum: http://www.si.edu/

Kids Discover: http://www.kidsdiscover.com/

PBS: http://www.pbs.org/

George Washington's Mount Vernon: http://www.mountvernon.org/

Works Cited

Allington, Richard L., and Peter H. Johnston. 2002. *Reading to Learn: Lessons from Exemplary Fourth-Grade Classrooms.* New York, NY: Guilford Press.

Anderson, Richard C. and P. David Pearson. 1984. "A Schema-Theoretic View of Basic Processes in Reading Comprehension." In *Handbook of Reading Research,* Vol 1. Edited by P. David Pearson, R. Barr, M.L. Kamil, and P. Mosethal, 255–91. White Plains, NY: Longman.

Cervetti, Gina N., Carolyn A. Jaynes, and Elfrieda H. Hiebert. 2009. "Increasing Opportunities to Acquire Knowledge through Reading." In *Reading More, Reading Better.* Edited by E. H. Hiebert. New York, NY: Guilford Press.

Goudvis, Anne, Stephanie Harvey, Brad Buhrow, and Anne Upczak-Garcia. 2012. *Scaffolding the Comprehension Toolkit for English Language Learners.* Portsmouth, NH: Heinemann.

Goudvis, Anne, and Stephanie Harvey. 2012. "Teaching for Historical Literacy." *Educational Leadership* March 2012: 52–57.

Harvey, Stephanie, and Anne Goudvis. 2005. *The Comprehension Toolkit: Language and Lessons for Active Literacy.* Portsmouth, NH: Heinemann.

Harvey, Stephanie, and Anne Goudvis. 2007. *Toolkit Texts: Short Nonfiction for Guided and Independent Practice* (Grades PreK–1, 2–3, 4–5, 6–7). Portsmouth, NH: Heinemann.

Keene, Ellin Oliver, Susan Zimmermann, Debbie Miller, Samantha Bennett, Leslie Blauman, Chryse Hutchins, Stephanie Harvey, et al. 2011. *Comprehension Going Forward: Where We Are and What's Next.* Portsmouth, NH: Heinemann.

Pearson, P. D., Elizabeth Moje, and Cynthia Greenleaf. 2010. "Literacy and Science, Each in the Service of the Other." *Science* April 23 (328): 459–63.

President and Fellows of Harvard College. 2007. *Interrogating Texts: Six Reading Habits to Develop in Your First Year at Harvard.* Available at: http://hcl.harvard.edu/research/guides/lamont_handouts/interrogatingtexts.html.

Lesson 1 | Read and Annotate
Stop, think, and react using a variety of strategies to understand

POSSIBLE TEXTS
Most of the articles in this resource would work to both model this lesson and for kids to practice. Annotation is foundational practice for reading in general. Some favorites include:
- "Intelligence, Counterintelligence, and Gunpowder"
- "The Famous Ride of Paul Revere"
- "Washington Makes His Move"
- "James Armistead: Master Spy"

ANNOTATING TEXT WHILE READING can be a powerful thinking tool. The practice of responding to the text—paraphrasing, summarizing, commenting, questioning, making connections, and the like—actively engages the reader in thinking about the main issues and concepts in that text. The purpose of this lesson is to encourage students to leave tracks of their thinking so they better understand and remember content information and important ideas.

RESOURCES & MATERIALS
- enough copies of an article for all students

CONNECT & ENGAGE
■ **Ascertain kids' prior knowledge about the text topic.**

Today we are going to read about [topic]. What do you think you know about this? Turn to someone near you and talk about [topic]. *[If the topic is unfamiliar, we project or post one or two images on the topic and allow all kids to engage in a discussion through observation and questions.]*

MODEL
■ **Show readers how to annotate thinking.**

When we annotate a text, we leave tracks of our thinking in the margins or on Post-its. I'll read a bit of the text out loud and show you my inner conversation, the thinking I do as I read. I'll annotate by taking notes to leave tracks of that thinking. These tracks allow me to look back so I can remember what I read and fully understand it. *[We read the beginning of the text out loud, stopping occasionally to ask kids to turn and talk about their own thinking and to model the following close reading strategies.]*
- Stopping to think about and react to information
- Asking questions to resolve confusion or to consider big ideas or issues
- Paraphrasing the information and jotting our learning in the margin
- Noting the big ideas or issues
- Inferring to fill in gaps in information in the text
- Bringing in prior knowledge that furthers understanding

Guide
- Monitor kids' strategy use.

[After reading a paragraph or two, we turn this over to the kids by asking them to read and annotate in pairs.] Now I want you to take over jotting your thinking on your copy of the article—or on Post-its if you prefer. I'll continue reading the text and stop to let you turn, talk, and jot down your thoughts. *[As we pause in the reading, we circulate among the kids to check to see if and how they are using the strategies we modeled and if they are coming up with their own thoughts and annotations.]*

Collaborate/Practice Independently
- Invite kids to finish the article.

Now I'll stop reading. Continue to read and annotate the article, either with a partner or on your own.

Share the Learning
- Invite kids to share, first in small groups and then as a class.

When you have finished the article, find two or three others who have finished. Form a group to share out your reactions to the article. Think about the important ideas in the article as well as any issues, questions, or thoughts you have. *[After groups have had time to discuss, ask kids to share out their thinking with the whole class, especially important ideas and questions.]*

Follow Up
- Kids might read related articles independently or investigate questions or gaps in information on this topic, continuing to annotate to leave tracks of their thinking.
- Inspire kids to assume the role of historians in search of information on a particular topic, locating information online or in print, annotating their thinking as they research, and summarizing what they learned for their cohistorians.

Lesson 2

Annotate Images
Expand understanding and learning from visuals

Visual literacy is critical to learning because graphic and pictorial elements often carry or enhance the message in print and digital media. In this lesson, we encourage close viewing and reading using a variety of entry points and aspects of visual images to gain historical information and to further understanding.

Possible texts
We select a variety of images on a particular topic that spur purposeful, interesting questions and discussion. The following images can be found with captions in the historical images pages in the book, as well as full size in the image bank. An article that has historical images and a map diagram for students to view for this lesson is "Washington Makes His Move."

- "Historical Image: Washington Crossing the Delaware"
- "Historical Images: Native American Warriors"
- "Historical Images: Olaudah Equiano"

Resources & Materials
- a copy of an image for each student (Use the images in the text to be read as well as those from the image bank or other sources.)
- Anchor Chart with three columns headed What We Think We Know, What We Wonder, and What We Infer
- Anchor Chart: Questions to Consider When Viewing an Image

Engage

■ **Invite students to study and respond to a shared image.**

[We choose one image and provide students with copies of that image or project the image for class discussion.] Look carefully at the detail in this image and really think about what you notice, infer, and wonder about it. Be sure to think about what you already know about this topic to help you understand.

■ **Chart students' thinking.**

Now turn and talk about what you know, wonder, and infer from the image. Also discuss questions and inferences that the image prompts you to think about. Keep in mind that we are always learning new information, and what we already know may be limited or even inaccurate, so be prepared to change your mind in light of new evidence. After talking, we'll come back together and share out our observations, inferences, and questions. *[We jot kids' thinking on a chart as we share out.]*

What We Think We Know	What We Wonder	What We Infer

L-3

MODEL

- Show students how to annotate the image with reactions, inferences, questions, and connections to prior knowledge.

[We use kids' responses to guide our think-aloud and annotate the image with some of the important information we want them to know.] Watch me as I jot down my inner conversation about this image—those are the thoughts that go through my head as I view it. Notice the language I use to jot my thinking—and how I annotate my thoughts right on the copy of the image. I might choose a small part of the image and view it more closely.

As I look at the image, I notice . . . and have a strong reaction to it. I think this is about. . . . When I read the caption here, it tells me more about what this is. Additional text will certainly add more important information. But I respond to the image first, to get a sense of what it's all about. And I ask myself some questions: What is the purpose of this document? What's the purpose of this image? Who created it and why? I can infer the answers to these questions, and I may get them answered when I read on, but I may even need to do further research when I am finished to get a more complete understanding.

GUIDE/COLLABORATE

- Encourage kids to work in pairs to annotate their copies of the image.

Now it's your turn. Choose from among the remaining images and work with a partner to discuss and record your thoughts. Annotate your copies of the image with your own ideas: what you notice, questions you have, connections to your background knowledge. You might want to look back at our original thinking about the image that we recorded on our chart. I'll come around and listen in on your conversations and post some questions you might consider as you annotate your image.

Questions to Consider When Viewing an Image

Who created this and why?

When I looked at this part of the image, I wondered. . . .

What can we infer from this image and other features?

What can we infer from other information we viewed or read?

How do images such as this help us better understand the topic?

Share the Learning

- Record kids' thinking as they share ideas and questions about the images.

Come back together now and let's discuss our background knowledge, questions, and inferences. *[We call kids' attention to the* What We Think We Know, What We Wonder, *and* What We Infer *chart we began earlier.]* Do we understand who created these images? Do we now understand some different perspectives on this topic? Turn and talk about how images such as these enhance our understanding of the topic. Did your thinking change after closely viewing these images and talking about them?

Follow Up

- Find more images for students to choose from that are related to the topic under study. (See the table of contents for the image bank for some possibilities.) Encourage kids to work in pairs or independently to study the images closely, guided by the *Questions to Consider When Viewing an Image* chart. As kids share out what they learned from each of the images, the whole class learns from multiple images.
- What images or artifacts of today will historians of the future study to learn about us? Invite students to create a time capsule of images—personal photographs, print images, artifacts—and imagine what future historians will infer about our times.

Lesson 3 | Build Background to Understand a Primary Source
Read and paraphrase secondary sources to create a context for a topic

Possible texts
Secondary sources that provide background for the upcoming study of a primary source are appropriate for this lesson.
- Thomas Thorp's Journal, 1775,
- A letter by Eliza Lucas, 1740
- Background for the Declaration of Independence, "A Quiet Room"
- Background for the Constitution, "A Republic, If You Can Keep It"

PRIMARY SOURCES can only be read in historical context. Just like working historians, students with background knowledge about the events, people, and ideas behind a primary source are far better able to interpret and understand it. Historians read secondary sources extensively to get a better understanding of historic events and ideas. Then they use the knowledge they have built to interpret and understand the primary source, ultimately using all sources to arrive at a more robust understanding. This lesson is preparation for Lesson 4; here, students build background knowledge by paraphrasing and getting the gist of secondary sources to prepare for study of a primary source document in Lesson 4.

Resources & Materials
- a copy of a primary source document or artifact to project or show
- several secondary sources related to the time period in which the primary source was created, enough copies for all students
- chart paper

Engage
Define primary source and surface background knowledge.

[We briefly project a copy of a primary source document.] What you see here is a copy of what is called a *primary source*. A primary source is an original document or artifact that is created at a specific point in history by someone who lived at that time. When we read or study a primary source, it's important to have some context for it—who wrote or said or created it, why was it written or created, and what historical events surrounded it.

This primary source was created by [creator] in [time period]. Turn and talk about what you know about this time period, this person, and what was happening at the time. *[Kids share background knowledge with a partner.]* Let's come back together and share out some of your prior knowledge about this. *[We list some of the ideas and information that kids come up with on a chart for all to see.]*

MODEL

- Demonstrate how to paraphrase and annotate secondary sources to build knowledge about a topic.

To prepare for studying this primary source, we'll be reading two articles about this person/this time period/these events. The articles are known as *secondary sources*; they are nonfiction articles written to inform us about a historical time. We'll use what we learn from reading them to inform our reading of this primary source.

As I read, I'm going to read for the essence of what's happening during this time period, with these people. My purpose is to get the gist—to capture the important events and big ideas to add to my store of knowledge. So I'm going to read a small section of the text, stop and think about it, and then write in my own words what is going on or what I learned from this section.

[We read the beginning of the text aloud.] After reading this part, I'm going to paraphrase, or put into my own words, what happened. I'll write a short phrase or two in the margin about this. Notice how I bracket this section of the text and jot down the gist as I read. From this section, I learned … and I'm thinking this will help me understand our primary source because I now have some historical context for it.

GUIDE

- Continue reading as kids paraphrase information and annotate in the margins of the text.

Now it's your turn. I'll keep reading aloud, but I'll stop to let you turn and talk, annotate your thinking, and write down the gist of this next section of the text. Remember to focus on the most important information and ideas that you think relate to the primary source we're going to read. *[We listen in to partner talk and glance at marginal annotations to make sure kids are getting the point. We then ask kids to share out what they have learned from the reading so far.]*

COLLABORATE/PRACTICE INDEPENDENTLY

- Invite kids to continue reading secondary sources to build background about the time period under study.

[We let students continue independently with the same article or—for more experienced classes—encourage them to choose among additional related secondary sources.] Keep reading about … , and continue to paraphrase and annotate in the margins as you read. Note that we don't always have to read sources word by word, but can skim and scan to find the parts that are most helpful to our purpose.

SHARE

- Chart students' learning.

Let's come together and discuss the information we found. We'll write down some of what you discovered as you read to get the gist. Remember, share out what you think will help us most with reading our primary source. I'll add to our list so we can keep this information and these ideas in mind as we read.

FOLLOW UP

- Read a primary source that relates to the information that students learned in this lesson. Use Lesson 4 to further support primary source reading.
- Challenge kids in pairs or teams to summarize—as historians might—the key information behind the topic under study and present their findings to the rest of the class in a creative, memorable format (e.g., art, diorama, poster).

Lesson 4: Read and Analyze a Primary Source
Focus on what you know and ask questions to clarify and explain

Possible Texts
Any of the primary source documents in this volume are suitable for this lesson. Here are some possibilities.
- "Historical Images: Boston Massacre"
- "John Tudor's Diary, 1770"
- "Captain Thomas Preston's Letter to a Friend, 1770"
- "Abigail Adams' Letter to John Adams, March 31, 1776"

PRIMARY SOURCE DOCUMENTS can offer unique insights into the time period students are studying, but they often present significant reading challenges. Created in different time periods and for a variety of purposes, these documents are often characterized by unfamiliar formats, arcane language—both archaic or unusual vocabulary and unfamiliar or difficult sentence structures—and content beyond the experience of today's reader. This lesson offers a strategy for approaching the reading of primary source documents. It is important to do Lesson 3 to build a historical context before we ask kids to analyze a primary source, because students need a great deal of background knowledge about the topic at hand. We would not consider having them read a primary source cold without any knowledge of the historical context.

Resources & Materials
- a primary source document, enough copies for every student
- Anchor Chart: Reading Primary Source Documents

Connect & Engage
■ Review the definition of primary source.

For a while we've been studying about [time period], right? So we already know a bit about it. One way to understand even more about that time is to read *primary source documents*. Who can remind us what a primary source is? *[We let students share their background knowledge and define primary source as "information—an original document or artifact—created at a specific point in history." They should know this from the previous lesson.]*

It's important to have a good deal of background knowledge about the people and events of the time period before tackling a complex primary source because these documents often have words and expressions that we don't use today. We call this arcane language. It's common for readers to come to an unfamiliar word or an idea and get stuck. Even if we read on to clarify understanding, reading on in a primary source sometime leads to even more confusion because there are so many unfamiliar words and concepts.

MODEL

- **Explain a strategy for reading a primary source containing arcane language.**

Let's take a look at this example of a primary source document. I'll read aloud the first couple of sentences. *[We read aloud enough to give kids a taste of the language.]* Wow. Pretty hard to understand, isn't it? That's why when we read primary sources we usually need to read it several times to make sense of it and get the right idea. However, just reading it over and over doesn't help. We need to read it closely and use strategies to understand what we don't know. We particularly need to think about any background knowledge we already have.

Have you ever come to a word or an idea you didn't understand when you were reading? Turn and talk about a time you remember that happening and what you did to understand what you were reading. *[Kids turn and talk and share out a few examples of ways they figured out difficult words and language.]*

One of the best ways to understand a primary source with a lot of unfamiliar words and ideas is to focus on what we *do* understand the first time we read it, perhaps think about what we have already learned about the content. Too often we get stuck on an unfamiliar word and that's it. So we focus on what we *do* understand the first time we read it and get a general idea of what the source is mostly about. Then when we reread it, we think about our questions and address those.

- **Model how to write notes on what you know and questions you wonder about.**

OK, so let's try it. *[We read a paragraph of the document.]* As I read this part of the document the first time, I don't have a clue what this word means, so I am not going to try to read it over and over. But I do understand this one, because I have some background knowledge about it. I can tell that the writer must have meant . . . when writing this. Thinking about what I know helps me get through this difficult text. So although there are quite a few words here that I do not understand, I can at least begin to get an idea of what this is mainly about by focusing on what I know. I'll also jot down any questions I have. We will get more information when we read this again.

So here is an Anchor Chart with some guidelines to help as we read primary sources. *[We review the process for each of the readings outlined on the Anchor Chart and then use the beginning of our document to model the first step. As we model, we make clear that any annotations focus on what we understand and on questioning difficult parts.]*

Reading Primary Source Documents

Reading #1: Focus on what you know. Annotate the text with what you do understand and ask questions about what you don't.

Reading #2: Use what you have come to understand to figure out the answers to your questions and infer the meaning of puzzling parts.

Successive Readings: Fill in the gaps by noting previous annotations, asking and answering questions, and making inferences for a more robust understanding.

Guide/Practice Independently
- Monitor kids' primary source strategy use as they continue on their own.

Now work in pairs to think through this primary source document. Continue reading it with a partner, thinking about what you already know to understand new information. Annotate any important ideas you understand and write questions about the parts you need to come back to figure out. *[We circulate to make sure students can actually annotate and make progress with the text, pulling them back together to tackle it as a group if not.]*

Share the Learning
- Call kids together to pool their knowledge and questions.

Let's get together and share our learning and our questions. *[We go back through as much of the document as students have read, noting our understandings, answering each other's questions, and making a chart of the questions we want to figure out in the next reading.]*

Follow Up
- The first reading of primary sources that contain particularly arcane language might take more than one session to finish. Give kids plenty of time to discuss things they understand. On subsequent readings, go back and model the process of reading for answers to questions and using known information to make inferences about the time period and the document's meaning.
- Involve kids in a reenactment—either dramatizing or creating a tableau—of the creation of the primary source.

Lesson 5 | **Compare Perspectives**
Explore the different life experiences of historical figures

POSSIBLE TEXTS

This lesson requires texts that reflect varying perspectives on the same events or time period. The following articles and primary source text deal with the experiences of different women during the American Revolution.

- "Elizabeth Burgin: 'Indefatigable'"
- "Just Say No! The Daughters of Liberty"
- "Following the Army"
- "Abigail Adams' Letter to John Adams, June 18, 1775"

When we learn about historical events or a time period, it is important to understand that historical time from a variety of different perspectives. History is very much about the "untold stories" of people whose perspectives and experiences may not get top billing in the history books and that too often go unrecognized. But history is about all of us, so an important goal of this resource is to include voices, people, and perspectives that can provide kids with a fuller understanding of historical times and the people who lived in those times. The purpose of this lesson is to provide students with opportunities to compare and contrast life experiences of people living in this period so as to better understand their perspectives.

RESOURCES & MATERIALS

- images of different people within a particular time period
- chart paper
- a three-column chart and matching Thinksheets for each student: Person/Experiences & Perspective/My Thinking
- articles reflecting different experiences of several people

CONNECT & ENGAGE

■ Introduce the idea of different perspectives.

[We post images of different people of the times—children, women, and men, for example.] Let's take a look at these different people. Turn and talk about what you notice about these pictures. Who do you see? What do you think you know about some of these people? Who is not here?

Even though all these people lived at the same time, let's consider how they might have experienced life in these times. Who has some background knowledge or some ideas about this? *[We record kids' background knowledge and thoughts on a chart, guiding them to understand that each person pictured experiences life in a different way.]*

We're going to read a variety of different articles today and compare and contrast the lives of different people who lived in this time period. We'll consider what might be similar about peoples' lives and what might be very different. Let's read part of one account together and then you'll read another account with a different perspective with a small group.

MODEL

- Record text evidence reflecting a person's experiences and perspective in a historical time.

[To prepare kids to compare and contrast different perspectives later in the lesson, we model how to think about a historical figure's experiences.] I'm going to read this article that is written from the perspective of [person or people]. The authentic information here shows us what these people's lives were like.

I'll begin by identifying who this is about and then read this account aloud. I'll read to find out what important experiences he or she had and how these shaped the person's perspective, or point of view. Using evidence from the text and perhaps the historical record, I'll also jot down my thinking about their experiences and point of view. I can organize my thinking on this chart:

Person	Experiences & Perspective	My Thinking

GUIDE

- Guide pairs to jot down text evidence for important aspects of a person's experience.

[We hand out a three-column Thinksheet—Person/Experiences & Perspective/ My Thinking—to each student.] Now I'll keep reading and ask you to work with someone sitting near you to ferret out more of these peoples' experiences as well as their perspectives on the times. You and your partner can discuss this and also record your thinking. Remember, the thinking column includes your interpretations and inferences as well as your questions from your reading.

COLLABORATE/PRACTICE INDEPENDENTLY

- Ask kids to work in small groups to study other historical people.

Now choose another article about a different person living in this same time period. Get together with three or four friends who are interested in the same article and record your thinking on your Thinksheets. As you read, think about how your historical characters' experiences affected their points of view, their perspectives on the times. Be sure to tie their experiences and perspectives to the text and also include your thinking.

SHARE THE LEARNING

- Invite students to talk about and compare individuals and their perspectives.

[Once students have surfaced a variety of perspectives, we reconvene the group to compare and contrast the different lives of the people they read about.] Now let's talk about the historical people in your articles. We consider how their experiences influenced their view of the world, and how people differ based on these life experiences. *[Kids love to work big, and large posters can be very helpful for sharing out the experiences/evidence information that kids have gathered.]*

Questions to guide sharing:
- What experiences did your person have?
- How did this person's experiences shape his or her perspective?
- How are his or her experiences like or different from other people we read about?
- Do you think this person's life experiences and perspective might have been, to some extent, "unrecognized" in general historical accounts of these times?
- Discuss why his or her perspective and life experiences are important to an understanding of people of this time period.
- Why do you think it might be important to consider a lot of different experiences and perspectives when studying history?

FOLLOW UP

- Provide additional groups of articles organized to highlight different viewpoints and perspectives on the same time period and engage students in comparing and contrasting different views.
- Ask students each to assume the role of a historical character they have read about. Put two or three different characters together and prompt them to discuss an event or condition of their time from the perspective of their character: What do you think about . . . ?
- Encourage students to conduct independent research on a lesser-known historical figure and craft a biography and portrait. Please see the student projects, "Unrecognized Revolutionaries", on pages L-31–L-32.

LESSON 6 | **Read Critically**
Consider point of view and bias

POSSIBLE TEXTS
This lesson is best taught with articles or primary source texts that have specific and clearly different points of view.
- "Loyalists in the American Revolution"
- "Patrick Henry's Speech to the Virginia Assembly, 1775"
- "A Bitter Debate"
- "Benjamin Banneker's Letter to Thomas Jefferson"

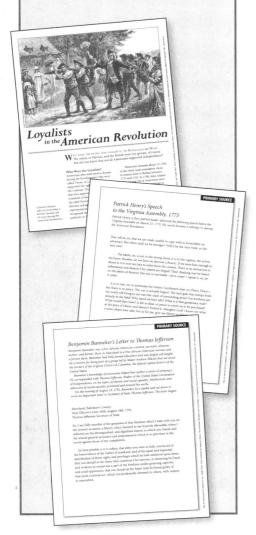

AS WE READ HISTORICAL SOURCES, it is important to read with a critical eye and a skeptical stance. Some articles provide balanced, "objective" information on a topic or issue. Several different perspectives and points of view are represented. Other articles may be written from a specific point of view with a definite perspective or even bias. Many articles fall somewhere in between. One way to support kids to become questioning readers is to show them how to discern the purpose of the sources they read. In this lesson, we help kids surface the author's intent and discuss why the article was written.

RESOURCES & MATERIALS
- Anchor Chart: Considering Point of View and Bias
- copies of two articles and historical images representing different perspectives on the same person, event, or time

CONNECT & ENGAGE
▪ Introduce questions that explore purpose, point of view, and bias.

[We project or share a copy of an article and discuss the title and its author. We pose questions to prompt kids to think about the point of view.] Before we read an article, it is helpful to discern whether the intent of the article is to be objective and offer information from several points of view or if it is written from a particular perspective. We ask ourselves questions like these.

Considering Point of View and Bias
- What is the author's purpose for writing the article? Is it written to inform us about a topic? To persuade us to have a particular opinion or view? For some other reason?
- Are several points of view or perspectives on the topic expressed? Or is there just one?
- What is the source of the information in the article or image?
- Can we detect any bias given the ideas in the article and the sources the author used to write the article?

Turn and talk about some of these questions. *[Kids do.]* This last question asks about bias. Who can tell me what *bias* is? *[We discuss the term* bias *and define it as "a preference or prejudice," noting that it usually refers to a point of view that doesn't recognize opposing or balanced views.]*

MODEL
- Read and think aloud to uncover the author's point of view.

[We hand out copies of an article to each student and read the beginning aloud, keeping in mind the questions posed on the chart. We think out loud about both the information and the point of view to begin to uncover the author's purpose for writing the article.] The author of this article is writing about [historical events]. Based on what's happening here, it sounds like the author has some strong feelings and a definite perspective. Now that I read on, I learn that the information we have about these events comes from [source of information]. The actual words make me think. . . .

From the information the author includes and the sources he or she references, I'm thinking the author may be biased. That's what I think so far.

GUIDE
- Guide students to read with a critical eye and a skeptical stance.

Now I'll keep reading. While I do, keep our questions in mind *[We reference the* Considering Point of View and Bias *Anchor Chart.]* and jot notes in the margins of your copy. What's the point of view? Can you detect any bias? What does text evidence tell you about the article's purpose?

PRACTICE INDEPENDENTLY
- Invite students to finish the article independently and/or read a second article with a different point of view.

Go ahead and read the rest of the article, jotting your notes in the margins. Keep our list of questions from the chart in mind.

SHARE THE LEARNING
- Listen in on small-group sharing.

Join together with two other people and share out your thinking about the questions on the *Considering Point of View and Bias* Anchor Chart. Did you all come to the same conclusions? What are some different points of view that you noticed? Why do you think people believed the way they did? How did their personal experiences affect their point of view?

Follow Up

- Provide kids with pairs or groups of articles, images, or combinations of both that depict the same event. Encourage them to compare these, focusing on the perspectives of their creators.
- Create a dramatic interpretation of a scene from the life of a particular person. Keep in mind the point of view of each character as you write the scene.

Lesson 7 | **Organize Thinking**
Create a question web

Possible texts

This lesson works well with a few related articles with images and text that spark kids' curiosity. Consider teaching this lesson with the following articles, historical images, and primary source texts.

- "Oney Judge: Washington's Runaway Slave "
- "Olaudah Equiano: Sailing from Slavery to Freedom"
- "Historical Image: Fraunces Tavern"
- "The Revolution's Frontier Front"
- "War in the West"
- "Stockbridge Indian Speech"

KIDS' HISTORICAL THINKING often begins with their authentic questions. We encourage kids' curiosity and engagement in history by keeping a list of their questions as we find out more about a topic or time period. We add to our knowledge of the topic as we find answers and create a list of lingering questions for research and investigation. This lesson suggests ways that students can organize questions for further study.

Resources & Materials

- an article containing illustrations, photographs, or other images as well as text that will stimulate students' questions
- a board or chart on which to create and display a question web
- a collection of articles on a variety of related topics

Engage

■ Let kids know that their own questions are the most important ones.

Sometimes when I read about an unfamiliar topic or learn new information, I find myself asking a lot of questions. Sometimes I ask questions to help me fill in gaps in my knowledge or explain something I don't understand. Other times I wonder what might have happened if circumstances were different, so I might ask, "What if . . . ?" or "What might have happened if . . . ?" Sometimes my questions go unanswered and require further investigation; we call those *lingering questions*. What I do know is that our own questions really help us dig deeper into a topic and further our understanding.

Model

■ Demonstrate how viewing and reading can prompt questions.

We're going to do some viewing and reading—and pay special attention to our questions while we do. First, let's take a look at the image in this article. What questions does it raise for you? Next, go ahead and look over the article to see what it's about. Turn and talk about your thinking. Maybe you have some background knowledge or some thoughts about this. *[Kids share out briefly.]*

I'm going to begin viewing and reading. I'm going to stop right here because I already have a question. I'm wondering. . . . I'll jot that down *[I write the question on one of the stems of the question web.]* and keep going. This section of the article leads me to wonder something else. *[Again the question is written on the web.]* As I think about these questions a bigger question comes to mind. I'm going to put that in the middle of what we'll call our *question web*—it's a visual map of our questions. My bigger question goes right in the middle here:

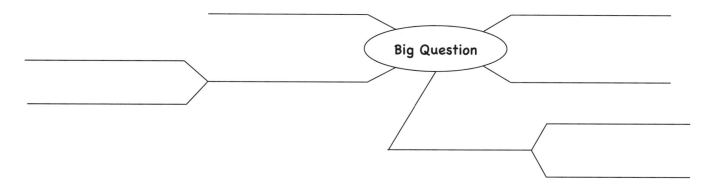

And then as I view and read, I'll add my other questions on stems around it—they are related to the big question—and put related questions near each other.

GUIDE/SHARE THE LEARNING

- **Read and view together, adding kids' questions to the web.**

[We read on, asking kids to turn and talk to surface their questions.] Let's keep reading and viewing together . . . . Let's stop here. Go ahead and turn and talk about your questions. Jot them on a Post-it so we can share them and add them to our web. *[Kids generate questions and jot these on Post-its. As they share, we have them put the questions on our group question web, guiding them to place related questions near each other.]* These are related to our big question, so we'll place them around our bigger question.

I noticed that as we kept reading, we were able to answer a couple of these questions. I can jot a short answer or response right on the web. It's just a brief thought to capture our thinking.

- **Share out questions that were answered as well as lingering questions.**

Now that we've finished the article, let's add any final questions to the web. Now go ahead and turn and talk with your partner and discuss if we've discovered some information that provides some insight into our big question. *[We discuss what we've learned about our big question, wrapping up the conversation by identifying lingering questions that remain.]*

COLLABORATE/PRACTICE INDEPENDENTLY

- Give kids a choice of investigations.

You're going to have a choice for continuing this work. Some of you seem quite intrigued by a couple of these lingering questions—questions that remain after our reading. If you'd like, go online and see if you can find a source or two that might give you some information about your question.

Another option is to read an additional source on a topic you choose. I have a whole bunch of articles right here, so if you'd like to tackle a different article or topic, come on up and peruse these. You can work with a partner, a small group, or on your own, but be sure to pay special attention to your questions. Try organizing them on your own web.

FOLLOW UP

- Question webs are great investigation starters. Kids often gravitate to questions and topics that matter to them, and researching answers provides the perfect opportunity for students to use their developing repertoire of reading and thinking strategies.
- Kids love to make their thinking visible. They can create many kinds of visuals—on posters, on the computer, with a collage of images and illustrations—to share the new information they are learning.

Lesson 8 | Read with a Question in Mind
Focus on central ideas

POSSIBLE TEXTS

Articles with obvious topics that are easily identified by scanning the title and features will facilitate generation of big ideas.

- "*Tinker v. Des Moines*"
- "The Five Freedoms"
- "America's Boldest Experiment"

OFTEN WHEN WE READ to understand big ideas and important information, we read with a question in mind. When we keep one or two focus questions in mind as we read, we can more easily zero in on the information and ideas that are most important to understand and remember.

RESOURCES & MATERIALS

- images related to the topic currently under study, some with labels or captions, others without
- Post-it notes
- copies of an article on the topic for every student
- Anchor Chart, Reading with a Focus Question in Mind, and matching Thinksheets for every student
- a selection of additional articles on the topic

CONNECT & ENGAGE

■ Engage students in a gallery walk.

[We post images at different points around the room.] We have placed a variety of images around the room, all of which relate to the article we will be reading. Move around the room, look at the images, and discuss what you notice or wonder with others gathered around each image. After talking, jot down on Post-its any inferences or ideas you have about the image as well as any questions that come to mind. Stick these right on the image. You might put your initials on the Post-its you write so you can keep track of your own thinking.

MODEL

■ Relate the kids' thoughts about the images they just observed to the topic of the article to be read. Show kids how to read with a question in mind and use a Notes/Thinking scaffold to take notes that will address the focus question(s).

Did you guess from the pictures in your gallery walk what topic we're going to begin studying today? *[Students name the topic.]* Right! Now, let's take a quick look at this article, its title and features. What is it mostly about? Are there one or two important ideas that stand out? Turn and talk about what you were thinking and wondering about as you looked at the images in our gallery walk. How do your questions and inferences relate to the topic of the article?

- Demonstrate how to turn the big idea of the article into a question—one that gets at the big ideas in the article.

So, from the images and a quick look at the text, I'd guess that one of the big ideas that is important to understanding this time in history is. . . . I can turn this big idea into a focus question and ask. . . . Keeping a focus question like this one in mind will guide us to find out important information about the topic.

[We hand out the Thinksheets and call attention to the matching Anchor Chart.] To keep my thoughts organized, I'm going to write our question(s) at the top of my *Reading with a Focus Question in Mind* page. It has two columns, *Notes* and *Thinking*, because both the information from the article and our thinking about it are important!

Listen and watch as I read and take notes on the article. I'll make sure the information I record relates to the focus question. So in the *Notes* column, I'll write facts and information about our question(s); in the *Thinking* column, I'll jot down what I think about the information—my reactions and responses. Maybe I'll have some additional questions or some background knowledge, all of which I can jot in the *Thinking* column. *[We read the beginning of the article, picking out information that relates to our question, writing it on the chart, and recording our responses.]*

Reading with a Focus Question in Mind

Focus Question: _____

_____

Title: _____

Notes	Thinking

Guide

- Continue to read the article aloud as kids take notes.

Now I'll keep reading this article while you take notes. Be sure to keep the focus question(s) in mind, jotting down only information that will help you understand the answers. Remember, including our thinking as we take notes means we'll process and understand the information more thoroughly. *[We continue reading, stopping occasionally to give kids time to turn and talk about the focus question before recording their ideas on the Thinksheet.]*

COLLABORATE/PRACTICE INDEPENDENTLY

■ Give kids an opportunity to study related sources, taking notes on and responding to the focus question.

On your own or with a partner, finish reading this article and writing down your notes and thinking about this article. Next, choose one of these other articles or images and continue to think about our focus question. *[We call attention to the images posted for our gallery walk as well as a collection of related articles.]* Does this new source add to your knowledge on this topic? Read it with the focus question in mind and take notes on it.

SHARE THE LEARNING

■ Ask kids to discuss the focus question in small groups, summarizing their learning.

[We help kids form groups of three or four, making sure that among the members of the group, they have read several of the articles so they can discuss each knowledgeably.] Let's get into groups to discuss what we have learned about our focus question. Get together with two or three other people; make sure that together you have read and taken notes on several articles and images. Share with your group your learning and thinking about the articles you have read.

After you discuss the focus question using each article, take a look at the questions and inferences you jotted on the images at the beginning of the lesson. How has your thinking changed? What do you know now that you didn't when you first viewed the images? What questions that you asked still linger?

FOLLOW UP

■ In small groups, have students do follow-up research to try to resolve any lingering questions. There are many websites rich with historical information; check out the recommended resource list on page xxv to get started. If their queries are still unanswered, students might try contacting historical museums or other institutions. Researchers are often willing to answer questions, especially those of engaged, curious students.

■ Kids love to share their new findings. They can give presentations or create short movies to share the new information they are learning.

Lesson 9 | **Surface Common Themes**
Infer the big ideas across several texts

> **POSSIBLE TEXTS**
> Any group of articles on the same topic will work for this lesson. A few suggestions are:
> - "Celebrating Citizenship!"
> - "Land of Opportunity and Obstacles"
> - Making Changes
> - "Excerpt from the Civics (History and Government) Questions for the Naturalization Test"

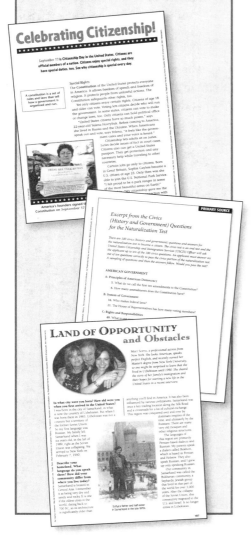

IN REAL-WORLD READING, we rarely read simply one text on a topic. Generally, we read a wide range of texts on a common theme to learn more about it and to understand a variety of perspectives. We infer the big ideas across these various texts to learn more about the overall topic or issue. The purpose of this lesson is to guide students to use evidence from several texts to infer broad historical themes.

RESOURCES & MATERIALS
- two-column Anchor Chart—Evidence from the Text/Big Ideas—and matching Thinksheets for each student
- a set of resources (e.g., an expository article, a piece of historical fiction, and an image) on the same historical topic for each group of three students

CONNECT & ENGAGE
▪ **Engage the kids and review what it means to infer.**

Today we're going to interact with several texts on a single topic to get more information. The more texts we read and the more images we view, the more we learn. To better understand the issues and information, we're going to infer the big ideas across several of these texts. Does anyone remember what it means to infer? Turn and talk about that. *[Kids turn and talk and share out some thoughts.]*

Inferring is the strategy we use to figure out information that is not explicitly stated in the text. To infer the big ideas, we need to think about what we already know and then merge our background knowledge with clues in the text to make a reasonable inference and surface some big ideas or themes about the topic or issue. If our inference doesn't seem reasonable, we can gather more clues and information from the text. If we ignore text clues and rely solely on our background knowledge, our inferences could be off the mark. So we're constantly looking for clues, text evidence, and more information to make reasonable inferences and come up with big ideas. Reading a number of articles gives us more background knowledge, which gives us more information upon which to base our inferences.

MODEL

■ **Model how to use text evidence to infer big ideas.**

[We display a two-column chart on which to record evidence and big ideas.] While I'm reading this article, I'll closely read the words, and I'll pay attention to the images and features, searching for clues to help me infer the big ideas. When I find some evidence that supports a big idea, I'll write it on the chart. We can find evidence for big ideas in words, pictures, features, actions, and details that are included in the text. Usually, there are several big ideas that bubble to the surface in an article.

Evidence from the Text (words, pictures, features, actions, details)	Big Ideas

[We read the article aloud, stopping when a big idea or theme is apparent.] I think these words are good evidence for the big idea of. . . . So I'll write the words from the text in the *Evidence* column and the big ideas that I infer in the *Big Ideas* column. Here, these images help me to infer the big idea of . . . , so I'll record information about the images in the *Evidence* column, too. Sometimes I look closely at the character's actions in historical fiction to infer the big ideas. My background knowledge may be helpful here. All of these clues are evidence for the theme of. . . .

GUIDE

■ **Invite kids to come up with text evidence for some big ideas.**

OK, now it's your turn. Let's read a bit together before you go off and try this in a small group. *[We read through a page of text.]* Now that I have read a page, turn and talk about what you think are some of the big ideas here. Look for clues and cite that as evidence for your big ideas. *[Kids share their ideas with a partner.]*

Who has a big idea they would like to share? What is the evidence for that idea?

Let's add to our chart. Sometimes the evidence came from words quoted directly from the text, and other times from pictures and features in the text.

COLLABORATE

▪ Support kids as they infer big ideas across several texts.

Now you can get together in groups of three. I have three pieces of text; they are all different, but they focus on the same topic. Since they are grouped around a common topic, they are likely to have some similar big ideas, and all will likely include evidence for those big ideas. As you read through these articles, they will add to your background knowledge, increasing the likelihood that you will make reasonable inferences when you are inferring the big ideas. Share your thinking with each other; note the text clues and the big ideas that occur to you based on your reading and viewing and jot them on your Thinksheets. *[We distribute three related resources to each group and* Evidence from the Text/Big Ideas *Thinksheets to each student.]*

SHARE

▪ Record kids' evidence and big ideas.

[We gather kids in a sharing session to talk about their group's big ideas and evidence.] What are some of the big ideas you inferred as you read and viewed? As you share them, I'll add them to the class' *Evidence from the Text/Big Ideas* Anchor Chart.

Did you find some similar ideas across all of the articles and images?

Great thinking about using text evidence to infer the big ideas. We can continue to make inferences beyond the book, especially if there is some good evidence to support them.

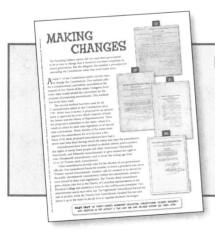

FOLLOW UP

▪ Add related resources to the original three and have kids continue to look for corroboration of their big ideas—or for new ones.
▪ Students might create dramatic tableaux to support their inferred themes: a series of frozen scenes carefully crafted to represent evidence of the big ideas.

LESSON 10 | **Synthesize Information to Argue a Point**
Use claim, evidence, and reasoning

Possible texts

This lesson requires texts that present information as evidence about an idea. You might consider teaching this lesson with the following articles and primary source text.
- "George Washington and Slavery"
- "Petitioning for Freedom"
- "James Armistead: Master Spy"
- "Benjamin Banneker's Letter to Thomas Jefferson"

A GOOD ARGUMENT expresses a point of view, uses information as evidence to support that view, and applies the information to persuade others. To make a good argument, the learner must turn information into knowledge, gathering evidence about the ideas in the text and synthesizing that information to make a claim that will convince others of the validity of the argument. To make a valid claim, however, the arguer must have some background about the issue; before making a claim and sharing the evidence, the claimant needs to have viewed or read several sources on the topic so that he or she knows enough to make a reasonable claim about it. As a result, this lesson on synthesizing information to argue a point is best taught near the end of a unit of study.

Resources & Materials
- several articles on the same topics or with similar themes (some read beforehand)
- three-column Anchor Chart with columns headed Claim, Evidence, and Reasoning and matching Thinksheets for each student
- Anchor Chart: Questions to Guide Effective Arguments

Connect & Engage

■ **Invite students to share what they already know about argument.**

How many of you have ever heard the word *argument*? Turn to each other and talk about what you know about arguing. *[Kids turn and talk, then share out, mostly about personal disagreements they have had with others.]* Today we're going to talk about a more formal kind of argument.

■ **Define the term *argument*.**

Have you ever believed in something so much that you have wanted to convince others to agree with you? It is common to feel that way. Sometimes it happens outside when we want to make rules for a new game. Sometimes it happens at home when we are trying to get one more dessert out of Mom. And sometimes it gets a little unpleasant, with people getting mad at each other. Well, the type of argument we are talking about today is about convincing others to see the issue from your point of view. But rather than getting mad and fighting about it, in this kind of argument we gather evidence to make a point and try to convince the other side based on valid information.

L-27

So writers make arguments all the time, and they do it without fighting. They share evidence that helps them make their case. They might argue that we should eat healthier foods and support their argument with statistics showing the health risks of eating junk food. Or they might argue that soccer is a safer game than football, and to make their case share information about the danger of concussions that come from getting tackled in football. This kind of argument is based on a claim—that we should eat healthier food or that soccer is a safer game, for example. Turn to each other and talk about something you believe and would like to make a case for or a claim about. Share evidence that would back up your case. *[Kids turn and talk and then share out.]*

MODEL

- **Read through a piece of text and show students how to use text evidence and reasoning to make and support a claim.**

When we make a claim, we need to provide evidence in support of the claim, valid evidence from a text or other source. And to make a decent argument, we need to know quite a bit about our topic. So we read about the issue or topic a bit and form an opinion. Then we merge the evidence in the text with what we already know to convince others of our claim. So let me show you how it works as I read through this article on. . . . I have an Anchor Chart here with columns headed *Claim, Evidence,* and *Reasoning.* As I read through the article, I'll collect evidence for the claim I'm making and add it to the first column.

Claim	Evidence	Reasoning

I have read a bit on this topic over the past week or so, and I already have a belief or opinion about it that I can turn into a claim. I'll state my claim—that is, the argument that I am going to try to make about the issue—in the first column. *[We write a claim in the first column and continue reading.]*

Here is some evidence for my claim. . . . supports my claim because. . . . I'll jot this in the second column.

Now in the third column, I'm going to show my reasoning—how I interpret the evidence to support my claim. I believe . . . because the evidence shows me that. . . .

It helps that I have learned about this topic beforehand. I already knew . . . from previous readings, so I can reasonably make this claim based on the evidence from this article as well as from my background knowledge.

Reasoning is an important part of this process because if my goal is to make a case for my point of view and convince others, I need to be able to reason through this issue or topic myself in order to understand it well enough to persuade others. And always remember, an argument is not just our opinion, but our point of view supported by evidence.

Guide/Collaborate

- **Encourage students to work in pairs to read through an article, make a claim, and support it with evidence and reasoning.**

So it's time for you to give it a whirl. With partners, choose one of these articles on [*the same topic or issue*]. Talk about what you already know about the topic based on the article we just read together as well as other things you've learned. Think about an argument, or claim, you would like to make. Write your claim on your Thinksheet. As you read this additional article, look for evidence that supports your claim and jot that down as well. And talk with your partner about your reasoning.

Questions to Guide Effective Arguments

- What is my point?
- Who is my audience?
- What might the audience already think about this argument?
- Does the evidence back up my claim? If so, how?
- Which evidence will most likely convince my audience of my claim?
- What would be a good counterargument? Is there evidence to support the other side? If so, what is it?

Think about some of these questions as you reason through the text. [*We display guiding questions and read them aloud.*]

Go ahead and get started. I'll come around and check in with your partnerships as you reason through the text, thinking about your claim and the evidence you find to support it. Remember, if you can't find evidence to fit your claim, you might need to revise your claim to fit the evidence!

Share

- **Bring kids back together to share their claims, evidence, and reasoning.**

[*Kids share their forms and we discuss their claims as well as possible counterarguments.*] Whenever we make an argument, we need to be prepared for a counterargument—a claim that contradicts our own. When faced with an opposite opinion, we need to address it with more evidence in support of our own claim or with evidence that disproves the opposite claim.

Follow Up

- This is an introductory lesson on synthesizing information to present an argument. Since making an effective case is a complex process, it requires repeated discussions and practice. So teaching this lesson with a wide variety of issues and articles comprises the next steps.
- Teaching kids to write a paper with a strong argument is an eventual goal. A good resource to support that process is available at the University of North Carolina Writing Center http://writingcenter.unc.edu/handouts/argument. This site will support you as you engage kids in claim-and-evidence writing, although it needs to be adapted for kids younger than college age.

"Unrecognized Revolutionaries"
A Project Created by Mariana X. McCormick

"To create a more diverse, inclusive, and accurate representation of Revolutionary America"

In a nutshell, that's the goal of a group of fifth graders in Mariana McCormick's history class. Through an unusual approach to the study of the Revolutionary War, these students learned to "think as researchers, act as historians." Not content to review the "usual suspects" of history, they created portraits—both visual and written—of individuals who have not received the attention they deserved for their roles in the Revolutionary War.

Using historical images, students viewed closely, drew inferences, and asked questions to think more carefully about how available sources, from both the past and present, shape our understanding of history. Realizing that there are many people left out of the typical history books, students delved into a scant and often hard-to-find collection of primary and secondary sources on less well-known men, women, and children. Experiencing the same excitement and obstacles that practicing historians face, students had to ferret out and often piece together information about the person. Students then painted portraits and wrote lively biographies of what they discovered about these unrecognized revolutionaries. Compiled into a class website, these portraits and biographies now serve as an original and engaging resource for their fellow students and a broader audience. (See http://unrecognizedrevolutionaries.blogspot.com/.)

Over the course of the project, students reflected on their research process in an Inquiry Journal, keeping track of their learning and insights about "doing history." This record of their experiences illustrates that when kids actively engage in inquiry with a genuine purpose, their interest, engagement, and skills as researchers soar!

STUDENT PROJECT

Peter Salem, Minuteman and Hero of Bunker Hill
By Kyley

Though Peter Salem is mostly known for his role serving at The Battle of Bunker Hill, he played a significant role in the Revolution that helped lead to America's success.

Peter Salem had a difficult childhood as an African-American slave. He was born in Framingham, Massachusetts in 1750. Salem was born into an enslaved family owned by Jeremiah Belknap. In around 1775, he was sold to Lawson Buckminster. The names and occupations of his parents are not known. Salem did not have a last name so his first owner, Jeremiah Belknap, is believed to name him Salem after his previous residence in Salem, Massachusetts. Lawson Buckminster freed Salem to let him enlist in Captain Simon Edgel's "minutemen." He was one of the only African-American men to be a part of the company.

Peter Salem successfully served in the American Revolution and participated in important battles. Salem fought in in four battles in all; The Battle of Concord, the Battle of Bunker Hill, the Battle of Saratoga, and the Battle of Stony Point. On June 17, Salem shot and killed British Major John Pitcairn during the battle of Bunker Hill. Many people recognized Salem's act, and the musket he used to kill Major Pitcairn is now in an exhibit at the Museum of the Battle of Bunker Hill.

Peter Salem had a quiet life after his service. Salem went to live in Leicester, Massachusetts, and built a cabin to live in after he finished serving in the army. He married Katy Benson in September, 1783. They did not have any children. After they married, they both became cane weavers. Peter Salem died on August 16, 1816, at age of sixty-six. In 1882, a monument was put up in Framingham, Massachusetts, his birthplace, to commemorate him at the Old Burying Ground.

Brave and successful, Peter Salem played a significant role in the American Revolutionary War that contributed to our country's freedom.

STUDENT PROJECT

Esther Reed
By Caroline

Although little is known about Esther Reed, she sewed through fabric and through the hearts of the grateful American soldiers.

Esther Reed had a very pleasant childhood. She was born on October 22, 1746 in London. She had a happy family, and loved to read. She lived in a wonderful house. She married Joseph Reed on May 31, 1770.

Esther Reed played a simple, yet important role in the Revolutionary war. She was the leader of a group called The Ladies Association of Philadelphia. They collected money and made clothes for soldiers. In all she collected $7000, and made 2000 shirts for soldiers.

When she died in 1780, Sarah Franklin Bache took Esther Reed's place, and became the leader of the group. Esther Reed changed the way people saw women. She inspired women to help out in the Revolutionary war.

Esther Reed sewed the clothes of freedom that the soldiers wore winning the battles for independence. Although she may not still be with us, Esther Reed taught us that just a little needle and thread can go a long way.

STUDENT PROJECT

Lydia Darragh
By Tatum

Sometimes great contributions to help one's country are made with just a few words.

Little is known about Lydia Darragh's early life. Darragh was born in 1728, in Dublin, Ireland. She married William Darragh in 1753 at the age of twenty-four. She immigrated to America, where she settled in Philadelphia before the Revolutionary War.

All because of Darragh, George Washington's army was prepared for a British ambush. Darragh was a Quaker, so the British wanted to use her household for meetings. At one meeting, the British demanded that the whole family stay in one bedroom. Suspicious, Darragh snuck out of the room and hid in a chamber closet. In the closet, she overheard the British talking about an ambush on Washington's army. Hearing that the meeting was concluding, she scurried back to the bedroom and pretended to be asleep. The British knocked on the door, but when she opened it, they did not suspect anything was wrong. The next morning, Lydia announced that she needed flour. Instead, she delivered the information to a general about the ambush. Washington's troops were ready for the ambush on December, 1777.

After the war, Lydia lived a normal life. Her husband died in 1783. In 1786, she moved to a new house and ran a store. Darragh then died on December 28, 1789. In 1827, her daughter Ann published a book on her mother's spy work.

Darragh's courage throughout the war proved that women can be just as good as men.

THE AMERICAN REVOLUTION and the Constitution

By the 1700s, America was making the transition from a colony of Great Britain to a country in its own right. As the colonies became more populated and started to establish their own trade and their own systems of government, they were getting impatient with many of the laws and taxes imposed on them by the British. The colonists started to fight back against King George III, and as tensions grew, events would spark the American Revolutionary War. Ultimately the United States of America would be created, but it would be a long and difficult road to get there.

American independence from Great Britain only happened because of the dedication of many patriots, from every part of colonial society. The Revolution, as with any period in American history, is the story of individual people who believed in the vision of an independent country, and fought for that vision in their own ways. Some of them became famous leaders, such as George Washington, John Adams, Thomas Jefferson, Benjamin Franklin, and John Hancock. Some sparked the fight for independence with their powerful words and actions: Thomas Paine, Patrick Henry, Samuel Adams, and Paul Revere. Others are less recognized, but made important contributions, including James Armistead, William Dawes, Abigail Adams, and Deborah Sampson, among many others. The colonists also received help from overseas in their struggle to become independent, with both France and Spain coming to their aid, either openly or in secret.

The American Revolution was a time of conflict for Native Americans. There were conflicts between the British and American settlers who were pushing them out of their traditional lands. Then, as war loomed between the British and Americans, the tribes were being pressured into supporting one side or the other. In 1775, the Iroquois, also called the Six Nations Confederacy, met to decide whom they would support. At first, the tribal leaders decided it was a private war and they should try to remain neutral. But ultimately, some leaders convinced others that taking sides was a necessity. The Mohawks, Senecas, Onondagas, and Cayugas sided with the British, fearing that if the American colonies became independent, they would take away

King George III

Samuel Adams

Abigail Adams

The Marquis de Lafayette, seen in this painting with George Washington, recruited men from the Oneida Nation. Native American officers and soldiers fought the British and their Native American allies in northern New York.

even more of their land. But the Oneidas and the Tuscaroras sided with the Americans and fought with them in several battles where other Iroquois nations were fighting alongside the British. George Washington even sent an army into Western New York State in 1779, to punish the Iroquois tribes that supported the British and stop their frontier raids. Called the Sullivan Campaign, it resulted in the destruction of many tribal villages, forcing the tribes to flee and clearing the way for American settlers after the war was over. Taking sides, tribe against tribe, split the Iroquois Confederacy, and after the Sullivan Campaign, the Confederacy was never again as strong as it once was.

The American Revolution did not just take place in the established colonies along the Atlantic coast, from New England to the Southern colonies. The war was also fought in the west, as the British struggled to hold on to their frontier forts in Illinois and Ohio. Soldiers fought in rugged terrain, in settled and cultivated areas, and at sea. Spies were able to gather much-needed intelligence. Women followed their men into battle, or even disguised themselves to fight alongside them. Many people remained loyal to the British crown and worked against the patriots and revolutionaries. But ultimately, the colonists were successful and the United States of America was officially born.

Any war has tremendous costs. There were over 24,000 deaths that took place on the battlefields of the American Revolution. Another 27,000 deaths were caused by diseases like scurvy and smallpox. Roughly 25,000 people were wounded in the war, and some were permanently disabled as a result. Property damage was common,

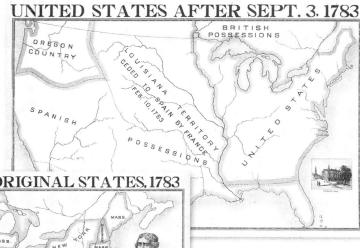

Maps showing the United States and the original thirteen states after the Revolutionary War (from H. C. Robertson's *Geographic-Historical Series Illustrating the History of America and the United States*).

Library of Congress Geography and Map Division

and many households lost valuable goods to looting by British soldiers. The aftermath of fighting and violence was also a legacy that would take many years for ordinary citizens to recover from.

Becoming a new country meant that there needed to be a system of government and a constitution to guide it. Along the way, the young United States struggled with issues such as slavery, religion, and, many years later, women's place in society. Would there be a king or a president? Who could vote? What rights would citizens have? Would there be an official religion? As the founding fathers created the United States Constitution, there were arguments and discussions about these and many other issues. The United States was a bold experiment in democracy, and the writers of the Articles of Confederation, and later the Constitution itself, knew how important it was to guarantee certain rights to their fellow citizens. They grappled with whether slavery should be illegal, what the role of religion should be in government, and other important issues that we still see the results of today in our Constitution. Many of the Supreme Court cases that have made huge changes in American society came much later, for example, abolishing slavery, giving women the right to vote, granting civil rights for African Americans, enforcing desegregation, and allowing freedom of speech in schools, are grounded in the work that the writers of the Constitution did hundreds of years ago.

The first page of the United States Constitution

We have the patriots and statesmen of this time period to thank for the foundation and framework of democracy that still guide us today. Each of them helped create the United States of America as we know it today. These are their stories: the stories of planners, leaders, spies, soldiers, merchants, and regular people, many of whose names will never be known. And we still benefit from their legacy every day, as citizens of what started out as—and continues to be—a great experiment in democracy.

The Declaration of Independence, a painting by John Trumbull in the U.S. Capitol Rotunda.

TIMELINE

THE AMERICAN REVOLUTION

and the Constitution

1760	George III becomes King of England
1764–1765	The Sugar Act and the Stamp Act, which are "taxation without representation," anger the colonists
1768	British troops arrive in Boston to enforce customs laws
MARCH 1770	During the Boston Massacre, the British fire on a crowd and kill five colonists
DECEMBER 1773	The **Boston Tea Party** takes place in protest against the Tea Act
1774	During Lord Dunmore's War, Virginia frontiersmen and Shawnee and Mingo Indians clash over territory
SEPTEMBER 1774	The first Continental Congress meets to consider action against British rule
APRIL 1775	The first battles of the Revolutionary War take place at **Lexington and Concord**, and Paul Revere makes his famous ride to warn the colonists about the British
1775	The Iroquois, or Six Nations Confederacy, meet to decide which side to support during the Revolutionary War. Some tribes side with the British and others with the colonists.
1776	**Thomas Paine** publishes *Common Sense*, which pushes the colonists toward independence
JULY 4, 1776	Congress ratifies the Declaration of Independence
1776	Washington crosses the Delaware River; Benjamin Franklin seeks help from France
1777	The Battle of Saratoga
1778	France signs a Treaty of Alliance with the United States
JULY 1778	George Rogers Clark and his men capture Kaskaskia from the British
FEBRUARY 1779	The British Fort Sackville at Vincennes, Indiana, surrenders to Clark and his men
1779	**George Washington** sends an army to Western New York to stop Native American raids on the frontier and to punish the Iroquois for supporting the British in the war
1780	The British capture Charleston, South Carolina
1781	At the **Battle of Yorktown**, British Lord Cornwallis surrenders the British Army
1783	Great Britain and the United States sign a peace treaty
1787	The **United States Constitution** is adopted
1791	The first ten amendments to the Constitution are ratified
1865	The 13th Amendment abolishes slavery
1920	The 19th Amendment gives women the right to vote

Boston Tea Party

Thomas Paine

Lexington and Concord

George Washington

Battle of Yorktown

U.S. Constitution

WAR in the West

The French and Indian War consisted of a series of small, bloody battles that pitted the French and their native allies against the British and their colonists. Below, Onandaga and British soldiers around a council fire.

Pelts are animal skins with the fur still on them.

To Americans in the 1770s, the West was a vast, heavily forested, and little-known wilderness. Lying between the Appalachian Mountains and the Mississippi River, the West's northern edges were bounded by the Great Lakes and British-held, but French-speaking, Canada. To its south was the Gulf of Mexico, while the western boundary—Spanish-held Louisiana—extended from New Orleans to the Missouri River and the Great Plains.

This area was thinly populated by many diverse groups of Native Americans. These tribes hunted, trapped, and farmed. They also traded with European colonists who lived in settlements and forts that were scattered across the region. The Indians offered **pelts** of fur-bearing animals in return for goods from the Europeans' home countries.

Controlling and protecting the profitable fur trade with the Native Americans became the focus of Great Britain's attention in the mid-1700s.

Battle for Land and Trade

Although the West was far from the main battlefields of the American Revolution, control of this huge area would decide the fate of what is today a large part of the United States. France originally claimed the land along the Mississippi River in 1682, but Great Britain also wanted to control the Ohio River valley and its valuable fur trade.

The struggle for power between these two nations set off a series of battles beginning in 1754 known as the French and Indian War. The Treaty of Paris, which ended the conflict, was signed in 1763. The French colony of Louisiana had been turned over to the Spanish by a secret treaty in 1762, but Canada, the Great Lakes, and the western land went to Britain. British troops took possession of the former French forts in the region. Some French-speaking inhabitants remained, but they became subjects of Britain's King George III.

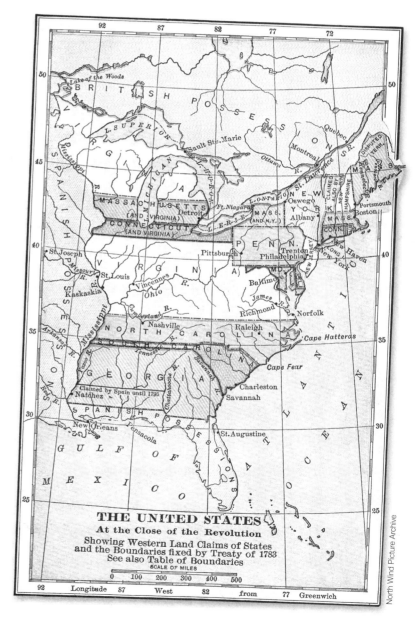

After the British lost the Revolutionary War, a number of American states quickly claimed pieces of the territory that extended into the West. Eventually, that vast land would be divided up into individual states.

Proclamation Line of 1763

The Proclamation of 1763 closed lands north and west of the Appalachian Mountains to settlement. The goal of the British was to put a stop to conflicts that had arisen between the Native Americans and the colonists due to the French and Indian War. This royal proclamation caused a furor amongst the colonists.

Garrisons are groups of soldiers based in, and ready to defend, towns.

Under British Control

Its victory over the French did not give Britain uncontested control of the West, however. Many American Indian groups had considered the French to be allies, so the arrival of British soldiers set off a widespread uprising in 1763. The Indians seized most of the small British forts and attacked frontier settlements in Pennsylvania.

In late 1763, to avoid more wars, the British changed their policies. That year, a royal proclamation attempted to keep American Indians and American settlers separated. It forbade British colonists from crossing the Appalachian Mountains and settling on western land. In addition, British soldiers monitored the fur trade to make sure the Indians were not getting cheated.

The western regions were very tempting to the land-hungry colonists of Pennsylvania and Virginia. Efforts by the British government to prevent settlement seemed unjust to the American colonists. Increasing numbers of settlers defied British troops and the Indians. Crossing the mountains, these colonists built homes in the rich valleys of present-day West Virginia and Kentucky, which were originally part of Virginia.

A New Alliance

This movement brought Virginia frontiersmen into open conflict with the Indians in what is known as Lord Dunmore's War of 1774. For the Native Americans, who feared the loss of their homelands, an alliance with British soldiers against settlers seemed to be in their best interest.

The fur trade made the West of particular importance to the British. American Indian hunters wanted manufactured goods—blankets, guns, knives, beads, and many other items—from Great Britain. Merchants throughout the West traded these for furs. The furs were shipped back to Britain, where many were turned into felt for the manufacture of hats. By the mid-1760s, British Canada's economy had come to depend on the fur trade. The presence in the West of American settlers angered the Indian trappers and threatened the end of the fur trade.

So, British control of the West depended on the goodwill of the Native Americans. It also required **garrisons** of British soldiers stationed along the Great Lakes at places like Fort Niagara, Detroit, and

Michilimackinac. These strong, well-defended posts guarded the fur trade routes from Canada.

Focusing their resources on several strategic locations meant that other parts of the vast new territory the British controlled had to be less defended. Only a few British agents and traders, local French-speaking militia, and Indian warriors guarded the important towns of the western territory farther south from the Great Lakes, such as Vincennes (in present-day Indiana), Cahokia (Illinois), and Kaskaskia (Illinois). By 1775, these settlements lacked large numbers of British soldiers and could not put up a strong defense.

An American Fights for the West

This was the western country into which George Rogers Clark and his tiny force marched in 1778. They were intent on protecting the American settlements within Virginia. But the British were just as determined to keep control of the West and its valuable fur trade. They organized raids against American forts and settlements. And many of the American Indians allied themselves with the British in an effort to keep their land and resist settlers from the East.

Clark, a surveyor and a major in the Virginia Militia, led a force of frontiersmen across southern Illinois and captured the British-controlled settlement of Kaskaskia, which then swore an oath of allegiance to America. His men went on to capture the British Fort Sackville at Vincennes on February 23, 1779. Winter campaigns were not common then, but Clark's men waded through half-frozen streams and camped at night without fires for cooking. His small forces, nearly frozen, still managed to attack the fort and force the British to surrender. Many historians called Clark's victory at Vincennes the most important event of the entire Revolutionary War west of the Appalachian Mountains. And George Rogers Clark himself was the most famous man to come out of this chapter in American history.

The American Revolutionary War in the West would prove to be a bitter fight of wilderness raids and attacks on forts, settlements, and native villages. At stake was the heart of the continent and the expansion of the new United States.

Decades after the Revolutionary War, George Rogers Clark was remembered as the most famous American in the West.

Contest for an Empire
1754 to 1763

Three hundred English settlers asleep in their beds were startled awake by shouts and the sound of axes smashing wood. Two hundred fifty Frenchmen and Abnaki, Caughnawaga, and Mohawk Indians from Canada swarmed through the small Massachusetts settlement of Deerfield on the edge of the wilderness. Many villagers who fought back were killed. Before the raiders were driven away by angry Englishmen, the invaders had taken 112 captives.

A Rivalry Around the World

The people caught in this attack were fighting for something much bigger than their small village. This small battle was part of a worldwide rivalry between France and Britain. In North America, where France held Canada (New France) and Britain held the colonies along the Atlantic coast, they were in competition for control of fishing areas and the fur trade. They argued over rights to the territory fed by the Ohio River. In Europe, they battled to keep each other from taking over other nations and controlling that continent. And in Africa, India, and other parts of the world, they fought for dominance in outlying colonies.

In all, four wars took place between 1689 and 1763. Each was fought in America, Europe, and other parts of

George Washington (on horseback) was a pivotal figure in the French and Indian War from the earliest days.

the globe. Other European powers—Spain, Austria, German states, Sweden, and Russia—also took up the battle. These wars changed not only the future of North America but also the future of the world.

Two World Powers Clash

France and Britain were equally powerful in America but in different ways. France had strong central control in its territory, whereas Britain had thirteen colonial governments that did not always agree. But when the wars began, the British colonies had more than two hundred thousand settlers, while New France had only twelve thousand colonists and traders. England had a stronger navy and more money to wage war, but the French had a widespread friendship with native inhabitants across half the continent.

These Indian alliances were important. Many tribes that profited from the fur trade joined the French. The six Indian nations of the Iroquois League fought with the British, but their alliance was not as strong as that between the French and other tribes.

These four wars came to be called the French and Indian Wars in North America. The European battles were given other names. The fourth war, which began as border skirmishes in 1754, erupted two years before war was officially declared. It is most commonly known as the French and Indian War.

Today historians prefer to call this conflict the **Anglo**, French, and Indian War. Only the British considered it a fight against the French and Indians. For the French, it was a fight against the British and Indians. If they had won, they probably would have called it the Anglo and Indian War. They also would have gained control of the North American continent, and you might be reading this in French instead of English.

Anglo is another word meaning British.

Above: A hand-colored woodcut of the French and Indian attack on Schenectady NY, winter of 1689–90.

Left: A Map of the British and French settlements in North America.

Breaking Up is Hard to Do

The American Colonies and the British government had a difficult relationship in the mid-1700s. England wanted the Colonies to obey its rules and recognize its authority. But the colonists were growing restless with the treatment shown them by the British Crown. To complicate matters, the Colonies were separated geographically from England by the Atlantic Ocean. During the eighteenth century, travel between the two countries/continents took months. Governing and being governed became very difficult for those on each side of the water.

The first British colonists who came to the New World in the early 1600s struggled to make their home in the new, unknown land. They came for different reasons—freedom of religion, the hope of finding riches, the chance of a better life. But many of these early settlers also shared some characteristics: They were adventurous risk takers and inclined

All was not well in the Colonies in the 1770s. In this view of the Boston Massacre, British regulars, surrounded by an angry mob, shoot to defend themselves.

This is one of the lanterns that hung in the Old North Church steeple. It signaled the start of a long night for alarm riders such as Paul Revere.

to independent mindedness. Those roots ran deep enough to carry over to the patriots of the next several generations.

The people who became embroiled in the Revolutionary War in 1775 still thought of themselves as British citizens. However, many of the people living in the Colonies in the mid-1700s had been born in the New World. Some had never even traveled to England. Their homes, families, and businesses—everything that was familiar—were in the Colonies.

Between 1689 and 1763, there had been constant warring among European countries over control of colonial North America. The American **militia** and British soldiers had fought side by side in this series of battles, known as the French and Indian Wars (1754–1763). But the cost of these overseas wars left the British government deeply in debt. The king and **Parliament** decided to raise badly needed money by imposing taxes on the Colonies.

The colonists viewed these taxes and other attempts to control them as unfair. Why should England be allowed to tax them when the colonists did not have any representatives in Great Britain who could convey their interests? Why was England sending soldiers to America at the colonists' expense? Why were the colonists being treated as second-class citizens? The rumble from these and other questions circulated by the colonists began to grow.

From 1764 to 1775, England enacted a series of taxes on the American Colonies. (See the timeline for more information about those specific events.) The men and women of Massachusetts particularly were opposed to England's policies. They formed political resistance groups, such as Boston's Sons of Liberty and Daughters of Liberty, and **boycotted** the taxed goods. But whenever the British government repealed one tax in the Colonies, it quickly introduced another.

Word of England's actions and its harsh treatment of the Bostonians spread beyond that colony's borders to other American cities and settlements. Individual colonies up and down the East Coast of America began to recognize that a break with England was looming. They also sensed that their strength to pursue such action would lie in supporting one another.

> A **militia** is an army made up of ordinary citizens, rather than professional soldiers.
>
> **Parliament** is the national legislature of Great Britain (among other countries).
>
> **Boycott** means to act together to stop buying or using something as a form of protest.

Stamps such as these were applied by the British to goods sold in the Colonies—with the cost of the stamp coming out of the colonists' pockets.

THE PATH TO WAR

A Timeline of Major Events

1764 — Sugar Act of 1764
British prime minister George Grenville introduces this tax, which reinforces a previous molasses sugar tax.

1765 — Stamp Act of 1765
This law is the first direct tax imposed on the American Colonies. Its purpose is to raise money for the military defense of the Colonies. It requires that all paper products (newspapers, legal documents, advertisements, and so on) bear a stamp. The colonists are angered by this "taxation without representation" in Parliament. They resist the law: It is repealed in 1766.

1766 — Declaratory Act of 1766
This is England's attempt to reassert its power over the American Colonies. The act states that the English government is the authority on all laws passed in the Colonies.

1767 — Townshend Acts of 1767
Named for British statesman Charles Townshend, these acts attempt to collect **duties** on items—such as glass, lead, paints, paper, and tea—coming into the Colonies from England. The Boston merchants refuse to pay the tax and boycott English goods. By 1770, most of the acts, except for the tea tax, are repealed.

1770 — Boston Massacre, March 1770
Massachusetts citizens resent the presence of British soldiers, who are sent to keep order in the restless colony and enforce the Townshend Acts. The colonists are physically and verbally abusive to the British **regulars**. Provoked by an angry crowd, the soldiers fire on the mob and kill five colonists.

A tax collector is tarred and feathered by colonists who are angry about the Tea Act.

Duties are taxes on imports that are charged by a government.

Regulars are soldiers who belong to a nation's permanent army.

1773

Tea Act of 1773
Introduced by Frederick, Lord North, the law attempts to save the financially strained British East India Company. It gives the company the right to pick merchants—those loyal to the king—in the Colonies to act as exclusive distributors of its tea. It also allows the company to export the tea directly to the Colonies instead of going to Great Britain first. The colonists refuse to support the tax.

Boston Tea Party, December 1773
Frustrated by the Tea Act, the people of Boston organize. They remove and destroy the tea being held on three ships in Boston Harbor.

The men in charge of the Boston Tea Party made every effort to destroy only the hated tea on the ships.

1774

Coercive Acts of 1774
Also known in the Colonies as the Intolerable Acts, these laws are enacted to punish Massachusetts for the Boston Tea Party. Boston Harbor is closed to all trade, and the colony's right to self-government is abolished. The people of Massachusetts are forced to **quarter** British troops. In addition, conflicts between the colonists and royal officials from then on are to be tried in England or another colony.

First Continental Congress, September to October 1774
Delegates from all the Colonies (except Georgia) meet in Philadelphia to discuss concerns over England's colonial policies. Petitions regarding major points of contention are composed and sent to the king.

> **Quarter** means to furnish with housing.

The Wigmaker's Boy and the Boston Massacre

Paul Revere created this engraving to protest the Boston Massacre.

In 1770, the wig shop where Edward Garrick worked was very busy. George III, king of England, had sent hundreds of soldiers to Boston, and each soldier wore a white wig. Six days a week, the teenage apprentices greased, curled, and powdered the long hair of the soldiers' wigs.

After work on Monday, March 5, Edward was standing on King Street. Captain John Goldfinch walked by. Weeks before, another apprentice in the wig shop had shaved this officer. The master had promised the captain's money to that boy, but Goldfinch was slow to pay.

Edward yelled, "There goes the fellow that won't pay my master!" The captain ignored Edward. He had paid his bill that afternoon, but he wasn't going to answer a greasy boy.

Later that evening, Edward was still grumbling about Goldfinch. "He's mean!" the boy complained to his friend, Bartholomew.

Hugh White, the private guarding the Customs House, answered back. "The captain's a gentleman," he told Edward.

"There are no gentlemen in that regiment," Edward cried.

White snapped, "Let me see your face!"

Edward stepped into the moonlight. Clonk! White hit him on the head with his musket. Edward staggered and started to cry. Bartholomew yelled: "What do you mean by abusing people like

By J. L. Bell, *Appleseeds*, © by Carus Publishing Company. Reproduced with permission.

that?" White jabbed his bayonet at the boys.

The apprentices ran away but came back with friends. They yelled "Lobster!" at the red-coated private. And then they threw snowballs.

The noise brought more people. Some had already been brawling with soldiers that night. They surrounded White's sentry box. Men from the Customs House ran for help. Soon more soldiers arrived.

Edward went home, but the crowd grew. People threw sticks and rocks. Angry and afraid, White and six other privates shot into the crowd of unarmed people. They killed five people and wounded six.

To many colonists, this unfortunate event proved that the king's army would kill the king's own people. To many British, it showed that colonists were rude and riotous. And the spark of that violence was just a young

Crispus Attucks

The first person killed by the British during the Boston Massacre was Crispus Attucks. Attucks was a sailor on a whaling ship. Not much is known about his life, but he may have been an escaped slave. Attucks led the group of men who hurled snowballs and debris at the British soldiers. Some accounts say that he threw a piece of wood that struck a soldier. This caused the British to open fire. But others say that he was leaning on a stick when the shooting started. Attucks was hit in the chest with two bullets and died immediately. His body was carried to Faneuil Hall in Boston. It lay in state until he and the other massacre victims were buried three days later.

Death of Crispus Attucks at the Boston Massacre, by James Wells Champney, 1856.

wigmaker who thought a captain hadn't paid for a shave.

Samuel Adams, an agitator who helped start the revolution, called this event the Boston Massacre and had Paul Revere engrave a picture of the scene. Revere, a dedicated Patriot and friend of Samuel Adams, created an etching that showed British officers firing at peaceful Boston citizens. Revere and Adams both knew that this wasn't the way it actually happened, but the drawing was seen all over the colonies and infuriated colonists. Everyone in America wanted to blame the British soldiers for the horrible violence. John Adams, Samuel's cousin, believed the soldiers deserved a fair trial, and represented the redcoats in court. A Boston jury ruled that six of the soldiers were not guilty and two were guilty of manslaughter.

When asked years later about the American Revolution, John Adams, who was later elected President of the United States, said that the most important revolution began even before the war itself. "The revolution was in the minds and hearts of the people," said Adams. John Adams was fighting for something more important than independence from England. He wanted a chance to form a totally new government based on fairness and self-government. Samuel and John Adams believed Americans could run their own nation and elect their own leaders. These cousins wanted to help form an American republic.

A section of a newspaper column with illustration by Paul Revere of four coffins bearing skull and crossbones and the initials of those killed: Samuel Gray, Samuel Maverick, James Caldwell, and Crispus Attucks.

Eager to share their own version of events with the government in Britain, Boston selectmen appointed James Bowdoin, Samuel Pemberton, and Joseph Warren to prepare an account of the Boston Massacre. Their narrative—together with an appendix containing ninety-six depositions—was published as a pamphlet a few days later, and copies were sent to England in response to military depositions.

John Tudor's Diary, 1770

John Tudor, a church deacon in Boston, supported the patriot cause, but disagreed with mob action. He recorded his account of the Boston Massacre in his diary.

On Monday evening the 5th, a few minutes after nine o'clock, a most horrid murder was committed in King Street before the customhouse door by eight or nine soldiers under the command of Captain Thomas Preston.

This unhappy affair began when some boys and young fellows threw snowballs at the sentry placed at the customhouse door. At this, eight or nine soldiers came to his aid. Soon after, a number of people collected. The Captain commanded the soldiers to fire, which they did, and three men were killed on the spot and several mortally wounded, one of which died the next morning.

PRIMARY SOURCE

Captain Thomas Preston's Letter to a Friend, 1770

Thomas Preston was a British officer who served in the Massachusetts Bay Colony. He commanded some of the troops in the Boston Massacre in 1770. Charges were brought against him and other soldiers, but he was acquitted in a trial held in Boston. John Adams was his attorney. It is still unknown whether or not Preston gave the order to fire on the colonists; many historians believe that he did not.

The mob still increased and were more outrageous, striking their clubs . . . against another, and calling out, come on you rascals, you bloody backs, you lobster scoundrels, fire if you dare . . . we know you dare not . . . At this time I was between the soldiers and the mob, [doing] all in my power to persuade them to retire peaceably, but to no purpose. They advanced to the points of the bayonets, struck some of them, and even the muzzles of the pieces and seemed to be [trying to start a fight] with the soldiers . . . While I was thus speaking, one of the soldiers having received a severe blow with a stick, stepped a little on one side and instantly fired, on which . . . asking him why he fired without orders, I was struck with a club on my arm . . . On this a general attack was made on the men by a great number of heavy clubs and snowballs being thrown at them . . . some persons at the time from behind calling out . . . why don't you fire. Instantly three or four of the soldiers fired, one after another . . . On my asking the soldiers why they fired without orders, they said they heard the word fire and supposed it came from me. This might be the case as many of the mob called out fire, fire, but I assured the men that I gave no such order, that my words were, don't fire, stop your firing.

Paul Revere created this image of the Boston Massacre to highlight British tyranny and stir up anti-British sentiment among his fellow colonialists.

Death of Crispus Attucks at the Boston Massacre, *by James Wells Champney, 1856, depicts Crispus Attucks in the Boston Massacre of 1770. Attucks, part African and part Native American, was the first person killed in the American Revolution after a mob attacked a British soldier in front of the Boston Custom House. An escaped slave and a seaman, Attucks was killed by British soldiers, who fired shots into the unruly crowd, killing four people; a fifth person would later die.*

Tea Troubles:
The Boston Tea Party

It was a cold December night in Boston in 1773. The three British ships, the Dartmouth, *the* Eleanor, *and the* Beaver, *were sitting in Boston Harbor, their holds full of tea that wasn't being unloaded because the angry residents of Boston were threatening not to buy or use the tea.*

Tea, Anyone?

The anger was directed at the government of Great Britain, which in May 1773 had passed the Tea Act, a law that almost guaranteed that the American colonists would buy tea from the East India Company. Why? The Tea Act imposed no new taxes on the colonies, but the law lowered the price on tea sold by the East India Company so much that it was way below the price charged by other tea companies. The Tea Act granted the British East India Company Tea an unfair **monopoly** on tea sales in the American colonies. Most American tea sellers would be put out of business.

Why did this law come about? The East India Company wasn't doing well financially and the British government wanted to help the company get back on its feet. The Tea Act was not intended to anger American colonists; instead, it was meant to help the British East India Company get out of massive amounts of debt.

Monopoly: Exclusive control by one group to produce or sell a good or service.

Above: The Destruction of Tea at Boston Harbor, 1773.

The Sons of Liberty

As relations with Britain worsened, a secret society of patriots decided to start taking action. In Boston in early summer of 1765, a group of shopkeepers and artisans who called themselves The Loyal Nine began preparing for **agitation** against the Stamp Act. This group, led by Sam Adams, came to be known as the Sons of Liberty. Members of this secret organization were not the leading men of Boston, but rather workers and tradesmen. The idea found success in many colonies, after the initial organizations in Boston and New York. By the end of 1765, the Sons of Liberty existed in every colony. After the Stamp Act was repealed a year after it was passed, the Sons of Liberty disbanded. But the patriotic spirit and the name remained. Groups of men, such as the ones who dumped the tea into Boston Harbor, were called Sons of Liberty.

This painting by F.A. Chapman shows the raising of a liberty pole in a village center on a festive occasion. There are many spectators, including some disgruntled loyalists. In the background, several men are removing a sign bearing the image of King George III.

Agitation: The act of attempting to stir up public opinion for or against something.

Other tea companies weren't happy about the Tea Act, of course, but the American colonists viewed it as another example of "taxation without representation." In effect, the Tea Act was putting a tax on tea sold by companies other than the East India Company. As with the Stamp Act and other unpopular taxes, they were all voted in by Parliament, which was thousands of miles away, and the American colonists had no way to influence the law or speak out against it while it was being debated in government.

From Anger to Action

So the colonists were angry. They wanted to do something else to let the British know about the unhappiness that the Tea Act was causing. Some people wanted to keep things nonviolent; others wanted bloodshed. The result was somewhere in the middle.

A group of colonists determined to make things change was the Sons of Liberty. Led by such impassioned patriots as Samuel

Adams and John Hancock, the Sons of Liberty had secret meetings at which they discussed how best to get their message across to Great Britain, that the American people wanted more of a role in governing themselves. Christmas was approaching in the year 1773, and the colonists faced another year of unopposed and unrepresentative taxes. The Sons of Liberty decided to take action.

Tea Overboard

On a chilly night of December 16, 1773, over 8,000 people gathered at the Old South Church in Boston. They came to hear fiery Sam Adams speak. He dared the crowd to take action. Later that evening, a large group of the Sons of Liberty disguised as Mohawk Indians stormed aboard those three unsuspecting British ships and dumped 342 crates full of tea overboard. These crates happened to be jammed full of tea, and so the companies that made that tea lost a lot of money that night.

Because the Sons of Liberty were disguised as Native Americans, they could claim that they were not guilty of dumping the tea. The British government knew better, of course, and grew angrier than ever at what it saw as Americans' ingratitude. The very next year saw the passage of what came to be called the Intolerable Acts, one of which closed the port of Boston entirely.

The Boston Tea Party was a symbolic act, an example of how far Americans were willing to go to speak out for their freedom. Two short years later, Americans were willing to give their lives for their freedom, as shots rang out on Lexington Green, signaling the start of the American Revolution.

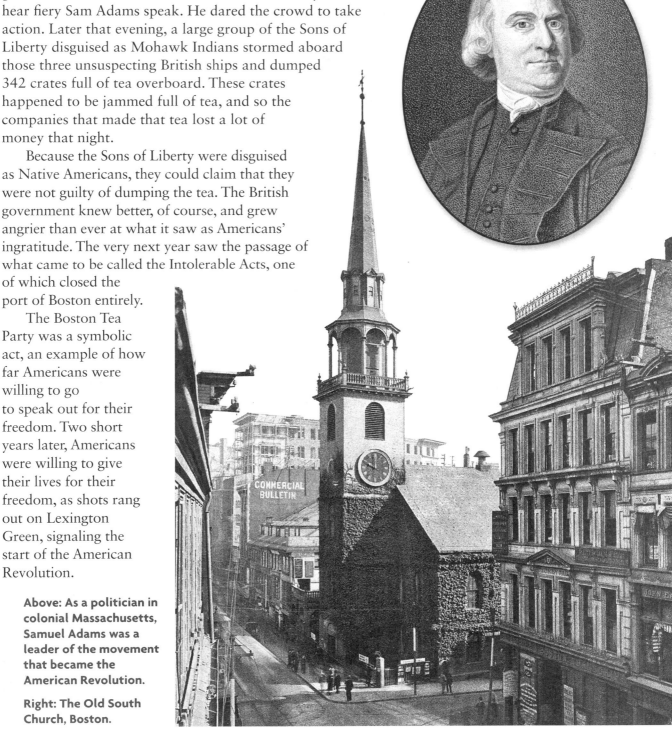

Above: As a politician in colonial Massachusetts, Samuel Adams was a leader of the movement that became the American Revolution.

Right: The Old South Church, Boston.

Just Say No! The Daughters of Liberty

During the American Revolution, women were not allowed to vote or fight in the army. But they found other ways to support the colonial fight for independence. For the first time, many women found a political voice. Some wrote letters and poems about politics, sending them anonymously to local newspapers. One writer criticized colonial men for not doing more to oppose unfair British laws. Her poem ended with the line, "Let the Daughters of Liberty nobly arise." Women were calling on each other to stand up and do their part.

To fight the British, these "daughters of liberty" used the power they had: the power to choose what not to buy.

The Stamp Act was one of the unfair laws women fought. To raise money, the British government passed a law saying that colonial citizens had to pay a tax on every piece of printed paper they used. Everything—from newspapers and marriage licenses to playing cards—was taxed. Many colonists felt that this Stamp Act tax was unfair.

Many women—among them, those calling themselves "daughters of liberty"—agreed to boycott British goods to protest the Stamp Act. These women refused to use

> To **boycott** is to refuse to do or buy something as a protest.

British cloth to make their clothes. Some women even refused to get married if their fiancés applied for a marriage license with a stamp on it! Eventually, the boycott was successful. When British merchants began to lose money because of the boycotts, the British government repealed—eliminated—the Stamp Act.

After the Stamp Act was repealed, the British put another tax on colonial citizens. Now, everyday items such as paint, tea, paper, shoes, and clothes were being taxed. Once again, the "daughters of liberty" said no to British goods. Women who had once bought British fabric now began to spin thread and weave cloth at home. They were proud to wear their homespun clothes as a symbol of their strength. The "daughters of liberty" were standing up to the British.

Then came the Tea Act in 1773. This law allowed British merchants to sell tea in the colonies for less money than anyone else. Many colonists saw this as an attempt by the British government to force other tea merchants out of business. Once the other tea sellers were shut down, the British would raise the prices on their own tea. To the colonists, this was unacceptable.

Patriotic women now refused to buy tea. Because they could not grow English tea in America, they used local plants to make "liberty tea." Using raspberry and mint leaves, verbena and lemon balm, even roses, violets, and goldenrod flowers, they brewed delicious hot drinks. Another popular drink was made from a

Sarah Franklin Bache, daughter of Benjamin Franklin, was well known for her own patriotism and public spirit. Sarah did extensive relief work during the Revolutionary War, raised money for the Continental Army, and acted as her father's political hostess after her mother died.

Esther De Berdt was born in London, England, but moved to Philadelphia after marrying Joseph Reed, an American who had studied law in London. Esther was exceptionally devoted to the revolutionary cause, organizing a women's group which raised money in support of the war and then used the funds to purchase linen and sew clothing for American troops.

plant that became known as New Jersey tea (Ceanthus americanus).

While colonial men fought the British with guns, women fought them with money. When they said no to British goods, they made the British government less able to pay its soldiers in the colonies.

Some people say that in the fight for freedom, the decisions women made when buying goods may have been as important as the decisions men made when they picked up their guns.

Patriotic colonial women spun to avoid importing British cloth.

Have a Cup of Tea?

IN THE COLD, DARK NIGHT of December 16, 1773, about 50 colonial men sneaked aboard three ships in Boston Harbor. Some say the plan was hatched in Sarah Bradlee Fulton's home. They also say it was her idea to dress some of the men in Mohawk Indian clothes and face paint.

The ships that the men boarded were owned by the East India Company and were loaded with tea. Working quietly, the disguised men threw 342 crates of tea into Boston Harbor. Then they sneaked away. Back at Sarah's house, she hid the disguises and scrubbed the red paint off the men. Today, Sarah is often referred to as the Mother of the Boston Tea Party for her help in making this plan work.

This "daughter of liberty" was also known for running messages for George Washington, caring for wounded soldiers, and stealing a load of firewood from British soldiers. Go Sarah!

Liberty Tea

To make your own liberty tea, you'll need to buy New Jersey tea, which can be found in an herb shop.

1. Ask an adult to help you roast the leaves in a 250° oven until they are crisp.
2. Steep 1 teaspoon of roasted leaves in 1 cup of boiling water for 5 minutes.
3. Add sugar or honey, if you like.
4. Now raise your cup to the women who helped fight for American independence!

Interview with Author Louise Borden

Louise Borden has written thirty books for children, including fiction, nonfiction, historical fiction, and biography. She uses extensive research, travel, and poetic prose to craft books about ordinary children experiencing extraordinary events, either historical or contemporary. We talked with her recently about *Sleds on Boston Common: A Story from the American Revolution.*

***Sleds on Boston Common* is such a great story! Tell us about how you got the idea for it.**

The seed for this book was planted in December 1987 when I was sitting in my dentist's office, reading an article about sledding in *Smithsonian* magazine. A few lines of the article mentioned an incident in Boston in 1775–76, involving local children wanting to sled on Boston Common, and a British general. I wrote down the date of the issue, put the scrap of paper in my pocket, and tossed it into an ideas file when I got home. I love snowy days and sleds, and you'll find that sleds appear in some of my other books. For several years after that dental appointment, I kept picturing those kids with their colonial sleds, and the British general in his red coat.

Years later, I called up *Smithsonian* and obtained a copy of the 1987 issue. Then I wrote to Peter Stark, the writer of the sledding article. A year went by. Finally, one day, I received a postcard in my mailbox from Missoula, Montana, from Peter, telling me he had just been forwarded my letter. From then on, I followed my research trail for a picture book.

For months, I was immersed in this Boston legend, trying to find out when and if it really happened. Other steps included corresponding via e-mail with the curators of Firle Place, General Gage's ancestral home in England. Imagine! E-mail research for a story about the American Revolution, a time when it took weeks or months for mail to reach America from England.

And we're curious, since it is historical fiction: what parts of the story are based on actual events? What is fiction?

My original intent was to write about Boston during the Revolutionary time period, Boston Common, and sledding. The story of the four Price children who want to sled ride, and who later meet General Gage, is totally from my imagination. During my own elementary school years in Cincinnati, students were allowed to bring sleds to school as we had a big hill on the campus and anytime we had a good snowfall, we'd enjoy an hour of sledding with our teachers.

After research, I slowly built the story, page by page. I decided to use Henry as the narrator. I felt his voice would make the story more immediate to young readers. *Voice.* It's so very important to me as a reader and as a writer. All kids can relate to school, a birthday present, family, and if they live in a colder climate, sledding. I used these familiar layers but also had the challenge of building the setting, and informing the reader via my text what was going on—that the British had closed Boston's harbor. I love maps, so it was fun creating the mapmaker William Price, his shop, and having his youngest son Henry help him.

I'm glad that SLEDS can help bring young readers into those Revolutionary times. When they open the book, and begin reading the first page, I want them to step into Boston in December of 1774.

Can you tell us about some of the ways you researched the authentic information in the book?

I researched at the New York Public Library, reading books about Thomas Gage, looking for archival papers from when he was stationed in New York City before going to Boston to quell the colonial unrest. I discovered primary documents signed by Gage at a university library. I read books about the Revolution, the history of Boston, Gage, colonial schools, and sledding. I read a few Boston newspapers from December 1774, so I could research the weather.

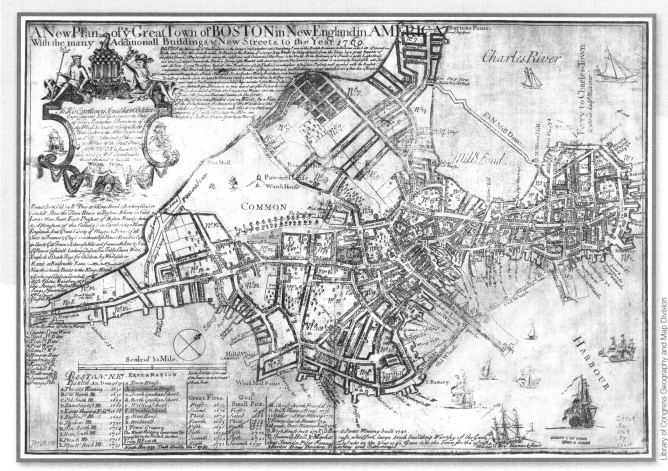

William Price's 1769 New Plan of the Town of Boston.

I looked at many maps of colonial Boston from 1750 to 1780. This map (above) from 1769 was my touchstone. I compared it with present-day maps of Boston, walking the streets around the Common to try to envision it in colonial times. I took details from that map, such as Province House, where Gage lived, and the Writing School on West Street. William Price, who printed and sold the map, was a well-regarded mapmaker. I used his name to honor his wonderful map that helped me so much in my research but I created fictional children whose names I made up. When reading about Thomas Gage, I found out he had a son named Henry, a total coincidence I was able to weave into the story.

Could you share some of your writing process, especially the idea of creating and crafting characters and story lines from primary sources and especially images?

Each book begins because I care deeply about something, such as the image of a young boy standing up to a British general. Each book involves research, whether it's a fictional story or a biography. So, I gather images, make notes about the most essential parts that I need to tell the reader and then I dive in, looking at that first blank page. Sometimes I've already thought about the structure of the book, other times I'm unsure but I know it will evolve as

I start writing pages. The first sentence is so important and often I make changes to that opening page again and again. *Where to begin.* Each book is different but every book helps me to write the next one. I have to hold on to my confidence as a writer—that eventually I will find the right voice, the right details, the right emotional resonance for the story.

Do you have any thoughts or advice for would-be historians? There are so many kids (and adults for that matter) who love things historical.

I attended an elementary school where curiosity was fostered in students. We were all explorers in my sixth-grade classroom, and my teacher wrote on my report card that she thought I would always enjoy research. Then she signed the card *Bon Voyage!* How did she know, this wise teacher, those many years ago?

Explorer. Pathfinder. Compass. These are words that inspire me during the research. And I always want to write a book that has not yet been written. As a student, I enjoyed social studies. I think a love of geography and maps, coupled with true stories in history, drew me into this area of study. Plus, I had some terrific history teachers along the way.

Perhaps, as a kid, I was able to find informational text, primary sources, and inspiring true stories to plant seeds for this lifelong interest. I have vivid memories of a guest speaker who came to our school each year and showed us slides of foreign countries and cultures. I became an armchair traveler in fourth grade.

Being a reader turned me into being a writer. Today I continually read a lot of nonfiction, biographies, etc. I enjoy working in the map rooms of the New York Public Library and the Library of Congress. I think reading widely about other places in the world, other times, and important world events, past and present, will help would-be historians chart their paths. But I've found my own way to add to the conversation about courage, perseverance, war, inventions, and ordinary people who grew up to do extraordinary things. I'm inspired by the people and the times that I choose to write about.

Louise Borden's writing room on a day of revision.

To read more about Louise, visit: www.louiseborden.com

Major Events of the American Revolution

For seven years, from 1775 to 1781, people of the 13 colonies fought a war to become independent from Great Britain. (The final peace treaty was signed in 1783.) The war is called the American Revolution, the Revolutionary War, and sometimes the War of Independence. You can locate some of the "hot spots" and events of the war on this map.

1 Massachusetts

Boston Boston was the center of protest against Britain. The Boston Massacre and the Boston Tea Party both took place here.

Bunker Hill/Breed's Hill Located across the harbor from Boston, these two hills were the scene of the Battle of Bunker Hill, where the Patriots were defeated by the British.

Lexington The "shot heard 'round the world" (the first shots of the war between the Patriots and the British) was fired on the Lexington town green. Paul Revere was on his way here during his famous midnight ride.

Concord The Patriots defeated the British in a battle at Concord's North Bridge.

2 New York

Saratoga The Battle of Saratoga was a turning point in the war. After the Americans won victories there, France gave its support to the colonies.

Ticonderoga Ethan Allen and the Green Mountain Boys captured Fort Ticonderoga from the British in 1775.

West Point The U.S. Military Academy is the country's oldest military post. In 1778, the Continental Army stretched a huge chain across the Hudson River to keep British ships from sailing there.

3 Pennsylvania

Philadelphia The colonies declared their independence here on July 4, 1776. It was also the site of the first Continental Congress, and the place where the founding fathers met to write the Constitution.

Delaware River General Washington, commander in chief of the colonial army, made his famous crossing here on Christmas night, 1776, to defeat British troops in Trenton, New Jersey.

Valley Forge General George Washington spent a hard winter here with his soldiers in 1778.

4 Virginia

Yorktown Site of the Siege of Yorktown, where colonial and French troops fought the British, who surrendered here on October 19, 1781. It was the last major land battle of the war.

Mount Vernon The site of George Washington's home and estate.

5 New Hampshire

New Castle In 1774, American patriots seized powder and ammunition from the British Fort William and Mary, which they gave to nearby towns to use against the British.

6 South Carolina

Charleston The British won an important battle here, but the Americans beat them in the southern countryside.

7 Rhode Island

This was the first state to declare its independence from Britain on May 4, 1776, two months before the Declaration of Independence was signed.

Illustration by Mark Mitchell, *Appleseeds*, © by Carus Publishing Company. Reproduced with permission.

Intelligence, Counterintelligence, and Gunpowder

Depots are storage places for military supplies and equipment.

The arrival of British warships in Boston Harbor in 1768 provoked Paul Revere to create this engraving, which shows large numbers of armed British regulars descending on the "peaceful" city of Boston.

After the Boston Tea Party in December 1773, nearly three thousand English soldiers were sent to occupy that Massachusetts city. General Thomas Gage, commander of all British troops in North America, established his headquarters in Boston and became royal governor of Massachusetts. He had orders to arrest patriot leaders and deal harshly with the Bostonians. But Gage thought that a better way to prevent revolution was to control the colonists' supply of gunpowder.

New England did not manufacture gunpowder, and imported supplies could be cut off. However, many arms **depots** still were available to local Massachusetts militias. Gage planned to bring them all under his supervision.

In the early morning of September 1, 1774, Gage sent troops to a powder depot six miles from Boston. Before the patriots could spread the word that British forces were on the move, the soldiers already had returned to Boston—with the gunpowder.

By Jerry Miller, *Cobblestone*, © by Carus Publishing Company. Reproduced with permission.

An Efficient Intelligence Network

The colonists were determined not to be surprised again. They created a system of alarm riders who would spread any future news.

But before information could be distributed, it had to be gathered. Colonial intelligence networks also were organized. "In the fall of 1774," Paul Revere wrote, "I was one of upwards of thirty . . . who formed ourselves into a committee for . . . watching the movements of British soldiers." This group reported to "[John] Hancock, [Samuel] Adams, Doctors [Joseph] Warren, [Benjamin] Church, and one or two more." Stablehands, barmaids, and others who could eavesdrop on British officers reported their findings to Revere.

The patriots received information from other sources as well. Warren had a highly placed informant (meaning one involved with high-ranking British officers) whose identity only he knew. These networks were so efficient that patriots sometimes knew the contents of orders from England before they even reached Gage.

The Counterintelligence Efforts

However, Gage also knew the colonists' plans. Army officers, royal officials, and **Loyalists** kept him informed. His best spy was actually one of the men to whom Revere reported: Dr. Benjamin Church was betraying his fellow patriots for money.

In December 1774, Gage decided to send ships to Portsmouth, New Hampshire, to bring back gunpowder that was stored in Fort William and Mary. The fort was guarded by only six British soldiers. But winter weather delayed the ships' departure. Traveling on horseback, Revere was able to notify the people of Portsmouth of Gage's plan. Patriot militiamen assaulted the fort and carried away the gunpowder and arms. Two slightly wounded **redcoats** were the only casualties.

Gage's next target was Salem, Massachusetts. By imprisoning some of Revere's "watchers," British troops were able to leave Boston without the patriots' knowledge. They were seen on the march, however, and alarm riders carried the message. By the time the British arrived in Salem, a drawbridge leading to the arms **cache** had been raised. The English troops were stalled. As colonial militiamen came pouring into Salem, the outnumbered British retreated empty-handed.

While Paul Revere certainly became the most famous of the alarm riders (shown here arousing townspeople along the road to Concord), he was just one of many colonists who helped carry the news about British plans.

> **Loyalists** were Americans who favored the British.
>
> **Redcoats** were British soldiers serving during the American Revolution.
>
> A **cache** is a hiding place used for storing provisions.

Samuel Adams (above left) was one of the first colonial leaders to push for a complete separation from Great Britain. He became an important man for the British to watch. British commander General Thomas Gage (center) grew frustrated at the constant leaking of secret information to the patriots. Patriot intelligence leader Dr. Joseph Warren (right) asked Paul Revere and William Dawes to set out on the night of April 18 to warn John Hancock and Samuel Adams that the British were headed their way.

Though Gage had failed twice, he was determined to try again. He sent two British officers to "walk the countryside" and discover whether a raid on Worcester or Concord would have a better chance of success. They reported that targeting Worcester would be too dangerous. Concord, by way of Lexington, was closer to Boston and would be safer.

British Plans Discovered

Although the officers wore disguises, their questions raised colonial suspicions. Their travels were watched closely, and Gage's plan was discovered. The one unknown, however, was when the British troops would move.

On April 18, 1775, Revere received several reports that British units were preparing to leave for Concord the next morning. Warren contacted his informant to verify the news. He learned that English troops would march the next day.

In an effort to keep Gage's plans secret for as long as possible, all exits out of Boston were guarded by the British. Twenty mounted English soldiers were sent to patrol local country roads and intercept any messengers. But Revere and William Dawes would try to get the news through anyway. In case they failed, it was determined that lanterns placed in the steeple of the Old North Church in Boston also would signal the message to a rider in Charlestown.

Riders Sound the Alarm

Both Revere and Dawes succeeded in slipping out of Boston. Then Revere managed to avoid capture by outriding patrollers just outside the city. Although they followed different routes, Revere and Dawes both arrived in Lexington around midnight. They warned Adams and Hancock that the British were on the move. Revere and Dawes then rode together toward Concord.

On their way, the men met Dr. Samuel Prescott, a young patriot who agreed to help them. Soon, several English patrollers stopped the three. Revere's horse was too exhausted to escape, and Dawes was thrown from his mount. Though Revere and Dawes were prevented from finishing their journey, the soldiers allowed them to walk away. Prescott got away by jumping over a stone wall. He took the news, gathered by so many, the last five miles to Concord.

John Hancock's home (upper right) was on Boston Common, a large grassy area in the city. With British troops stationed there, each side could watch the comings and goings of the other.

Watchful Eyes in Boston

The city of Boston was a dangerous place in the 1770s. Unruly mobs roamed the streets. They threatened violence to supporters of England. Meanwhile, British soldiers armed with guns patrolled the city.

The patriots were gathering equipment for war. At the same time, more and more British soldiers were arriving in Boston. Each side wanted to figure out what the other was going to do.

Because the British and the patriots were living in the same city, they could watch each other. Because they spoke the same language, they could listen to each other. They could also use spies.

Some of the Americans living in Boston supported the British. They were known as Loyalists. Some were merchants, some were farmers, and some were craftsmen. They lived among the patriots. But often they were not publicly known as Loyalists.

On the patriot side, Paul Revere joined a group of craftsmen who held meetings at a Boston tavern. They took turns wandering the city streets at night to watch the movements of British soldiers.

Unknown to Revere and his friends, there was a Loyalist spy in their midst. Dr. Benjamin Church was trusted by Revere's group. But secretly he was giving information to the British about patriot activities.

Two British soldiers, disguised as civilians, walked around the countryside outside Boston to learn about military planning by the patriots. The spies were quickly identified as British agents. They were closely watched during their entire journey by keen-eyed patriots.

Watchful ears and eyes gave Revere a signal to begin his "midnight ride." Some historians say that a patriot who worked in a Boston stable heard two British soldiers talking about their plans to march on Concord. He passed the word to Revere, and the patriots' warning system went into high gear.

By Mike Weinstein, illustrated by Tim Foley, *Appleseeds*, © by Carus Publishing Company. Reproduced with permission.

The Famous Ride of Paul Revere

Paul Revere loved his children and grandchildren. (He had at least 51 grandchildren!) He called them his "little lambs." Imagine that you are sitting with Paul Revere and some of those grandchildren, hearing about the famous ride of April 18, 1775. Listen!

The British were going to march, our spies told us. Soon, they would cross the Charles River. From there they could capture Samuel Adams and John Hancock, who were in Lexington planning the fight against the British. Then they could march on to capture our patriot weapons, stored in Concord. Adams and Hancock had to be warned. The townspeople had to be warned, too, so that they could defend our weapons. The Regulars—the British soldiers—were coming, and people needed to know!

I had a plan already. First, I hurried to Christ Church, to give a warning to those waiting across the river. We had agreed on a code: one lantern would be lit in the church steeple window if the British were to leave Boston by land, two lanterns would be lit if they were to leave by the river. Light two lanterns, I told my friend who waited in the steeple.

Two friends were waiting to row me across the river to Charlestown. But in the excitement, I had forgotten my spurs! Then I noticed that my little dog had followed me. I wrote a quick note to your grandmother, tied it around the dog's neck, and sent the dog home. The dog returned shortly—carrying my spurs.

Again we were about to start, when we realized that we had not brought a cloth to muffle the squeak of the oars. One of the men had a sweetheart who lived nearby. He whistled at her window. I heard whispers and a rustle of clothing. Then the lady tossed down her petticoat! It was still warm as we wrapped it around the oars.

In Charlestown, my friends met me with a horse. I set off immediately. Once, two soldiers on horseback chased me. But they were no match for the fine horse I rode. In Medford, I woke up the captain of the militia, our patriot soldiers. Then I raised the alarm at every house from there to Lexington: "The Regulars are out! The Regulars are out!" I cried.

I arrived in Lexington around midnight. Sam Adams and John Hancock had been staying there with Hancock's relatives. I warned them that the British soldiers were coming. I had only a short time to rest my horse. Then I set off for Concord to alarm the people there. William Dawes, another Boston messenger, came with me. Soon we met up with Samuel Prescott, a local doctor.

Paul Revere's Horse

Paul Revere was a fine horseman, but he didn't ride his own horse on the night of April 18, 1775. John Larkin, a wealthy patriot, loaned Revere his finest, fastest horse. Even after all these years, we still are not sure of the horse's name. Revere simply called it "a very good horse." Larkin family history tells of a brown mare named Brown Beauty. Was that the horse Revere rode, a horse with the speed and endurance of an Arabian stallion?

Revere reached Lexington safely, but on the road to Concord, he and the horse were ambushed by a British patrol.

"I know what you are after and have alarmed the country . . . ," Revere said.

Eventually, the Redcoats took Paul Revere's horse, and he had to walk the rest of the way. The horse was never returned. Paul Revere's borrowed horse was the first prisoner of the Revolution.

We had gotten about halfway to Concord. Suddenly, I saw a group of officers ahead. In an instant, we were surrounded. The officers ordered us into a pasture. One of my companions jumped his horse over a stone wall. The other got away, too. But I was caught.

A British officer pointed a pistol at me and began to question me. I told him that I knew what they were after. "I have alarmed the country," I said. "There will be 500 Americans here soon!" I could see that my words surprised them.

The officers marched me back toward Lexington, all the while calling me a rebel. Just as we neared the town, we heard gunshots. "What was that for?" one of them asked. I answered that it was to alarm the town. Well, this worried them so much that they let me go—but not before taking that fine horse!

I trudged back to Lexington and found Sam Adams and John Hancock preparing to leave. Mr. Hancock asked me to fetch a trunk he had forgotten. That was what I was doing when I saw the British troops march in, all red coats and brass buttons! Not minutes later, I heard a shot, then two. Then there was a roar of gunfire. I had just heard the first shots of the American Revolution!

But that is a story for another time. Good night, my little lambs!

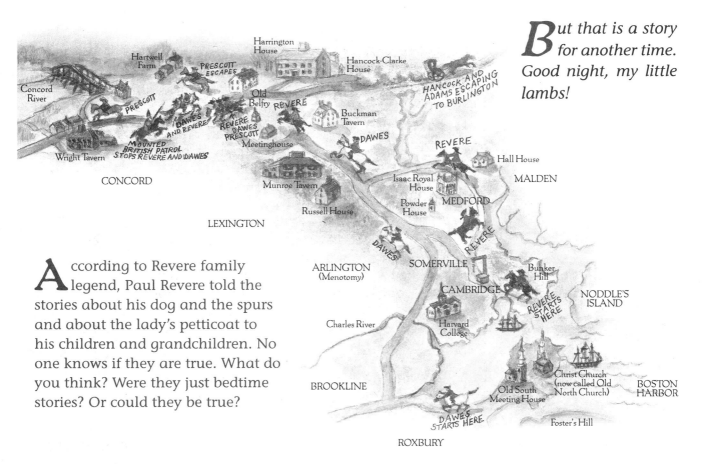

According to Revere family legend, Paul Revere told the stories about his dog and the spurs and about the lady's petticoat to his children and grandchildren. No one knows if they are true. What do you think? Were they just bedtime stories? Or could they be true?

They Rode, Too

It's true that Paul Revere has gotten most of the credit for the famous April 1775 ride. But William Dawes and Samuel Prescott played important roles, too.

William Dawes

Joseph Warren contacted me on that famous April night. He instructed me to take the land route out of Boston, and to warn the towns of Roxbury, Cambridge, and Menotomy [now called Arlington]. Then I was to travel on to Lexington and warn Samuel Adams and John Hancock of the British threat. I had made a few rides for the freedom fighters before, but my face was not as well known as that of Paul Revere, so Warren thought my chances of being recognized by the British were less. Actually, I had befriended some of the British guards, since I traveled frequently, and some of them allowed me to slip through the checkpoints. I am also, if I say so myself, a fair actor, and several times I pulled on a big hat and changed my voice to sound like a drunkard or a country farmer. By 12:30 AM, I had reached Lexington and joined Revere. We continued on toward Concord. We met up with young Dr. Samuel Prescott and rode together until a British patrol stopped us. We all tried to break free, and in the confusion, I yelled out in as many different voices and accents as I could that I had captured some of the American Regulars! In this way I was able to escape. I lost my watch and my horse, but I was able to walk back to Lexington.

Samuel Prescott

I had just been to visit my fiancée and was enjoying a quiet ride home on that warm April night. Suddenly two men came galloping toward me out of the darkness. I learned that it was Paul Revere and William Dawes, and that they had been sent to warn the citizens and **Regulars*** that the British troops were on the move. Well, since I was local to the area and knew all the roads well, I offered my help to spread the word. When the British patrol intercepted us, I leaped over a nearby wall and made my escape. I made my way back to the main road and continued on, warning each house that I passed. I made it to the town of Concord—the only one of the three of us who did—and warned them as well.

* **Regulars** were paid professional soldiers who fought for the colonies.

PRIMARY SOURCE

Paul Revere's Letter to Dr. Jeremy Belknap, 1798

In this letter to Dr. Jeremy Belknap, Paul Revere summarizes his activities on April 18 and 19, 1775. He recounts how Dr. Joseph Warren urged him to ride to Lexington to warn John Hancock and Samuel Adams of British troop movements, how he had previously arranged with some fellow Patriots to signal the direction of those movements by placing signal lanterns in the steeple of Old North Church, and how he left Boston from the "North part of the Town," was rowed across the Charles River by two friends, and there borrowed a horse and began his ride. In this excerpt, he describes how he avoided British soldiers and reached Lexington.

I set off upon a very good horse; it was then about eleven o'clock and very pleasant. After I had passed Charlestown Neck, I saw two men on horseback under a tree. When I got near them, I discovered they were British officers. One tried to get ahead of me, and the other to take me. I turned my horse very quick and galloped toward Charlestown Neck, and then pushed for the Medford Road. The one who chased me, endeavoring to cut me off, got into a clay pond near where Mr. Russell's Tavern is now built. I got clear of him, and went through Medford, over the bridge and up to Menotomy. In Medford, I awaked the captain of the minute men; and after that, I alarmed almost every house, till I got to Lexington.

Militias and Minutemen

Many myths surround the first battle of the American Revolutionary War. Chief among these is that the victorious Americans were just a bunch of embattled farmers who, without training or leadership, hid behind trees and took shots at the retreating British.

Today, historians tell a different story. They point out that the battle was won as battles have always been won: by bringing superior force to bear on an enemy. The American patriots had twice as many soldiers as the British. And these men were able to assemble with astonishing speed. In addition, not all the New England fighters were simply farmers; the patriots had many trained soldiers in their ranks.

Militias

Beginning in the 1600s, Massachusetts towns established militias. These were to be available at the local governor's discretion. Made up of able-bodied males between sixteen and sixty years old, these men voted for their officers and **mustered** four times a year for training, usually on the local village **green**. The town, which paid for the training and some of the weapons, often stored its militia's ammunition.

Initially, the purpose of the militias was to provide forces capable

Compared with the British regulars (inset), the militiamen (top) did not have the organized "look" of an army with uniforms and all the same weapons, but their experience in the French and Indian Wars made them worthy opponents.

Mustered means called troops together.

The **green** is a grassy area usually located in the center of a town and set aside for common use.

By Malcolm C. Jensen, *Cobblestone*, © by Carus Publishing Company. Reproduced with permission.

Smoothbore means having no spiral grooves within the barrel of a gun.

Flintlock is a device in which a flint in the hammer of a gun produces a spark that ignites a charge.

Paper cartridges were tubes in which gunpowder and musket balls were wrapped together to speed up loading.

Minutemen in Stockbridge, Massachusetts, set out for Lexington and Concord once the news reaches them about the fighting there.

of defending the towns and the outlying farms against Indian raids. As the Colonies grew, the militias became an instrument of attack. Towns began to coordinate small groups of militias from a wide area into a larger force, which then would be sent long distances to destroy Indian settlements.

Minutemen

Out of the militias sprang an elite group within each town that was selected for special training. The minutemen were required to be ready to arm themselves and gather "at a minute's notice." They were mostly young men in their twenties, who often selected their own officers. The officers were usually among the most respected members of the community. They had had previous military experience, which was gained fighting alongside English regulars in a series of wars against the French and their Indian allies.

Neither the typical British officer (usually upper class) nor the typical British soldier (mostly lower class) understood the colonial militia. They looked down on the militiamen as men who lacked the courage to march into battle against volleys of gunfire. Yet, an average company of militiamen was made up of a cross-section of New England middle-class society. Most militiamen and officers could read and write. They often were propertied taxpayers or the sons of prosperous families. Many had some specialized skill or trade—furniture making, medicine, milling, blacksmithing, or innkeeping—that gave them income, status, and a voice in the community.

Lexington and Concord

In the winter and early spring of 1775, many colonial militias knew that war was approaching. It was an unusually mild winter, and the militias took advantage of it by calling for additional training. Some companies of minutemen trained four half-days each week. This training paid off. The militias were more disciplined under fire than the British regulars.

The militiamen and officers at Lexington and Concord understood that it was important for the English to fire first. This had been stressed often by Massachusetts leaders such as Samuel Adams, John Hancock, and Dr. Joseph Warren. They wanted Americans to be seen as the victims of British violence, not the cause of it.

For the most part, the colonial militiamen and the British soldiers were outfitted with much the same types of weapons—**smoothbore flintlock** muskets, bayonets, and **paper cartridges** for rapid firing.

By Malcolm C. Jensen, *Cobblestone*, © by Carus Publishing Company. Reproduced with permission.

While both sides were trained to aim when firing their weapons, the militiamen clearly aimed at individual targets—particularly British officers, who were easy marks. Often the English shot high, which military experts today consider a sign of poor training.

Once the fighting began, some militia companies broke ranks and took shots at the British anytime they could. Others, such as Captain John Parker's men, continued to function as a unit and later ambushed the British **column**. Other militiamen rode their horses to a weak point along the British column, fired, and then rode on to find another good location.

Some colonists, though too old to join the militia, took up arms anyway. Samuel Whittemore, a seventy-eight-year-old veteran of the French and Indian Wars, took his musket, two pistols, and a saber, and positioned himself close to the British line. He killed three men, and then was shot and bayoneted more than a dozen times by a charging group of British soldiers. He was left for dead, but Whittemore lived eighteen more years, dying at the age of ninety-six.

Regarding the English belief that the colonists were a **ragtag** group of soldiers, Hugh Lord Percy wrote following the battles: "Whoever looks upon [the militiamen] as an irregular mob, will find himself very much mistaken. They have men amongst them who know very well what they are about. . . . Nor are . . . their men devoid of . . . spirit . . . for many of them advanced within 10 yds to fire at me & other officers, tho' they were morally certain of being put to death themselves in an instant."

Between 47 and 55 different militia regiments mustered to fight in the battles of Lexington and Concord.

Column, in this case, means a formation of troops in which all elements follow one behind the other.

Ragtag means diverse and disorderly.

Thomas Thorp's Journal, 1775

During the Battle of Lexington, eight patriots were killed and ten were wounded; only one British soldier was wounded. The British then marched to Concord. The patriots had enough warning to hide most of the supplies and weapons. In Concord, the British split up to occupy the village, guard a bridge, and search for weapons. The minutemen, outnumbered by the British, retreated through the village, crossed the bridge, and took positions behind stone walls. Minuteman Thomas Thorp described the scene in his diary.

We found a great collection of armed men, from Concord and other towns. There were several hundreds, cannot say how many . . . Our officers joined the others. Three companies of redcoats was on the other side of the north bridge and a few begun ripping up planks from the bridge . . .

At the same time, several Concord men shouted "Smoke! The redcoats are torching our town . . ." Captain [Isaac] Davis returned to [us] and drew his sword, and said to the company, "I haven't a man that is afraid to go," and gave the word "March!"

The redcoats run from the bridge and others shot toward us, dropping shots meant to warn and I saw where a ball threw up the water about the middle of the river.

Their next shots was to kill for I heard our young fifer cry out he had been hit, and a major near me shouted "Fire, fellow soldiers! For God's sake, fire."

HISTORICAL IMAGE

An excerpt from
The Battle of Lexington
BY LEMUEL HAYNES

For Liberty, each Freeman Strives
As it's a gift of God
And for it willing yield their Lives
And Seal it with their Blood

Thrice happy they who thus resign
Into a peacefull grave
Much better there, in Death Confin'd
Than a Surviving Slave . . .

—Lemuel a Young Mollato

LEMUEL HAYNES *was a prolific author of essays, poems, and sermons. An excerpt from his poem, "The Battle of Lexington," appears above.*

Haynes, the abandoned child of an African father and a white woman, was born in 1753 at West Hartford, Connecticut. Five months later, he was bound to service until the age of 21 to David Rose of Middle Granville, Massachusetts.

With only a basic education, Haynes developed a passion for books, especially the Bible and books on theology. As a young man, he frequently held services at the town parish, sometimes reading sermons of his own.

When his indenture ended in 1774, Haynes enlisted as a minuteman in the local militia. While serving in the militia, he wrote a lengthy poem about the April 1775 battle of Lexington. In the title of the poem, he refers to himself as "Lemuel a young Mollato who obtained what little knowledge he possesses, by his own Application to Letters." Although the poem emphasized the conflict between slavery and freedom, it did not directly address the slavery of African Americans.

After the war, Haynes turned down the opportunity to study at Dartmouth College, instead choosing to study Latin and Greek with clergymen in Connecticut. In 1780 he was licensed to preach. He accepted a position with a white congregation in Middle Granville and later married a young white schoolteacher, Elizabeth Babbitt. In 1785, Haynes was officially ordained as a Congregational minister.

HISTORICAL IMAGE

Deborah Champion's Cloak

In September 1775, twenty-two-year-old Deborah Champion of Connecticut was asked by her father, Henry Champion, the Continental Army's commissary general, to deliver messages from her father to General George Washington in Boston. Riding on horseback with the family slave, Aristarchus, Deborah headed north and then east, crossing enemy lines in Massachusetts.

She hid the papers for General Washington under the bodice of her dress, and fastened her neckerchief over the bodice. Deborah's mother insisted that she wear a silk hood that fit snugly, and an oversized bonnet to cover her head. Deborah later conceded that her mother's advice was wise. When approached by a soldier wearing a red coat, Deborah covered her face with her bonnet up, and the British soldier let her pass, remarking that she was "only an old woman." The red wool cloak that she wore on her mission is pictured here.

Deborah Champion recounted this adventure in a letter to a friend.

Deborah Champion's Letter to a Friend, 1775

My Dear Patience,

I would have answered your last letter long before now, but I have been away from home. I know that you will hardly believe that such a stay-at-home as I should go and all alone too, to where do you think? To Boston! I will tell you all about it . . .

So, dear Patience, it was finally settled that I should start in the early morning. Before it was fairly light, mother called me, though I had seemed to have hardly slept at all. I found a nice hot breakfast ready, and a pair of saddle-bags packed with such things as mother thought might be needed. Father told me again of the haste with which I must ride and the care to use for the safety of the messages.

The British were at Providence, in Rhode Island, so it was thought best I should ride due north to the Massachusetts line, and then east to Boston. Hiding my papers in a small pocket in the saddle-bags under all the eatables mother had filled them with, I rode on. I was determined to ride all night. It was very early in the morning that I heard the call of the sentry. Now, if at all, the danger point was reached.

Pulling my bonnet still father over my face, I went on. Suddenly, I was ordered to halt. I did so. A soldier in a red coat proceeded to take me to headquarters. I told him it was too early to wake the captain, and to please let me pass. I said I had been sent in haste to see a friend in need. That was true, if misleading. To my joy, he let me go. Evidently he was as glad to get rid of me as I of him.

That is the only bit of adventure that befell me in the whole long ride. When I arrived in Boston, I was so very fortunate to find friends who took me at once to General Washington. I gave him the papers, which proved to be of great importance.

He complimented me most highly on the courage I had displayed and my patriotism. Oh, Patience, what a man he is, so grand, so kind, so noble. I am sure we will not look to him in vain to save our fair country for us.

PRIMARY SOURCE

Patrick Henry's Speech to the Virginia Assembly, 1775

Patrick Henry, a fiery patriot leader, delivered the following speech before the Virginia Assembly on March 23, 1775. His words became a rallying cry during the American Revolution.

They tell us, sir, that we are weak; unable to cope with so formidable an adversary. But when shall we be stronger? Will it be the next week, or the next year?

. . . The battle, sir, is not to the strong alone; it is to the vigilant, the active, the brave. Besides, sir, we have no election [choice]. If we were base enough to desire it, it is now too late to retire from the contest. There is no retreat but in submission and slavery! Our chains are forged! Their clanking may be heard on the plains of Boston! The war is inevitable—let it come! I repeat it, sir, let it come.

It is in vain, sir, to extenuate the matter. Gentlemen may cry, Peace, Peace—but there is no peace. The war is actually begun! The next gale that sweeps from the north will bring to our ears the clash of resounding arms! Our brethren are already in the field! Why stand we here idle? What is it that gentlemen wish? What would they have? Is life so dear, or peace so sweet, as to be purchased at the price of chains and slavery? Forbid it, Almighty God! I know not what course others may take; but as for me, give me liberty or give me death!

PRIMARY SOURCE

Excerpt from The Declaration of Independence

The Declaration of Independence is the statement adopted by the Continental Congress on July 4, 1776, which announced that the thirteen American colonies, then at war with Great Britain, regarded themselves as thirteen newly independent sovereign states, and no longer a part of the British Empire. Instead they formed a new nation, the United States of America. A committee consisting of Thomas Jefferson, John Adams, Benjamin Franklin, Robert Livingston, and Roger Sherman was appointed to draft the declaration. On July 2, Congress voted unanimously for independence. Fifty-five delegates from all thirteen colonies signed the declaration.

In CONGRESS, July 4, 1776

The unanimous Declaration of the thirteen united States of America,

When in the Course of human events, it becomes necessary for one people to dissolve the political bands which have connected them with another, and to assume among the powers of the earth, the separate and equal station to which the Laws of Nature and of Nature's God entitle them, a decent respect to the opinions of mankind requires that they should declare the causes which impel them to the separation.

We hold these truths to be self-evident, that all men are created equal, that they are endowed by their Creator with certain unalienable Rights, that among these are Life, Liberty and the pursuit of Happiness. That to secure these rights, Governments are instituted among Men, deriving their just powers from the consent of the governed. That whenever any Form of Government becomes destructive of these ends, it is the Right of the People to alter or to abolish it, and to institute new Government, laying its foundation on such principles and organizing its powers in such form, as to them shall seem most likely to effect their Safety and Happiness.

Prudence, indeed, will dictate that Governments long established should not be changed for light and transient causes; and accordingly all experience hath shewn, that mankind are more disposed to suffer, while evils are sufferable, than to right themselves by abolishing the forms to which they are accustomed.

But when a long train of abuses and usurpations, pursuing invariably the same object evinces a design to reduce them under absolute Despotism, it is their right, it is their duty, to throw off such Government, and to provide new Guards for their future security.

Such has been the patient sufferance of these Colonies; and such is now the necessity which constrains them to alter their former Systems of Government. The history of the present King of Great Britain [George III] is a history of repeated injuries and usurpations, all having in direct object the establishment of an absolute Tyranny over these States. To prove this, let Facts be submitted to a candid world.

. . .

He has refused his Assent to Laws, the most wholesome and necessary for the public good.

He has forbidden his Governors to pass Laws of immediate and pressing importance, unless suspended in their operation till his Assent should be obtained, and when so suspended, he has utterly neglected to attend to them.

. . .

He has kept among us, in times of peace, Standing Armies, without the consent of our legislatures.

. . .

We, therefore, the Representatives of the United States of America, in General Congress, Assembled, appealing to the Supreme Judge of the world for the rectitude of our intentions, do, in the Name, and by the authority of the good People of these Colonies, solemnly publish and declare:

That these United Colonies are, and of Right ought to be Free and Independent States; that they are Absolved from all Allegiance to the British Crown, and that all political connection between them and the State of Great Britain is and ought to be totally dissolved; and that as Free and Independent States, they have full Power to levy War, conclude Peace, contract Alliances, establish Commerce, and to do all other Acts and Things which Independent States may of right do.

And for the support of this Declaration, with a firm reliance on the protection of Divine Providence, we mutually pledge to each other our Lives, our Fortunes, and our sacred Honor.

Following the Army

Jenna Grilli knows her way around a 1700s battlefield (top)... and is comfortable in the 21st century, too (above)!

About 13 years ago, Jenna Grilli made a decision: "I decided that the best way to learn about life in previous centuries was to experience it firsthand." So she took up reenacting. "I was always very interested in what life was like for people in other historic eras. I spent lots of my time reading primary sources about women's lives in the 18th century," she says. "In my studies, I found that many more British women followed the army than did American women." We asked Grilli to tell us more about her role as a Revolutionary War camp follower.

What was life like as a camp follower?

It was very difficult. The people who followed the army were expected to live almost the same life as a soldier except for fighting in battles or doing fatigue duty, such as cutting down trees. They were expected to travel on foot for quite long distances. Their shoes often wore out, which meant they had to walk barefoot. The family members that followed the army had to be very tough to endure this life.

What sorts of jobs might a camp follower do?

It was rather varied. A woman might have worked as a laundress, nurse, seamstress, or **sutler**. The only official job that would be part of an army organization would be as a nurse. Women were expected to do a rotation in the hospital. During that time, they received full rations—normally they received only half rations. They also were paid by the army for this service. One thing that women were not expected to do was to cook for the men—the soldiers cooked for themselves.

By Andrew Matthews, *Cobblestone*, © by Carus Publishing Company. Reproduced with permission.

Were camp followers official members of an army unit?

In a sense, yes. A specific number of followers was permitted and recognized by the army, and they were provided rations by the army. They were expected to follow army rules and could even face **courts-martial** if they broke any rules.

Imagine cooking every meal outdoors over an open campfire!

Were they paid?

They were paid by the soldiers for individual jobs. For example, a camp follower would be paid for laundering clothing. If she made, repaired, or altered clothing, she would be paid by the piece for that work.

What motivated a woman to sign up for this?

Most men who served in the British army were from the lowest social class and did not own land or real property. This would result in a very uncertain future for a woman's family when her husband left to fight in a war. Following the army provided a British woman with a way to keep herself and her children fed. A majority of the American soldiers, however, did own their own land, so their wives and children were expected to stay at home to keep the households and farms operating while the men were off fighting.

A **sutler** is someone who sold goods to the soldiers.

Courts-martial are courts that try cases in the military services.

Is it true that children also were camp followers?

Absolutely. Children would have been a very large part of the camp follower population. They made their way with the army just like their parents did. No special accommodations were made for children.

Tents (right) offered an army protection from the elements, but lots of people were packed inside each one.

Following an army around resulted in a lot of worn-out shoes (below).

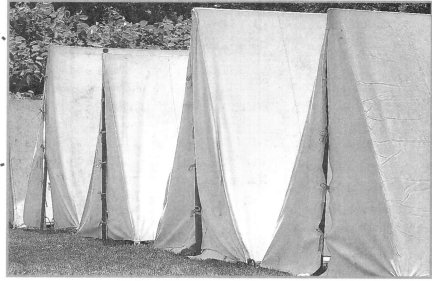

Photos above and top courtesy of Jenna L. Grilli-Schnitzer; boots: Fanfo/Shutterstock.

By Andrew Matthews, *Cobblestone*, © by Carus Publishing Company. Reproduced with permission.

Playing the Bad Guy

In the world of Revolutionary War reenactments, "living historians" portray soldiers on both sides of the conflict. Some choose to portray patriots fighting for America's freedom, while others choose to play what might be considered a more "sinister" role . . .

Two lines of soldiers stand face-to-face on the Lexington town green, eyeing one another warily through the early morning mist. An advance guard of British regulars, on the march from Boston to Concord in search of rebel weapons, are confronted by a crowd of local militia.* The townspeople of Lexington, previously alerted by Paul Revere, have been up all night awaiting the redcoats' arrival and now stand stubbornly in their path. Tensions rise as the British officer orders the Lexingtonians to disperse. Angry words are exchanged between the two groups; this is not the first time rebellious colonists have expressed their defiance toward the king. Commanders on both sides step in to calm their men and de-escalate the confrontation. Just as it appears the colonial militia are about to stand down, a shot rings out. Immediately, chaos takes over. Muskets fire on both sides: from the redcoats in attack, and from the militia in retreat. The British charge forward with their bayonets raised, and the heavily outmanned rebels run for their lives. Then, seemingly as quickly as it started, it is over. The British troops reassemble on the green to continue their march to Concord, and the townspeople rush to assist the fallen colonial soldiers: eight dead and ten wounded.

This confused skirmish is repeated every year, on the third Monday of April, as part of the Patriots' Day holiday to commemorate the battles of Lexington and Concord in 1775. Historians consider these battles to

---

*Although "minutemen" companies—elite militia units that could be ready at a minute's notice—eventually became synonymous with the soldiers of Lexington, in 1775 the town did not have such a company. The local militia at that time was simply known as the "Lexington Training Band."

Scott Thornbury portrays a light infantryman in the 4th King's Own Regiment, which figured prominently in the battles of Lexington and Concord. Members of the 4th wore red coats trimmed with blue. Light infantrymen were expected to be highly agile in order to outflank the enemy.

Manny Gonzales takes on the role of a grenadier in service of His Majesty's 10th Regiment of Foot. The grenadiers, selected for their imposing stature, are known for their tall hats, trimmed with genuine bear fur.

Mary Stone, also in the 10th Regiment of Foot, is fife major in the military band. Musicians were distinguished from soldiers by having the colors of their coats and trim reversed. While women would never have been in uniform in the 18th century, they are welcome to join modern reenactment groups.

For further information about the reenactment organizations featured here . . .

The Lexington Minute Men: www.lexingtonminutemen.com
The 4th King's Own Regiment: www.kingsown.net
His Majesty's 10th Regiment of Foot: www.redcoat.org

be the start of the American Revolutionary War. The scene is carefully choreographed to occur just as it did over 200 years ago. Dozens of experienced reenactors work together to portray both soldiers and townspeople to make the event as realistic and as historically accurate as possible. In order to participate, reenactors must be members of one of several societies dedicated to recreating the life and times of the Revolutionary War period.

One of the most popular reenactment societies, appropriately named the Lexington Minute Men, represents the colonial soldiers (and their families) fighting on the side of rebellion against King George. In the words of the organization's website, "The Lexington Minute Men are dedicated to honoring those brave Patriots who have made the ultimate sacrifice in defense of our Nation's freedom." Other groups recreate the military units that fought on the British side. Among them are the "4th King's Own Regiment" and "His Majesty's 10th Regiment of Foot." These organizations are committed to faithfully represent the soldiers who fought in service of the British Army during the "American War for Independence." So why would a modern American choose to fight on the side of the British in a reenactment? Who would want to play the bad guy?

Several reenactors on the British side stated that they initially began the hobby by portraying members of the colonial militia, but as they became more involved, they grew fascinated by the rich history of the British regiments and by the intricacy of their uniforms. The British soldiers may have all been referred to as redcoats, but in fact there were many subtle differences in uniform between regiments, including trim colors, insignia, and equipment. Each reenactor is responsible for creating his or her own historically accurate uniform, which is entirely handmade using authentic materials. It is a labor of love, requiring many hours of work and research.

Another attractive aspect of portraying a redcoat is the British drill and discipline. Unlike the colonial militia, the British troops were professional soldiers, with a highly regimented routine. British army reenactors spend a lot of time performing field drills. They also emulate the same command hierarchy that existed in an 18th century British regiment. As it so happens, many among the redcoat ranks were former members of the military in their real life; they appreciate reliving the regimental life of a different era.

Many British regiment reenactors cited their desire to better understand the British point of view during the Revolutionary War. As avid historians, they have read deeply about the competing interests and influences at work in colonial America in the late 18th century. Putting themselves in the shoes of a British soldier helps them explore a more nuanced view of the circumstances that led up to the explosive events of April 19, 1775.

Any other reasons? "Well," said one with a wink, "Sometimes it's just fun to play the bad guy."

A Soldier's Gear: Colonial Militia

A The **flintlock musket** was the most common weapon used in battle during the late 1700s and early 1800s. Skilled soldiers could reload and fire a musket three or even four times per minute.

B A musket is loaded by pouring a premeasured amount of gunpowder into the **muzzle**, followed by the musket ball.

C The **flintlock mechanism** ignites the powder to fire the weapon. Pulling the trigger causes the hammer to swing down, scraping a piece of flint against a steel plate to create a spark.

D Soldiers carried a **cartridge box** that held 20 to 30 premade charges of powder and a musket ball, individually wrapped in paper.

E A **powder horn** holds extra gunpowder and keeps it dry.

F A **haversack** is a small pouch used to hold food and personal items. While sometimes made of leather, it was more commonly linen or cotton.

G A **knapsack** holds a blanket and bulkier items.

A Soldier's Gear: British Regiment

A The British Army all used the same standard issue **flintlock musket**, nicknamed the "Brown Bess."

B A **cartridge** is a premeasured packet of gunpowder and a lead ball, wrapped in paper. To load his musket, the soldier tears the top of the cartridge off with his teeth, then pours the contents into the muzzle.

C The **ramrod** is stored beneath the muzzle of the musket. The soldier thrusts it into the muzzle to pack down the gunpowder, musket ball, and the wad of paper from the cartridge.

D Officers in the British Army could be identified by a decorative metal pendant called a **gorget**. It was engraved with a design unique to that officer's regiment.

E The **bayonet** was a fearsome part of 18th century British weaponry. Normally holstered on the hip, the sharp-pointed blade could be affixed to the end of a musket for fighting at close range.

F Only officers were allowed to wear a **sword**, slung on the left hip.

G A **whistle** could be effective in directing soldiers under an officer's command.

Daniel Granger
Boy Soldier

Going to war is dangerous—too dangerous for youngsters. You must be at least 18 to join the Army. But during the American Revolution, a few underage soldiers slipped in. One, Daniel Granger, was only 13 years old when he first served in the Army. Daniel arrived at the camp of the Continental Army near Boston in November 1775. He intended to pick up his sick older brother and bring him home. Instead, Daniel took his brother's place.

"The Weather was extremely cold," wrote Daniel, when he recorded his memories as an old man. *"And Winter Hill was a high bleak & cold place."* Daniel was issued a musket. He had the scary duty of standing guard at camp overnight. *"About eleven or twelve oclock, the Sentinal that was placed above me, heard the ice trickle down from the Rocks as the Tide fell off, which frightened him, I heard him hale, at the Top of his voice, 'Who comes there' twice I beleave, and then fired off his Gun and ran off,"* Daniel recalled. *"I could hear the Drum beating at the guardhouse to turn out the Guard. I cocked my Gun, looked and lissaned, but could see nor hear anything but the trickling of the Ice on the Shore."*

Daniel returned home in the spring to work on the family farm. A year later, young Daniel—now 15—again enlisted in the Army. The Army was marching across the countryside. The soldiers traveled everywhere by walking. They cooked their own food, washed their own clothes, and often slept under the open sky. *"About Nine Oclock, we were halted on a fine Plain, a dense*

Wood on our left hand, and were told that we should have twenty Minutes To take our breakfast. And it was my turn to cook for the Mess. We struck up a fire by a large Stump, on with Kittle, to make some hasty Pudding, & another Kettle to heat water to steep some Tea."

Daniel's march of almost 200 miles brought him to Saratoga, New York. The colonial troops *"were arranged on both sides of the Road, Drums & Fifes playing Yankee doodle, Cannon roaring in all quarters,"* Daniel wrote. *"The whol World seemed to be in motion."* The Battle of Saratoga was a great American victory. After the excitement, Daniel walked home to Massachusetts. On his way home, he awoke one morning to find himself covered with five or six inches of snow.

About a year later, Daniel again joined the Army—this time as a musician. After the war, Daniel returned to the family farm. Later, he became a teacher. But he never forgot his experience as a boy soldier.

Diary excerpts from an article in the *Mississippi Valley Historical Review* (now the *Journal of American History*).

Drummer Boys

Young boy soldiers carrying drums and playing fifes (small flutes) had an important role in the Continental Army. Tired men were cheered by tunes like "Yankee Doodle." Fifers and drummers also spoke a special "language" with their instruments. Different rhythms meant different orders, such as wake up, march, set up camp, and take up arms. Musicians wore special uniforms, usually a reverse of colors from the troops. That way, commanding officers could find them during a battle to tell them what to play next.

From *The Pictorial Field-Book of the Revolution*, by Benson J. Lossing, 1860.

Saving the Day

Fighting in South Carolina, American General Nathanael Greene needed to get an important message to General Thomas Sumter, asking him to join him so that the two generals could mount an attack. Gen. Greene searched for someone brave enough to carry the message through enemy territory, but no one was willing to take the risk. Finally, Emily Geiger, being a good patriot, volunteered to carry the message. Emily left on horseback, under the guise of visiting a relative. She was riding through forests and swamps when suddenly, British soldiers surrounded her. Emily was scared. If the British found the letter, they would arrest her. So she quickly memorized it . . . and then tore it into tiny pieces and ate it! Since there was no evidence indicating that Emily was a spy, the British let her go. Emily was able to continue her mission, and once she reached Gen. Sumter, she delivered the message verbally. Gen. Sumter was able to join Gen. Greene, and the Americans won a big battle thanks to Emily. Emily was truly a heroine during the Revolutionary War.

Battle of Bunker's Hill, June 17, 1775, is a painting by John Trumbull. Painted many years after the revolution, it commemorates the battle that Trumbull considered to be the earliest important event in the war. The painting depicts the death of General Joseph Warren, an influential Massachusetts politician. (Peter Salem, an African American patriot who fought in the battle, appears in the bottom right corner of the painting.)

African Americans joined in every major battle of the American Revolution, showing bravery and loyalty to their fellow soldiers.

Peter Salem, an African American patriot who received his freedom with he enlisted in the Continental Army, fought at the Battle of Bunker Hill in June 1775, at the start of the Revolutionary War. Salem shot and killed British major John Pitcairn, commander of the British troops at Lexington, forcing British soldiers to retreat.

This commemorative stamp honors Salem Poor. Salem Poor was another African American minuteman who fought alongside Peter Salem. He was a free black man who shot and killed British lieutenant colonel James Abercrombie, and was recognized as a brave and gallant soldier in a petition for his heroic deeds to the General Court of the Massachusetts Bay Colony by his white commanders in December 1775.

Colonel John Fitzgerald's Diary, 1776

Colonel John Fitzgerald, one of George Washington's aides, recorded the events of December 25 and 26, 1776 in his journal. During these two days, Washington led his army across the Delaware River and attacked a Hessian regiment in Trenton, New Jersey. Shortly after this important victory, Washington gained another victory over a British force in the Battle of Princeton, driving the British and Hessians out of New Jersey.

Christmas, 6 P.M.—The regiments have had their evening parade, but instead of returning to their quarters are marching toward the ferry. It is fearfully cold and raw and a snowstorm setting in. The wind is northeast and beats in the faces of the men. It will be a terrible night for the soldiers who have no shoes. Some of them have tied old rags around their feet; others are barefoot, but I have not heard a man complain. They are ready to suffer any hardship and die rather than give up their liberty. I have just copied the order for marching. Both divisions are to go from the ferry to Bear Tavern, two miles. They will separate there; Washington will accompany Greene's division with a part of the artillery down the Pennington road. Sullivan and the rest of the artillery will take the river road.

Dec. 26, 3 A.M.—I am writing in the ferry house. The troops are all over, and the boats have gone back for the artillery. We are three hours behind the set time. Glover's men have had a hard time to force the boats through the floating ice with the snow drifting in their faces. I never have seen Washington so determined as he is now. He stands on the bank of the river, wrapped in his cloak, superintending the landing of his troops. He is calm and collected, but very determined. The storm is changing to sleet and cuts like a knife. The last cannon is being landed, and we are ready to mount our horses.

Dec. 26, noon—It was nearly four o'clock when we started. The two divisions divided at Bear Tavern. At Birmingham, three and a half miles south of the tavern, a man came with a message from General Sullivan that the storm was wetting the muskets and rendering them unfit for service.

"Tell General Sullivan," said Washington, "to use the bayonet. I am resolved to take Trenton." . . .

[After the battle:] We have taken nearly one thousand prisoners, six cannon, more than one thousand muskets, twelve drums, and four colors. About forty Hessians were killed or wounded. Our loss is only two killed and three wounded. Two of the latter are Captain [William] Washington and Lieutenant [James] Monroe, who rushed forward very bravely to seize the cannon . . .

Dec. 27. It is a glorious victory. It will rejoice the hearts of our friends everywhere and give new life to our hitherto waning fortunes. Washington had baffled the enemy in his retreat from New York. He has pounced upon the Hessians like an eagle upon a hen and is safe once more on this side of the rivers. If he does nothing more, he will live in history as a great military commander.

HISTORICAL IMAGE

Washington Crossing the Delaware *is a painting by German American artist Emanuel Gottlieb Leutze. George Washington crossed the Delaware River on Christmas night 1776, and captured the enemy garrison at Trenton, New Jersey, the following day. The victory was significant because many of Washington's soldiers' enlistments were due to expire on December 30. This victory improved morale and convinced soldiers to reenlist.*

Loyalists in the American Revolution

Colonial citizens (above) drumming a British Loyalist out of town during the American Revolution.

WHO WERE THE PEOPLE WHO FOUGHT IN THE REVOLUTIONARY WAR? The rebels, or Patriots, and the British were two groups, of course. But did you know that not all Americans supported independence?

Who Were the Loyalists?

Americans who were loyal to Britain during the Revolutionary War were called Tories, or Loyalists. They supported the right of Britain to rule the Colonies. This does not mean that they approved of the Crown's treatment of the Colonies. Many, like the rebel Patriots, were for individual liberties and against taxation without representation. But the Loyalists recognized the king's ultimate authority in America.

Historians estimate about 15–20% of the white male population chose to remain loyal to Britain between 1775 and 1783. In 1780, John Adams believed that 5% of Americans were loyal, but he revised his estimate in 1815 as he reflected on the struggle for independence. He concluded that about one-third of the people opposed the Revolution. Loyalism was weakest in the oldest, best-established colonies, such as Connecticut and Virginia. But although Loyalists were a minority in

By Jean K. Potratz, *Cobblestone*, © by Carus Publishing Company. Reproduced with permission.

every colony, there were enough of them to forestall an American victory.

Why Did They Support the British?

Colonists chose loyalism for many reasons. Although there were exceptions, most Loyalists were landowners, professionals, or government officials, and many were wealthy. In many cases, they remained loyal in an attempt to preserve their standing in the community. Others were influenced by particular circumstances. For instance, in New York, if a landlord supported the rebels, his tenants usually backed Britain. Or if a man's property was plundered by rebels, the owner usually took the other side. Thomas Brown was a Georgia planter who attended rebel meetings in Augusta. He did not agree with the rebels' actions, so he joined a group of Tories and led guerrilla attacks in Georgia's sparsely populated areas, called the backcountry. In contrast, one Loyalist broke his oath of allegiance to the Crown after his plantation was plundered by Tories. Some Loyalists fought not for the king but against men who had wronged them.

How Did They Support the Crown?

Although many Tories protested being drafted by the Crown, about thirty thousand Loyalists wore the British uniform. The Carolina King's Rangers, Tory Rangers, Tarleton's Legion, Rawdon's Volunteers, St. Leger's Loyal Greens, and Pennsylvania Loyalists were some famous Loyalist regiments. Some of these troops fought alongside British regiments, while others hauled supplies and firewood for the British Army. The British rarely organized, supported, or rewarded Loyalist regiments.

In the backcountry of some colonies, fighting was reduced to guerrilla warfare. One Patriot tavern keeper, Colonel Nathaniel Heard, was called the "Tory Hunter." He tracked fleeing Tory judges, lawyers, and doctors to force them to yield to the Continental Congress. He killed some and imprisoned others in camps in the Connecticut hills. Likewise, Loyalists, both individually and in groups, terrorized the countryside.

How Were Loyalists Treated?

The formation of Committees of Safety was authorized by the Continental Congress in 1774. Their purpose was

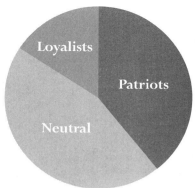

Choosing Sides
Chart showing Loyalist and Patriot sentiments among white men.

Colonel Benjamin Pickman was a Loyalist from Massachusetts.

to relay information, promote the rebel cause, protect patriot property, and identify Tories. They required voters to take an oath of loyalty to Congress or lose their voting rights. In Queen's County, New York, Tory resistance was so strong that travelers had to have passes issued by the local Committee of Safety. Committee members watched for tax evaders, antirebel speeches, and men who refused to serve in the militia. In New York, they stifled freedom of the press by burning all copies of a rebuttal to Thomas Paine's pamphlet *Common Sense*.

Some early Patriots expressed their mixed loyalties in this stamp, which supports both liberty and the king.

The committees arrested and tried many suspected Loyalists. In extreme cases, committee members whipped offenders or applied tar and feathers, a very painful punishment. Loyalists convicted of treason were executed. Little oversight existed to ensure just treatment in committee operations, and some members used their power to settle personal grudges.

Men found guilty of disrupting enlistments were imprisoned, and their property was confiscated. Frederick Philipse was the owner of fifty thousand acres in Westchester, New York. When he fled the country, his property was sold to 287 new owners, most of whom were former tenants.

Loyalists sent to prison suffered the most. The first Continental prison was Simsbury Mine, an abandoned copper mine north of Hartford, Connecticut. Anglicans (members of the Church of England) who were Loyalists, other Tories, army deserters, and felons were sent there. In the jail in Litchfield, Connecticut, William Franklin (royal governor of New Jersey and Benjamin's son) was in solitary confinement for nearly eight months with no furniture or toilet facilities. He even had to pay for his own food.

To escape persecution, thousands of Loyalists fled to British-held cities for protection. When the British evacuated a city, the Loyalists had to either follow the army or remain with the rebels. When the British left Boston in 1776, nearly one thousand Loyalists crowded onto British ships, leaving property and families behind. Those who stayed found life extremely difficult. After the British departed from Charleston in 1782, rebels forced some remaining Loyalists out of their homes, and many were imprisoned, tarred and feathered, or whipped.

Many Loyalists gathered at a large refugee camp on Long Island, New York. Loyalists felt secure there because the British Army occupied New York City. As many as ten thousand Loyalist troops were stationed on Staten Island. About eighty to one hundred thousand Loyalists also fled to England, Canada, and the West Indies. In May 1775, the leaders of the Anglican Church in the Colonies left for England because of religious and political persecution. More than seven thousand Loyalists sailed from New York Harbor on April 26, 1783.

The Loyalists were caught in the middle in the War for Independence. They supported the king of England because they felt that was the best course for the Colonies, but their loyalty cost them their freedom, their property, and in some cases their families and lives.

The Royalist Press

On a bright, sunny day in 1765, members of the House of Burgesses in Williamsburg, Virginia, crowded together, discussing a startling speech given by Patrick Henry. Henry had denounced the Stamp Act that had recently been passed by the British government. But although the delegates found Henry's speech startling, ultra-Royalist* Joseph Royle, editor of the *Virginia Gazette*, refused to print what Henry said because it contradicted his belief that the colonists must remain loyal to the Crown.

The large, literate population of the Colonies eagerly read the many newspapers of the times, and the Stamp Act divided the press throughout the Colonies. Both patriot and Royalist groups used the newspapers as an outlet for their opinions, and as the dispute between the groups became more heated, so did newspaper coverage of the issues. For example, in the late 1760s, John Mein, editor of the *Boston Chronicle*, tried to suppress pro-Revolutionary, anti-British sentiment by making his newspaper a vehicle for bitter attacks on the patriots. Mein eventually was forced to leave the colonies.

Not only did Royalist press face boycotts because of strong pro-British comments, but individual newspapers also suffered physical attacks. For instance, in 1775, editor James Rivington's press for the *New York Gazetteer* was destroyed by Connecticut militia that did not agree with his articles. The patriots dismantled his equipment and melted it down for bullets.

As the war progressed, several Royalist papers, mainly supported by the British government, were started in the Colonies. Hugh Gaine's *New York Mercury* was published in New York from 1776 to 1783, and James Humphrey's *Pennsylvania Ledger* was pubished from December 1777 to May 1778 in Philadelphia. There were fewer Royalist presses in the South, but toward the end of the war, the *Royal Gazette* (Charleston, South Carolina) and the *Royal Georgia Gazette* (Savannah) were published.

James Rivington fled to London after the attack on his press in 1775, but he returned to the Colonies in 1777 to start the *New York Royal Gazette*. Acting as the king's printer in the Colonies, Rivington made the *Gazette* the greatest Royalist newspaper during the war. Rivington later became a double agent, supplying information about the Royalists to General George Washington.

During and after the war, most of the Royalist printers were forced to leave America. The Royalist presses were then taken over by Patriots, who used them to promote the new American republic.

* Royalist is a synonym for Loyalist.

Royalist editors, working in the years before freedom of the press was guaranteed, faced many attacks. James Rivington's press was destroyed by people who disagreed with his articles.

Stockbridge Indian Speech

A member of the Stockbridge tribe gave the following speech to the Massachusetts congress in Western Massachusetts in 1775.

Brothers!

You remember, when you first came over the great waters, I was great and you were little—very small. I then took you in for a friend, and kept you under my arms, so that no one might injure you. Since that time we have been true friends: there has never been any quarrel between us. But now our conditions are changed. You are become great and tall. You reach to the clouds. You are seen all around the world. I am become small—very little. I am not so high as your knee. Now you take care of me; and I look to you for protection.

Brothers! I am sorry to hear of this great quarrel between you and old England. It appears that blood must soon be shed to end this quarrel. We never till this day understood the foundation of this quarrel between you and the country you came from. Brothers! Whenever I see your blood running, you will soon find me about to revenge my brothers' blood. Although I am low and very small, I will grip hold of your enemy's heel, that he cannot run so fast, and so light, as if he had nothing at his heels.

Brothers! You know I am not so wise as you are; therefore I ask your advice in what I am now going to say. I have been thinking, before you come to action, to take a run to the westward and feel the mind of my Indian brethren the Six Nations, and know how they stand—whether they are on your side or for your enemies. If I find they are against you, I will try to turn their minds. I think they will listen to me, for they have always looked this way for advice, concerning all important news that comes from the rising sun. If they hearken to me, you will not be afraid of any danger from behind you. However their minds are affected, you shall soon know by me. I think I can do you more service in this way than by marching off immediately to Boston and staying there. It may be a great while before blood runs. Now, as I said, you are wiser than I; I leave this for your consideration, whether I come down immediately or wait till I hear some blood is spilled.

Brothers! I would not have you think by this that we are falling back from our engagements. We are ready to do anything for your relief, and should be guided by your counsel.

Brothers! One thing I ask you, if you send for me to fight in my own way. I am not used to fight English fashion; therefore you must not expect I can train like your men. Only point out to me where your enemies keep, and that is all I shall want to know.

The British persuaded thousands of Native Americans to fight on their side in the war. In this painting, British General John Burgoyne addresses warriors from several nations in July 1777, as he begins his invasion of northern New York.

Native Americans from several small tribes in New England and the South volunteered to fight for the Americans early in the war. This may have given the Marquis de Lafayette, seen in this painting with George Washington, the idea to recruit the Oneida Nation to send 49 men to fight in May 1778.

George Washington was deeply impressed by the courage of the Oneida and their fighting abilities. The next year, warriors from the Oneida Nation and the Tuscarora Nation were commissioned as American lieutenants and captains. For the rest of the war, these Native American officers and soldiers fought the British and their Native American allies in northern New York.

Other Native peoples to fight on the American side were the Stockbridge Indians of Massachusetts, the Mashpee of Cape Cod, and the Catawba of the western Carolinas. But the Oneida Nation made the greatest contribution; an estimated three thousand Oneida warriors fought for the United States. Despite severe retributions by the Mohawk Indians and other tribes who sided with the British, the Oneida Nation remained loyal to the Americans until the end of the war. When peace came in 1783, the thankful Americans gave Oneida officers and men grants of land for their courage and devotion during the struggle for freedom.

Secret Help from Spain

Early in March 1776, a French secret service agent named Pierre de Beaumarchais wrote to Jerónimo Grimaldi, Spain's foreign minister. Beaumarchais' letter was simple and direct. France would provide money and supplies to help the American colonists in their fight against England. Would Spain do the same?

Grimaldi wasted little time in answering. "It is certainly desirable to us that the revolt of the people keep up," he wrote in reply. An agreement was reached. That summer, Grimaldi delivered one million French **livres**, along with instructions to use the money to arm the American rebels, to Beaumarchais.

This transaction was the first of many secret payments made throughout the Revolutionary War by Spain to the colonists. Those most instrumental in providing the support were two Spanish foreign ministers: Grimaldi at the start of the war in 1776, and José Moñino y Redondo, Conde de Floridablanca, beginning in 1777.

Livres were a currency worth a pound of silver each, formerly used in France.

Aristocrats are members of a ruling class or nobility.

Bayonets are blades made to fit the end of a rifle, used in close combat.

Oddly, Grimaldi and Floridablanca were not enthusiastic supporters of the American rebels and their fight for independence. As **aristocrats** who served kings, Grimaldi and Floridablanca disapproved of popular revolts. As officials of a country that held New World territories of its own, the two had little sympathy for rebellious colonies. Instead, both men supported the Americans out of national self-interest. Neither had any love for England, a longtime enemy of Spain. An exhausting, drawn-out struggle would weaken the English military, the ministers reasoned. This result would be good for Spain.

In addition, the ministers feared that a new American nation might threaten the land that Spain had claimed around the New World colonies. A colonial war with England would reduce the chance of attacks on Spanish holdings. "We ought to want the English and [the colonists] to exhaust themselves," wrote Grimaldi.

Grimaldi and Floridablanca provided enough equipment and money to the weaker American side to keep the war going. Before leaving office, Grimaldi arranged for delivery to the New World of more than 200 cannon, 4,000 tents, and up to 30,000 uniforms for the soldiers. Floridablanca continued this policy by sending **bayonets**, shoes, and blankets. And Spain provided the colonists with funds from its national treasury. Obtaining loans from Spanish banks was made easy for the Americans, as was repayment when the colonial governments found it difficult to do so.

However, Grimaldi and Floridablanca were careful not to give the colonists so much support as to risk ending the war in America's favor. Unlike France, Spain remained neutral

Covert means covered up or hidden.

at first. It provided **covert** aid while publicly working to negotiate a peace treaty. After Spain entered the war in 1779, Floridablanca paid for American diplomat John Jay to spend two years in Madrid, Spain. However, the minister complained that Jay kept repeating the same two pleas: "Spain, recognize our independence; Spain, give us some money."

Exactly how much the two Spanish ministers allowed to be spent is unknown: Most of the money was given in secret. Some money was routed through other countries, making its origin hard to trace. Other monies were disguised as loans. Privately, Grimaldi told the colonists that one such payment, officially seen as a loan, really was a gift. "His majesty would do these things out of the graciousness of his royal disposition," he said, "without stipulating any return." Historians estimate that about five million dollars was provided to the Americans.

At a minimum, the Spanish government under Grimaldi and Floridablanca provided the American patriots with many hundred thousand dollars' worth of weapons, clothing, and other materials—all with the king's approval. Nearly the same amount was offered in currency for the Americans to use as they wished.

All in all, it was a fair trade. The Spanish ministers got a war that weakened the British, and the Americans obtained their independence.

Spain's Agenda

Spain hoped to achieve several points as a result of its involvement in the American Revolutionary War. They were: the return of the Floridas in North America, the Mediterranean island of Minorca, and the Spanish coastal land of Gibraltar; control of the Bahamas and Jamaica in the Caribbean; and the end of British presence along the Mississippi River and in Central America. The Spanish were successful in all their positions except Gibraltar and Jamaica.

By Stephen Currie, illustrated by Tim Foley, *Cobblestone*, © by Carus Publishing Company. Reproduced with permission.

The French Alliance

The Marquis de Lafayette was in his 20s when he came to America and helped the Colonies fight for independence.

In late summer, 1777, a young French nobleman introduced himself to General George Washington at an army camp in Pennsylvania. The Marquis de Lafayette had waited a long time for this meeting. When he first arrived in America, he was snubbed by Congress. He was told that America needed supplies and money, not an arrogant Frenchman with little training as a soldier. But Lafayette persuaded Congress that he wanted America's happiness as much as any personal glory. In America's struggle, he saw the best hope "for honesty, tolerance, equality, and a quiet liberty."

A Courageous Frenchman

Washington welcomed Lafayette into his circle of friends. Within a short time, Lafayette was fighting for the American cause. When a musket ball struck his leg in a battle at Brandywine Creek on September 11, 1777, Lafayette continued rallying his men. When Washington reported his bravery to Congress and news of his courage made its way back to France, Lafayette became the link between a great world power and the struggling new United States.

Lafayette had come to America to help fight France's long-standing enemy, Great Britain. His own father had died fighting the British. It was natural that France paid attention when war broke out between Britain and its Colonies in America. A weakened Britain was in France's interest.

A Tenuous Union

As early as December 1776, American commissioners (government officials), including Benjamin Franklin, arrived in Paris seeking French support. King Louis XVI approved money for weapons and supplies, but then problems developed. Commissioner Silas Deane made a nuisance of himself badgering the French ministers of state. British spies stole secret letters. When American privateers* began brashly using French ports, France had had enough. The French were still rebuilding their navy after the last war with Britain and did not want to plunge into another war

*These ships, privately owned and manned, were authorized by the government during wartime to attack and capture enemy vessels.

prematurely. On top of this, news arrived of the British capture of Fort Ticonderoga in New York.

But America needed France's help, and Franklin advised patience. He was rewarded with news of an American victory at Saratoga (October 17, 1777), where a British army of five thousand men surrendered. The fact that the Americans could strike a serious blow against Britain impressed King Louis. Also, rumors were flying that Lord North, Britain's prime minister, might offer peace to keep the Colonies joined to Great Britain, something France did not want.

A Treaty of Friendship

With their navy finally up to strength, the French prepared to make a move. In early January 1778, negotiators began working toward a treaty of alliance. On February 6, France and the United States agreed to a treaty of friendship and commerce, though this was kept secret for another month. Both countries pledged to continue the war until America was fully independent. Neither would make peace with Great Britain on its own. Meanwhile, France hoped to persuade Spain to join the allies. King Louis hoped this would be "for the good of both nations."

When news of the treaty reached Lafayette on June 1, he excitedly kissed Washington on both cheeks. Here, at last, was real help from his homeland—men, money, supplies, and, most important, the French navy.

Both countries hoped the French fleet under Admiral d'Estaing would make short work of the British navy and force the British out of New York with a blockade. Lafayette acted as a go-between for d'Estaing and the American generals John Sullivan and Nathaniel Greene. But no one got along. Worse yet, after several failures, d'Estaing sailed for the French West Indies without capturing or destroying a single British ship.

When the British opened a second front in the South, d'Estaing was again unsuccessful. So far, the alliance had produced only failure and bad

French and American troops soundly defeated the British at Yorktown, Virginia, on October 19, 1781, ending the Revolution.

feelings. But then, in July 1780, came a turning point. A new fleet arrived carrying five thousand French soldiers and the Comte de Rochambeau.

With their beautiful uniforms and equipment, the French awed their ragged allies. But many months passed before Rochambeau and Washington met and began making plans for the summer campaign of 1781. During these bleak times, France bolstered the bankrupt America with new loans.

A Successful Alliance

Washington favored driving the British from New York. Meanwhile, Lafayette was in Virginia using his smaller force to harass the British army there. Any plan depended on the French fleet, now commanded by the Comte de Grasse. In the end, it was Grasse who decided where to strike. When the French sailed to the Chesapeake Bay, Washington and Rochambeau hurried their forces to Virginia. With the French navy blocking the British escape and preventing the arrival of reinforcements, the allies defeated Lord Cornwallis at Yorktown.

Yorktown was the beginning of the end. In early 1782, peace talks began. For a year, Franklin and others pressed for points such as recognition of American independence, acceptable boundaries for America, and fishing rights. The peace treaty, signed September 3, 1783, acknowledged America's independence. The British came out surprisingly well. They kept strong trade bonds with the former Colonies and still wielded great power. It is not unusual after a war for former enemies to work together, which is what happened with Great Britain and the new nation.

France, however, was nearly bankrupt and on the brink of its own revolution. Although Lafayette inherited these difficulties when he later became a leader in his homeland, his friendship with America never wavered. On several visits to the United States, his old allies welcomed him as a hero, remembering his great part in France's contribution to American independence.

Three years after the surrender at Yorktown, Lafayette visited Washington at Mount Vernon, his home (above). Lafayette remembered, "Our meeting was very tender and our satisfaction was mutual."

In this French print (left), George Washington holds two important documents—the Declaration of Independence and the Treaty of Alliance.

WORLD TURNED UPSIDE DOWN

FAST FACT
THERE IS A LEGEND THAT THE MARCHING TUNE *THE WORLD TURNED UPSIDE DOWN* WAS PLAYED DURING THE SURRENDER. RECENT SCHOLARSHIP CANNOT CONFIRM THIS, BUT THE TITLE CERTAINLY EXPRESSES THE FEELINGS BOTH SIDES MUST HAVE EXPERIENCED THAT DAY.

A red-coated British drummer boy climbed alone to the top of a defensive wall. Standing in full view of his enemy, he began beating a slow, steady drumroll. The horrifying artillery **barrage** going on around him made it impossible to hear the drum. Fortunately, Continental Army soldiers could see and understand what they could not hear: The boy was beating the call to **parley**.

RAISING THE WHITE FLAG

When the American artillery finally ceased, a British officer waving a white handkerchief climbed up from the trenches. He was blindfolded and taken to General George Washington's headquarters. It was 10 a.m. on October 17, 1781.

Earlier that morning, British general Charles Cornwallis had inspected his defenses, which were being assaulted by 100 cannon firing from close range. Cornwallis had realized these defenses could be demolished before the end of the day. He would have to surrender or see his army destroyed. He chose the former.

Many homes and buildings were badly damaged during the American bombardment of the British defenses in Yorktown.

A barrage is a heavy shower of artillery fire in front of friendly troops to screen and protect them.

Parley means to discuss or confer, especially with an enemy.

Conceding means yielding or granting.

Cornwallis undoubtedly was aware of the date. Exactly four years earlier on October 17, 1777, an entire British force commanded by General John Burgoyne had surrendered to the Americans at Saratoga, New York. Until this October 17, Saratoga had been the Continental Army's greatest victory and Britain's bitterest memory.

NEGOTIATING THE SURRENDER

The British officer carried a letter to Washington. In it, Cornwallis asked for a 24-hour cease-fire in order to discuss surrender terms. Realizing that Cornwallis still was hoping for reinforcements to arrive in time to save him, Washington granted a two-hour cease-fire and told Cornwallis to present surrender conditions within that time. Cornwallis stalled for time and replied with unacceptable terms in order to prolong the negotiations.

For two days, messengers went back and forth between the British and American camps. Cornwallis argued for easy terms while watching and hoping for relief forces totaling 6,000 troops and 44 ships. Washington tried to hurry the negotiations without **conceding** too much. At 11 a.m. on October 19, the two sides signed a final agreement. Washington ordered that the surrender ceremony be held just three hours later.

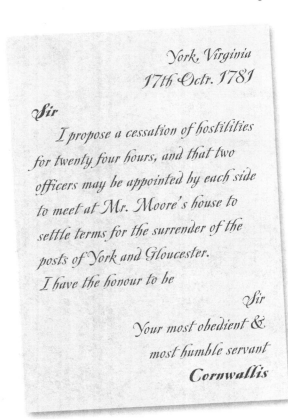

York, Virginia
17th Octr. 1781

Sir
I propose a cessation of hostilities for twenty four hours, and that two officers may be appointed by each side to meet at Mr. Moore's house to settle terms for the surrender of the posts of York and Gloucester.
I have the honour to be
Sir
Your most obedient & most humble servant
Cornwallis

By one o'clock, the road leading out of Yorktown was lined with French and American troops. The French looked magnificent with their beautiful uniforms and splendid equipment. Although thin, ragged, and badly equipped, the Americans appeared impressive in victory. Crowds of civilians gathered behind the armies. To pass the time, bands took turns playing marches.

At two o'clock, the British and Germans arrived. They were in fresh uniforms and led by General Charles O'Hara. Cornwallis, claiming illness, had sent his second in command to handle the official surrender. The defeated army, with their own bands playing, marched slowly though the ranks of the victors.

O'Hara had no intention of surrendering to a "colonial." He rode directly to the French general, the Comte de Rochambeau, and offered his sword. Rochambeau shook his head and directed O'Hara to Washington. Frustrated, O'Hara then offered his sword to Washington, who refused it and passed O'Hara on to General Benjamin Lincoln, Washington's second in command. The British attempt to snub the Americans had failed.

The defeated troops then gave up their weapons. The first British soldiers violently threw down their rifles in an attempt to ruin them. Lincoln quickly put a stop to that and made certain that the rest of the guns were stacked properly. The British then marched back to Yorktown: More than 7,000 soldiers and 840 sailors were prisoners of war. Most of the British army eventually was transferred to prisoner of war camps in northern Virginia, Maryland, and Pennsylvania. The majority of those soldiers remained confined for two years.

ANNOUNCING VICTORY

That night, Washington wrote to the Continental Congress announcing the victory at Yorktown. He asked

French and American officers watch as British general Charles O'Hara makes a formal surrender to American general Benjamin Lincoln. When General Charles Cornwallis left the job of surrender to his second in command, General George Washington appointed his second in command to receive it.

Lieutenant Colonel Tench Tilghman to carry the message to Philadelphia, Pennsylvania. Though ill, Tilghman accepted the honor.

Tilghman boarded a fast sailboat traveling up the Chesapeake Bay toward Philadelphia. Unfortunately, the skipper ran the boat aground, and Tilghman was stranded for a night. Then the wind died, and again, the boat could not sail. Finally, Tilghman got ashore, borrowed a horse, and, riding furiously over wet, muddy terrain, arrived in Philadelphia at 3 a.m. on October 24. He delivered his message and collapsed into bed at an inn, exhausted and sick with chills and fever.

While Philadelphia celebrated, Tilghman asked Congress to pay his bill at the inn because he had no money—but neither did the national treasury. Each congressman personally donated one dollar to pay Tilghman's expenses.

The British forces sailing to reinforce Cornwallis did not hear of his surrender until October 24, when they finally reached the Chesapeake Bay. These sailors sent a messenger ship to London with the news, and then returned to New York. Lord North, England's prime minister, received word one month later. He threw out his arms as if he had been shot. "Oh God!" he cried. "It's all over!"

Meanwhile, some of the American regiments were redeployed to General Nathanael Greene's army in the Carolinas, while others returned to winter camps in New York. The French army remained in Yorktown and Williamsburg, Virginia, until the following spring. When news of the British surrender reached France, the French were ecstatic: No victory could be sweeter than one over the British.

THE PAINTING "SURRENDER OF LORD CORNWALLIS" BY JOHN TRUMBULL IS ON DISPLAY IN THE ROTUNDA OF THE U.S. CAPITOL.

By Jerry Miller, *Cobblestone*, © by Carus Publishing Company. Reproduced with permission.

Partisans Spring into Action

American partisans in the South used their personal knowledge of the land to keep the British on their toes.

A **partisan** is a member of an irregular military group that harasses the enemy.

After the British captured Charleston, South Carolina, on May 12, 1780, the future looked bleak for the American cause. Fortunately, the Swamp Fox and the Carolina Gamecock rode to the Revolution's rescue.

Francis Marion (the Swamp Fox) and Thomas Sumter (the Carolina Gamecock), along with Andrew Pickens, led **partisan** bands of farmers and frontiersmen in hit-and-run raids on British and Loyalist troops in North and South Carolina. Their daring attacks on enemy outposts, patrols, and supply wagons kept the British off balance, giving the Continental Army opportunities to regroup.

British military strategists had expected the South to be its key to victory. Reports of Loyalist strongholds in Georgia and South Carolina had convinced the British to launch a new campaign in the spring of 1780. They reasoned that when those two colonies were back under British control, it was only a matter of time until North Carolina, Virginia, and then the North fell to them, too. Through the spring and summer of 1780, the British army under General Charles Cornwallis pushed Continental forces out of

South Carolina and advanced toward North Carolina.

But the British plan to rely on homegrown military men backfired. When Loyalists took up arms against **patriots**, waves of violence were triggered. A bloody conflict erupted, with people in the same towns and even from the same families choosing opposing sides and fighting against one another.

Some of the Loyalists who signed up to fight used the war as an excuse to settle old scores. Raiders killed and stole from those they despised for personal reasons. In addition, plantations were **plundered** by British and **Hessian** soldiers, and stories of prisoners being butchered by their captors further inflamed both sides. In time, many colonists who might have preferred to stay neutral were drawn into the conflict. And usually, they cast their allegiances with the American militia.

Meanwhile, Marion, Sumter, and Pickens led their partisan militia bands in **guerrilla warfare** against the British, attacking without warning and withdrawing quickly. They also served as scouts and spies for the Continental Army. Though their numbers were few, they had an advantage in fighting in familiar territory and focusing on their enemy's weaknesses.

Marion tormented the British in places he knew well, such as the coastal marshes near South Carolina's Santee and Pee Dee rivers. Riding with anywhere from 20 to 200 men, he spearheaded raids that targeted enemy supplies and communications. Marion was so effective that Cornwallis ordered British lieutenant colonel Banastre Tarleton to find and destroy him.

In November 1780, Tarleton's cavalrymen chased Marion through the marshes for 26 miles. The hunt ended when Tarleton finally cried, "Come, my boys! Let us go back, and we will find the Gamecock. But as for this . . . old fox, the Devil himself could not catch him!"

So, Tarleton switched tactics and went after the Gamecock. The feisty Sumter, skilled at recruiting and leading partisans, had formed his own group of militiamen after Tarleton's forces torched his home in May 1780. Sumter went on to make trouble for British and Loyalist troops in western South Carolina and won battles for the Americans at Fish Dam Ford and Blackstock's Ford. He suffered serious defeats, however, at Fort Granby and Quinby Bridge.

> **Patriots** are those who support and defend their country.
>
> **Plundered** means robbed of goods by force.
>
> **Hessians** were professional German soldiers hired by the British.
>
> **Guerrilla warfare** is when small units of militia harass and undermine the enemy, as with surprise attacks.

Sumter's Legacy of Service

Although Thomas Sumter fought as a partisan leader in the American Revolutionary War, his name is associated more closely with the Civil War (1861–1865).

After the Revolution, Sumter represented South Carolina in the U.S. House of Representatives (1789–1793 and 1797–1801) and Senate (1801–1809). In 1829, the United States honored Sumter's service by naming a new fort at Charleston Harbor, South Carolina, for him.

On April 12, 1861, the first shot of the Civil War was fired at Fort Sumter. Federal troops surrendered, and the fort flew the Confederate flag for most of the war. Fort Sumter became a national monument in 1948.

Both sides engaged in looting during the Revolutionary War. In this painting (*Advance of the Enemy,* by Alfred Wordsworth Thompson), a family watches helplessly as a British and Hessian advance party raids their home.

Pickens had risen to prominence in 1779 at the Battle of Kettle Creek in northern Georgia, where his 300-man militia had crushed a British force more than twice its size. Captured at Charleston, South Carolina, Pickens was released on the condition that he would cease fighting. But when Loyalists terrorized his family and destroyed his plantation, Pickens and his men resumed guerrilla activities near the Georgia border.

Francis Marion's knowledge of the land—and swamps—frustrated British attempts to capture him.

British major general Patrick Ferguson felt the force and fury of the partisan fighters on October 7, 1780, at Kings Mountain, South Carolina. Ferguson had ordered settlers in western North Carolina and eastern Tennessee to declare their allegiance to the British crown, or he would "hang their leaders and lay waste the countryside with fire and sword."

The threat spurred Tennessee backwoodsmen to cross the Blue Ridge Mountains and surprise Ferguson at the border of North and South Carolina. Joined by militia from those two colonies and Virginia, the "overmountain men" killed Ferguson and defeated his highly trained Loyalist troops.

On the heels of that battle came news that American major general Nathanael Greene was assuming command of American forces in the South. Greene issued a call for "men who love their homes, wives, and children and will fight to protect them."

Brigadier General Daniel Morgan and his Virginia Riflemen answered the summons. On January 17, 1781,

Morgan faced 1,100 of Tarleton's well-trained British troops at Cowpens in western South Carolina. Morgan made the most of his 1,000-man force, which included frontier sharpshooters, Continental soldiers, and militia led by Pickens. The result was an overwhelming victory for the Americans.

In an effort to drive Cornwallis from the Carolinas, Greene continued to count on the Swamp Fox, the Carolina Gamecock, and other partisan fighters. With their help, Greene accomplished what he called "flushing out the bird" that General George Washington eventually caught in Yorktown.

Hated British Raider

A portrait of Lt. Col. Banastre Tarleton, with a medallion featuring a cavalry scene below.

Dragoons were heavily armed 17th- and 18th-century troops on horseback.

When Lieutenant Colonel Banastre Tarleton returned to England in 1782, the British hailed him as a hero. To Americans, however, he was known as "Ban the Butcher" and "Bloody Tarleton"—one of the most hated figures of the Revolutionary War. Historian Christopher Ward said of Tarleton, "He wrote his name in letters of blood all across the history of the war in the South."

Tarleton commanded the British Legion, a cavalry and light infantry unit. His **dragoons** used surprise, speed, and skill to crush American soldiers on the battlefield. They also burned crops, plundered homes, and terrorized civilians in raids throughout the southern countryside.

Tarleton's bloody reputation was sealed on May 29, 1780, at Waxhaws on the North and South Carolina border. When Colonel Abraham Buford's Virginia Continentals tried to surrender, Tarleton's men continued their assault with bayonets and sabers: They slaughtered 113 Americans.

After that massacre, "Remember Tarleton's quarter!" became a rallying cry for Americans. Typically, a soldier who requests quarter is asking for mercy—that is, not to be killed upon surrender. "Tarleton's quarter" was just the opposite—no mercy. Some patriots began using "Tarleton's quarter" to justify their own mistreatment of British and Loyalist prisoners.

Tarleton eventually was captured at Gloucester Point, Virginia. Afraid of trusting his fate to the angry Americans, he surrendered to French forces, who permitted him to sail home.

Washington Makes His Move

In August 1781, British general Charles Cornwallis and his troops were settled in at Yorktown, Virginia. The general's decision to stay in this peninsula town, near where the York River flows into the Chesapeake Bay, would prove to be an important step in bringing about the end of the American Revolutionary War.

The war that began in 1775 with the Battles of Lexington and Concord (Massachusetts) had been raging for six years. Most of the major fighting during that time had occurred in New England or the Middle Atlantic (from New York to Maryland). Each side had won some battles, but neither the Americans nor the British seemed able to deliver the decisive blow that would destroy the other's will to continue.

In late 1778, General Henry Clinton, commander in chief of the British army in America, was bottled up in New York. Positioned around the city, General George Washington and his Continental Army maintained a close eye on the British army's land movements, keeping the two armies at a standstill. So, Clinton moved his military **campaign** south by ship to take advantage of the larger **Loyalist** population in those colonies. He believed that he was on the path to victory after his army won a series of battles against America's Continental Army in Georgia and South Carolina.

Converging on Yorktown, George Washington and his generals dealt the final blow of the Revolutionary War.

Map labels:
- About 4,500 troops with Lafayette, including over 3,000 militia.
- About 8,000 troops under General Washington, including a French force of more than 4,500 commanded by the Count de Rochambeau.
- Cornwallis entrenched with an army of about 7,500 (British, German, and American Loyalist forces).
- The French fleet with 3,000 troops under the Count de Grasse which blockaded the sea approaches to Yorktown.

By Kip Wilson, *Cobblestone*, © by Carus Publishing Company. Reproduced with permission.

HOW DID THEY STACK UP?

WASHINGTON

Let's compare the generals of the opposing armies at Yorktown. Perhaps the biggest difference between the two can be found in each man's overall objective. Washington saw Yorktown as an opportunity to deal a decisive blow to the British military, forcing it to consider surrendering. Clinton's order to Cornwallis, meanwhile, was simply to hold the British position in Virginia until reinforcements arrived or Cornwallis' troops were relieved.

CORNWALLIS

George Washington	Charles Cornwallis
realistic	optimistic
trained on the job	highly trained and educated
risk taker	sure and steady
sought victory by any means	played by the rules
believed in the American cause	no personal stake in the war
American/French forces amounted to as many as 19,000 troops: 8,000 Continental, 8,000 French (infantry and navy), and 3,000 Virginia **militia**	British forces amounted to about 7,500 troops
benefited from cooperation with French allies Rochambeau and de Grasse	suffered from a lack of coordination with Clinton

Washington: Library of Congress; Cornwallis: *Dictionary of American Portraits*, Dover Publications, Inc., 1967.

Circumstances changed, however, once Clinton headed back to New York and left Cornwallis in command in the South. Cornwallis decided to concentrate on crushing Virginia in the spring of 1781. He led the Marquis de Lafayette, a French nobleman fighting with the Continental Army, on a wild-goose chase through the colony. Finally, Cornwallis occupied and fortified Yorktown, and then waited for the British navy to bring new supplies.

Since all signs pointed to a looming American attack on British forces in New York, Cornwallis believed he would be spared a large assault. He relaxed—until August 30, when French ships arrived in the Chesapeake Bay.

The sight of the French navy in the bay was the first hint that Washington had a definite plan in mind. A French army led by Lieutenant General the Comte de Rochambeau had arrived in America in 1780, and Washington had hoped to lead a large-scale assault on New York with Rochambeau's help.

But when Washington learned that Cornwallis' large force had **dug in** at Yorktown and that a French fleet under Admiral the Comte de Grasse was

A **campaign** is a series of military operations enacted to achieve a common goal.

A **Loyalist** was someone who remained loyal to the British throne during the American Revolutionary War.

A **militia** is an army composed of ordinary citizens rather than professional soldiers.

Dug in means built trenches in the earth for protection.

The British surrendered their arms to General Washington after their defeat at Yorktown in Virginia in October 1781.

on its way to the Chesapeake Bay, he changed his mind. The French army and navy would give the Americans the strength in numbers to trap and overwhelm the British army at Yorktown.

While American and French forces headed south, a small number of Continental Army troops were left behind in New York to make it appear as if an attack there were imminent. By the time Clinton and Cornwallis realized that both the French navy and the American army were converging on Yorktown, it was too late: There was no escape from the peninsula that Cornwallis had chosen to defend. Yorktown would be the last stand for the British army.

The battle between the French and British fleets in the Chesapeake Bay sealed the fate of General Cornwallis and his British troops at Yorktown. The French surprised the British fleet at the mouth of the Chesapeake, forcing the British navy to retreat to New York, leaving General Cornwallis stranded.

By Kip Wilson, *Cobblestone*, © by Carus Publishing Company. Reproduced with permission.

James Armistead: Master Spy

Characters

Narrator 1

Narrator 2

Marquis de Lafayette: a 23-year-old French nobleman who came to America to volunteer his services to the Continental Army

George Washington: the commander of the Continental Army

James Armistead: a 21-year-old enslaved man from Virginia

James Armistead (above), an enslaved African American, enlisted in the Revolutionary War under General Lafayette. Working as a spy, Armistead gained the trust of General Cornwallis and Benedict Arnold, providing information that allowed American forces to prevail at the Battle of Yorktown.

Introduction:

Narrator 1: In 1781, General George Washington sent a small force of about 1,200 soldiers under the command of the Marquis de Lafayette to stop British troops who had invaded Virginia.

Act I

Narrator 2: General Washington's headquarters, April 1781. Lafayette enters the American leader's library. Washington rises to greet him and shakes his hand. The two are meeting to discuss stopping British raiders from looting and burning their way through Virginia.

George Washington: Welcome, my friend. I am anxious to hear of your progress in Virginia. Come and have a seat by the fire.

Marquis de Lafayette: Thank you, sir. I am afraid that all is not going well. I have encountered more difficulties than I thought I would.

Narrator 2: Washington and Lafayette sit facing each other in wing chairs in front of the fireplace.

Washington: What difficulties do you talk of?

Lafayette: Governor Jefferson warned me that Virginia was a state of "mild laws and a people not used to prompt obedience." He was right.

Washington: I know that Virginians have their own way of doing things.

Lafayette: I have tried to get horses for my troops from farmers, but they hid them and their wagons.

Washington: They probably want to save what horses they have left for farm work because the British have already stolen so many of them for their own troops.

Lafayette: My soldiers are also hungry. The farmers will not sell us meat and grain, and they refuse to exchange their produce for American paper money because they claim it is almost worthless.

Washington: That has been a problem with which we have all had to deal.

Lafayette: In addition, I have had to contend with two British armies. These well-trained soldiers have been moving swiftly through the state, burning and looting everywhere they go. They have burned Richmond and many warehouses full of tobacco, weapons, and food. They have even chased many members of the Virginia legislature across the state.

Washington: I heard that Governor Jefferson just barely escaped being captured and that he resigned from office.

Lafayette: The government of Virginia has no power. The British can easily invade such a land.

Washington: Especially with leaders such as Cornwallis and the traitor Benedict Arnold.

Lafayette: I refuse to give up, though. Do you have any advice for me?

Washington: Yes. Have your soldiers watch every movement the British make. But, do not get too close. You are not strong enough to win a battle just yet. Send spies into their camps. I need all the information I can get.

Lafayette: Where can I get more help?

Washington: Recruit black troops. You should be able to enlist several hundred. They could help you find more horses for your soldiers.

Lafayette: I will begin at once. The next time we meet, I will have better news to report to you.

Narrator 2: Washington smiles as the determined young Frenchman leaves the room.

Act II

Narrator 1: Lafayette's headquarters one week later. The general is interviewing an enslaved person named James Armistead. He has volunteered to serve as a soldier and spy. Armistead stands at attention before Lafayette.

Lafayette: What is your name?

James Armistead: James, sir.

Lafayette: And your last name?

Armistead: Armistead, after my master, William Armistead.

Lafayette: Where are you from?

Armistead: My master's farm near the town of Williamsburg in New Kent County.

Lafayette: How old are you?

Armistead: Twenty-one years old, sir.

Lafayette: Why did you come to our camp?

Armistead: I asked my master for permission to enlist under you, General Lafayette.

Lafayette: Why me?

Armistead: Your fame has spread throughout Virginia, and I have heard that you need recruits. You are fighting to help America become free from British rule, and I, too, want my freedom someday.

Lafayette (impressed by Armistead's sincerity): Are you willing to risk your life as a spy for us in the British camp of Benedict Arnold?

Armistead: Yes, sir.

Lafayette: You must understand that I cannot promise you your freedom, even if you do this for us. Only your master or a decree from the General Assembly of Virginia can declare you a freeman.

Armistead: I know, sir. I am willing to take my chances.

Lafayette: I can see that you are a brave and intelligent young man. I think you will be loyal to the Americans and a good spy.

Armistead: Thank you, sir.

Lafayette: I want you to make your way to Arnold's headquarters. Offer him your services. Tell him you want to earn your freedom. I am sure he will believe you. Volunteer to serve his officers as a guide on the country roads. Learn all that you can about the British and follow their every move. Then, report everything you see and hear to me as often as possible.

Armistead: Yes, sir.

Lafayette: You may leave today. We have no time to waste.

Narrator 2: Armistead makes his way to Arnold's headquarters and soon wins the confidence of the British. He sends reports to Lafayette almost daily. Using some of this information, American troops sneak into the British camp and nearly capture Arnold. Even after this incident, the British continue to trust Armistead so much that they asked him to spy on the Americans! As a double agent, Armistead gave useful information to Lafayette while giving false information to the British.

Act III

Narrator 1: George Washington's headquarters, July 1781. Lafayette reports his progress. The two generals stroll about the camp on the warm summer evening discussing what has happened since their last meeting. General Arnold has returned to the North, and Armistead is now serving at the headquarters of General Cornwallis.

Washington: So Benedict Arnold has left Virginia. Now, you have only one British general with whom to contend, and a capable, cautious general at that. Have your spies had any success with Lord Cornwallis?

Lafayette: I have a very loyal and able slave, James Armistead, who volunteered to spy against the British. He sent me a great deal of information when he was in Arnold's headquarters.

Washington: Is he now with Lord Cornwallis?

Lafayette: Yes, but he is having a much more difficult time obtaining secret reports. Cornwallis is so careful with his maps and orders that my spy sometimes cannot get at them.

Washington: Have you been able to follow the British through Virginia?

Lafayette: I have often had to guess at the movement of the enemy. They seem to travel as fast as the wind. I have to admit that I am devilishly afraid of this cautious and intelligent general.

Washington: You must not lose track of him.

Lafayette: Our small army followed a few miles behind Cornwallis when he marched west through Virginia to the Blue Ridge Mountains and then back to the coast. He knew we were behind him, but I told my men that we were chasing them. This lifted their morale.

Washington: That was clever of you. Do you think Armistead will be able to get much information to you?

Lafayette: He spends a lot of time in Cornwallis' tent, but pretends not to understand their plans. He also serves the general and his officers their food and drink. They would not allow his presence at meals if he were not trusted.

Washington: How does he get word to you?

Lafayette: He tells what he has overheard to black men in the camp who have the liberty to come and go. They bring me the secret information a couple of hours later.

Washington: Where is Cornwallis now?

Lafayette: He and his army have moved to the city of Portsmouth near Chesapeake Bay. Armistead tells me that a fleet of British sailing ships is anchored in the harbor. The ships seem ready to carry the enemy troops to a new location, but I have received no news that Cornwallis and his men have sailed.

Washington: Keep reporting all your news to me. I am anxious to keep track of Cornwallis. His capture would contribute greatly to the success of our war efforts.

Lafayette: With the help of my trustworthy spy, I am sure we will be victorious.

Narrator 2: Lafayette leaves to return to his camp in Virginia. He wants to be present if any critical news should arrive from his spy and scouts.

Act IV

Narrator 1: Lafayette's headquarters, early August. Armistead himself reports to the young French general.

Lafayette (surprised): I am glad to see you, James. But why have you come in person?

Armistead: General Cornwallis has sailed with his army from Portsmouth.

Lafayette: Do you have any other information?

Armistead: I could not find out where they are going.

Lafayette: I will send scouts to find out his destination. I must notify General Washington at once. We are grateful to you for your service and devotion to the American fight for liberty. I will do whatever I can to assist you in your quest for freedom.

Armistead: Thank you, sir. When the war is over, I plan to petition the General Assembly of Virginia to declare me a freeman.

Lafayette: Let us hope this war will be over soon.

Narrator 2: It is not long before Lafayette learns from his scouts that Cornwallis and his army have landed at Yorktown, a small port on the York River near Chesapeake Bay. This news is reported to Washington, who tells Lafayette and his army to keep the British from leaving the port. By September, American and French troops surround Cornwallis. On October 19, the British general surrenders. The final battle of the American Revolution is over.

One year after the peace treaty is signed by the United States and Great Britain, General Lafayette writes a certificate praising the loyalty and wisdom of James Armistead. Armistead sends this certificate, along with a petition to declare him free, to the General Assembly of Virginia. The Assembly agrees to pay his master, William Armistead, a fair price for his freedom. In appreciation for the trust and assistance given him by General Lafayette, Armistead changes his name to James Armistead Lafayette.

Your Life as a Farmer

A **yeoman** is an independent farmer with property.

Imagine you are a farmer in rural Massachusetts in the mid- to late 1700s. Earlier settlers had established farms near the Connecticut River because that land was the most fertile. When you arrived, you set out to establish a farm on land that was hilly, rocky, and sometimes infertile. But hard work has never deterred you: You achieved your goal to become a **yeoman**.

Yours is a simple life, filled with plenty of hard work. You own a large tract of land but cultivate only a small part of it because farming takes a tremendous amount of time and energy. You try to hire laborers to help with the planting and harvesting, but the region's isolation makes it difficult to find workers.

Fortunately, your father, brothers, and uncles—as well as some members of your wife's family—have farms in the same community. You, your extended family, and your neighbors help one another sow the fields and gather the crops. Families and friends coming together socially for common tasks such as cornhusking, logrolling, quilting, and barn raisings develop strong ties to the community.

You grow most of your own food and get water from a well or nearby spring or brook. Your family grows an assortment of vegetables, such as peas, turnips, potatoes, and carrots. Corn—used for animal feed or ground into flour—wheat, and rye are the main crops, so you grow more of them. Their surplus can be used to obtain goods that you cannot produce on your farm—like salt—or to buy small luxuries.

Of course, buying products in this part of western Massachusetts may not involve the exchange of cash. Bartering is the preferred method. For example, in exchange for medical services for his family, a blacksmith might offer to shoe a doctor's horse. Or, two bushels of corn from one family might be traded for one bushel of wheat from another farm. You might offer to help a neighbor seed his farm in exchange for the loan of his plow and team of horses for use on your land.

Although industries such as logging, weaving **flax**, and raising livestock exist in rural areas, the goods that are derived from these businesses have to travel long distances—either carried over rutted roads or sent down the Connecticut River—in order to be traded or sold. That takes time, and the earnings from the sale of these items are not always immediately seen.

> **Flax** is the fine, light-colored textile fiber that is obtained from the plant of the same name and woven into thread.

By Anne de Ocejo, illustrated by Mark Mitchell, *Cobblestone*, © by Carus Publishing Company. Reproduced with permission.

You have recently returned from fighting in the Revolutionary War. Your family was barely able to produce life's necessities while you were gone. Without surpluses, you eventually are forced to claim **bankruptcy** and **mortgage** your farm.

Part of your financial problem stems from the location of your farm: Western Massachusetts is isolated from the large eastern commerce centers. Coastal city dwellers—including merchants and shippers—were not as hard hit because they were able to continue trading with other colonies during the war. With an emphasis on wealth and profits, cities do not foster the same community spirit as rural areas. As trader Samuel Collins told his brother in a dispute over a transaction, "It is a common saying, business before friends." Bartering and sharing labor have no place in such a society.

Accustomed to communal support and a system of exchanging goods, you become frustrated when you come up against eastern businessmen who focus on cash transactions and profits. You are forced to sell horses, plows, and even livestock—often for less than their true value—just to pay your debts. You need that equipment for your livelihood, but you are threatened with jail if you do not pay what you owe. If you go to jail, your chances of working and earning money to improve your situation are diminished considerably. How can you make the government understand how difficult your circumstances are?

> **Bankruptcy** is the situation of being completely unable to pay debts.
>
> A **mortgage** is a temporary pledge of property to a creditor as security for repayment of a debt.

East vs. West

	Western Massachusetts	Eastern Massachusetts
Geography	Rural settlements	Urban towns and cities
Economics	Small family farms	Merchants and businesses
Commerce	Barter for goods	Cash transactions

By Anne de Ocejo, illustrated by Mark Mitchell, *Cobblestone*, © by Carus Publishing Company. Reproduced with permission.

Yankee Doodle

The favorite march song of Americans was "Yankee Doodle." The term "Yankee" was an insulting label for New Englander, and "Doodle" meant a fool. While historians believe the song was originally sung by British officers to mock the disorganized colonials who served in the French and Indian War, Americans seemed to take pride in "Yankee Doodle" during the revolution.

Father and I went down to camp
Along with Captain Gooding,
And there we saw the men and boys
As thick as hasty pudding.

Yankee Doodle keep it up,
Yankee Doodle Dandy,
Mind the music and the step,
And with the girls be handy.

There was Captain Washington
Upon a slapping stallion
A-giving orders to his men—
There must have been a million.

"The Flutist," an oil painting thought to be of Barzillai Lew, attributed to an unidentified artist, after Gilbert Stuart. Barzillai Lew was a fifer in the same patriot regiment as Peter Salem and was with him at the Battle of Bunker Hill, where he played "Yankee Doodle Dandy" to rally the Continental troops against the British.

HISTORICAL IMAGE

Fraunces Tavern, a national historic landmark, museum, and restaurant in New York City, played an important role in the American Revolution. One of General Washington's loyal New York supporters was Samuel Fraunces, a free black man from the West Indies, who was the owner of Fraunces Tavern in New York City. The tavern was the meeting place at different times for both American Patriots and British Loyalists. The Sons of Liberty, a secret group of Patriots, met at Fraunces Tavern frequently and planned a tea party protest inspired by the Boston Tea Party. Samuel Fraunces also became a spy for General Washington, providing him with valuable information. Fraunces Tavern was also the setting for General Washington's Farewell Address to his troops at the end of the American Revolution in 1783. When Washington became the first president of the United States, Samuel Fraunces became the first steward of the White House.

From *The Pictorial Field-Book of the Revolution*, by Benson J. Lossing, 1860.

A DIFFICULT DECADE

When militiamen left to fight for the future of the Colonies, they risked the welfare of their homes and families.

The **backcountry** refers to a sparsely inhabited rural region.

One would think that the years after the American Revolution (1775–1783) would have been good ones for the people of the new United States. After all, they had just won a war against England, a mighty European country. The new country had plenty of land and natural resources. Now that they also had political independence, the American people could set up their own form of government and run their nation as they pleased.

But in fact, the years following the Revolutionary War were difficult ones. Many Americans, especially poorer citizens, former soldiers, and people of the **backcountry**, were unhappy with their lives and their government. They felt that the Revolution had promised much but delivered little. By 1786, frustration had spilled over into outright rebellion.

ECONOMIC HARDSHIPS

Much of the anger stemmed from the Revolution itself. Before the war, most soldiers had been making decent livings as farmers or craftsmen. When the fighting was over, however, they came home to fields overgrown with weeds and workshops in ruins. It would take a lot of time and energy to make them profitable again. Three years after the end of the war, many soldiers still had not returned to their earlier standard of living.

Earnings from active duty during the war were another issue for soldiers. Colonial governments had very little money during the Revolution, so they offered soldiers very low wages, most of which were not even paid in cash. Instead, soldiers received notes, or promises, that they would be paid—someday. The men took the notes, hoping they eventually would receive what they were owed.

Most of the notes still had not been paid by 1786, however. Many states—particularly ones like Massachusetts, where much of the fighting had taken place—simply did not have the funds. As a result, the notes were practically worthless. Disgusted, many soldiers sold them to rich merchants for one-tenth or less of their face value. The ex–military men could not wait for their state governments to pay what they owed: Their farms and homes required improvements, and their families needed to eat. The wealthier merchants could afford to buy the notes at the greatly reduced price and wait until the government had money. Then, they would redeem the notes, at a great profit to themselves.

A proclamation by the State of Pennsylvania offering a reward for Daniel Shays and three other rebellion ringleaders, signed by Benjamin Franklin.

> **Having a hard time picturing Daniel Shays?**
> Shays was an American soldier, revolutionary, and farmer best known for being one of the leaders of Shays' Rebellion, an uprising against oppressive debt and tax policies in Massachusetts. A pivotal event in American history may be named for him, but during the time in which he lived, he was viewed as an outlaw and troublemaker. He was certainly not the kind of person that the Massachusetts leaders of that time wanted to see remembered and studied in future generations. So very little is truly known about Daniel Shays, and we don't have any physical description or actual images of how he looked. Just goes to show you that fame is not just skin deep!

A WEAK FEDERAL GOVERNMENT

As time went on, some soldiers argued that the responsibility of paying the debts should belong to the federal government instead of to the states. Since the war had been a national effort, their argument made sense. There was one major problem with it, though: The relatively new national government was weak.

Although Americans had joined together during the war, most saw themselves primarily as citizens of their state or even their town. And the new political structure of the United States reflected this notion. Under the **Articles of Confederation**, the individual states held most of the power. The central government could not form an army, for example, and had no power to collect taxes for national use. Thus, it had no method of paying the debt owed to the Revolutionary War soldiers.

Not being paid for their military service frustrated many of the soldiers, but problems with the economy angered more Americans. People who lived at the western edges of states such as Massachusetts barely made a living on small farms. When times were bad, as they were in 1785 and 1786, these folks were hit especially hard—some came close to starvation. Most Americans believed that their states were not doing enough to help them. They charged that the governments were prejudiced against the citizens of their respective states.

A STATE DIVIDED

In some cases, their complaints were correct. The Massachusetts state constitution, for instance, strongly favored the rich merchants of eastern cities like Boston. These were the same men

> The **Articles of Confederation** were the system of government used by the United States before the Constitution.

COLONIAL CURRENCY

The colonists used various forms of "money"—including Spanish coins, Native American wampum, cash crops such as tobacco, and colonial notes and coins. The value of these currencies differed depending on the part of the country you were in. Then, in 1764, Great Britain forbade the colonists from issuing any paper money, creating a shortage. The Americans, however, printed money called "continentals" to help finance the Revolutionary War, but the continentals became worthless after the war. These factors, combined with the burden of high taxes, made for difficult economic times in the years after the war. It was not until 1792 and the passage of the Coinage Act that the United States adopted an official unit of currency—the dollar.

Facsimile of the first money coined by the United States.

American artist John Trumbull portrayed the British surrender at Yorktown in 1781, in which British general Charles Cornwallis' sword was presented to General George Washington's second in command, General Benjamin Lincoln. Before the end of the decade, Lincoln would be the commander of the Massachusetts militia that tried to end Shays' Rebellion.

who had bought up the soldiers' undervalued notes. In addition, these merchants had played a big role in forming the Massachusetts state government. They supported laws that raised taxes and made it a priority to pay off the notes.

Before the Revolutionary War, the colonial government of Massachusetts had left the western part of the state more or less alone. This was no longer true after the war. The state government began demanding high taxes, which the people simply did not have the means to pay. It forced rural residents to obey laws that had been passed far from their communities and refused to issue more paper money to help lighten the debt. The changes made the western Massachusetts citizens resentful—and angry.

Massachusetts was not the only place where discontent grew in the years after the Revolution. Other states also experienced problems, mostly for similar reasons. But the lack of pay for soldiers, the unfair state constitution, and the poor economy all combined to make the situation in Massachusetts especially explosive.

Eliza Lucas Pinckney
A NEW CROP FOR A NEW COUNTRY

WHAT IS INDIGO?

Indigo is a plant that belongs to the same family as peas and beans. It is a tall shrub with hairy leaves and small light purple flowers. The leaves are the part of the plant that produces indigo dye. The leaves are picked and left to ferment in tanks of water until a blue sludge forms at the bottom of the tank. This sludge is dried into indigo "cake," and is then cut into cubes or formed into balls. Indigo was used to dye the denim for blue jeans until it was replaced with synthetic dyes. Today people are more interested in natural dyes again, and indigo is making a comeback.

Eliza Lucas Pinckney is known to us through her letters and journal, which we can still read today. But imagine what it would be like to hear Eliza tell us her story. This is what she might say:

Everyone said that I couldn't do it. They should know better than to say such a thing to me! It only makes me try harder to prove them wrong. And in this case, I knew that indigo was a crop we could grow in the Carolina colonies. Father moved us here when Mother fell ill, that she might enjoy a milder climate. When Father left us here in South Carolina in 1738, that he might sail for his military duty in Antigua, where he commanded British naval forces, I wished I too could travel with him, back to the West Indies where I had been born. But it was not to be. Instead, Father left me in charge of the 600 acre plantation on Wapoo Creek, and another 1,500 acres at Garden Hill. I might only have been 17, but Father knew I could look after the family, our business, and our slaves as well as any man. I preferred the business of farming to an idle, gossipy life of balls and society in Charleston. And perhaps I turned down several good marriage prospects while he was gone, but I also much preferred hard work and independence to being a lady of leisure. When Father offered to make a match between me and an elderly man whom he claimed would be perfect for me, I respectfully replied, "A single life is my only choice and if it were not that I am yet but Eighteen, I hope you will put aside the thoughts of my marrying for two or three years at least."

It was clear to me that the plantation needed new crops if we were to survive and prosper. I experimented with ginger, figs, cotton, cassava, and alfalfa. Then I arrived at the idea of growing indigo. Indigo was the source of the valuable blue dye that everyone thought only the French could grow on their Caribbean islands. I felt certain that

A photo of Snee Farm, the plantation home of the Pinckney family in South Carolina, built in 1754.

we could grow indigo here, and make the dye ourselves, freeing our new colonies from having to trade with the French. As I wrote in my journal, I had greater hopes from indigo than any of the rest of the things I had tried.

Of course, it was not easy. My first crop froze in the fields, and the second was ruined by worms. The third crop was small, only a hundred plants. I finally learned how to make indigo grow well, but making the dye turned out to be much more difficult. Father sent an expert from Montserrat to help me, but the miserable man sabotaged the first batch of dye by adding too much lime and spoiling the color. His name was Nicholas Cromwell, and it seems he was afraid that if we were able to grow indigo and make the blue dye here, we would harm the economy of his Caribbean island home. I threw him out of my house as soon as I discovered his treachery, and hired his brother Patrick in his stead. By 1744, I was able to send seventeen pounds of quality indigo dye to Britain! I also gave the seeds of my indigo plants to other Carolina growers, that we might all share in this new crop. Together, we would produce all the indigo that the colonies might possibly want. For thirty years, South Carolina thrived on indigo.

By the time I reached the age of 21, I was a wealthy and successful plantation owner in my own right. I married Charles Pinckney, a lawyer from Charleston, and we raised three children, including two fine sons, Charles and Thomas. I am proud to say that my sons were heroes of the Revolutionary War against Great Britain. And my son Charles was one of the first planters to grow long-staple cotton, which became the economic basis of the entire South. And it was all because of my stubbornness!

Postscript

When Eliza died in 1793, George Washington himself offered to be one of those who carried her coffin at her funeral.

PRIMARY SOURCE

A Letter by Eliza Lucas, 1740

Eliza Lucas Pinckney changed agriculture in colonial South Carolina, where she developed indigo as one of its most important cash crops. Its cultivation and processing as dye produced one-third the total value of the colony's exports before the Revolutionary War. As manager of three plantations at age 16, Pinckney had a major impact on the economy.

We are about seventeen miles by land and six by water from Charles Town [later Charleston]. We have about six agreeable families around us with whom we live in great harmony. I have a little library in which I spend part of my time. My music and the garden, which I am very fond of, take up the rest that is not employed in business. Of that my father left me a pretty good share, and indeed 'twas unavoidable . . .

I have the business of three plantations to transact, which requires much writing and more business (and fatigue of other sorts) than you can imagine . . . Much of my time is spent on my experiments with indigo—the plant which produces such a beautiful blue dye . . . I have also taken pains to bring the ginger [and] cotton . . . to perfection [but] have greater hopes from indigo (if I could have the seed earlier next year from the West Indies I would have greater success).

The Wild Colt: Abigail Adams

Small, pale, and often sick, little Abigail loved books. Her dark, wide eyes sparkled when she read. More than anything, Abigail wanted to go to school, but her mother, Elizabeth, wouldn't let her. In those days, school education was just for boys. Girls were supposed to learn how to keep the house going, make household goods, and take care of a family.

Abigail was born in 1744, in the seaside village of Weymouth, in colonial Massachusetts. Back then, daughters and married women had few rights. They weren't allowed to vote or own property. Everything, including their clothes, belonged to their fathers or their husbands.

Abigail's mother wouldn't let her go to school, but her father, Reverend William Smith, taught Abigail to read and write. (He taught her two sisters and brother, too.) Abigail loved learning and read every book in her father's library. When she was ten, she began to learn about farming. After her father gave her a lamb, she spent half her time in the barn, to her mother's dismay; Elizabeth thought both reading and farming were unladylike. But Abigail's Grandmother Quincy just smiled and said, "Wild colts make the best horses."

When Abigail was 20, she married a young lawyer named John Adams. John liked Abigail's gentleness and the way she argued with him. John made Abigail laugh, and she liked the way he always tried to do the right thing. They had six children, but two died as babies. For a while, the Adams family lived in Boston, but their farm in Braintree—just outside the

The great distance between us makes the time appear very long to me.
—Abigail wrote to her husband

Our house... is a scene of confusion... Soldiers coming in for lodging, for breakfast, for supper, for drink, etc. Sometimes refugees from Boston, tired and fatigued, seek asylum for a day, a night, a week. You can hardly imagine how we live.
—May 24, 1775

The day—perhaps the decisive day—is come, on which the fate of America depends.... The constant roar of the cannon is so distressing that we cannot eat, drink, or sleep.
—Sunday, June 18, 1775

bustling port town—was the place they called home. (Later, Braintree was renamed Quincy.)

When American colonists began to pull away from the control of Great Britain, John Adams was right in the middle of the conflict. For months at a time, he was away from home. At first, John served as a member of the Continental Congress, representatives of the colonies who were trying to resolve the conflict. They met in Philadelphia—300 miles and 19 days away by horseback. Later, he sailed to Europe to help the colonies.

Abigail took care of the children and managed the farm by herself. Abigail missed her husband and was sometimes afraid, but she wanted America to be free. She nursed her family through illnesses, melted her pewter spoons to make bullets, and fed and sheltered both colonial soldiers and homeless colonists. When colonial soldiers lost a battle, Abigail cried. When George Washington's army drove the English out of Boston, she cheered.

By Leigh Anderson, illustrated by Mark Mitchell, *Appleseeds*, © by Carus Publishing Company. Reproduced with permission.

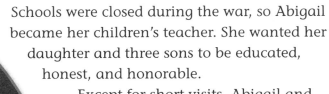

Schools were closed during the war, so Abigail became her children's teacher. She wanted her daughter and three sons to be educated, honest, and honorable.

Except for short visits, Abigail and John were apart for ten years. Abigail wrote to John often, telling him the local news and offering her opinions. Embarrassed by her poor spelling and grammar, Abigail frequently asked John to burn the letters she wrote. John told her that she was his best reporter and most trusted advisor. He kept her letters, perhaps because he knew they told the story of the birth of a new nation.

After the war, now with Abigail at his side, John continued to serve his nation. They traveled to France and England as John fulfilled his duties as American **ambassador** to those countries. When George Washington became the United States' first president, John Adams became the first vice president. Eight years later, John was elected as the nation's second president.

Abigail Adams was the first First Lady to live in the White House. She visited the family farm whenever she could, but John said he needed Abigail's advice, so she didn't stay away long.

During one trip home, Abigail arranged for a black servant boy, James, to attend school. When neighbors complained, saying a black child didn't belong there, Abigail became angry. She believed that everyone had a right to get an education. James remained at school.

Abigail never stopped speaking her mind, but her words and actions didn't always agree. She said she believed that a woman's job should be to take care of the home. But what she did was different: As an educated woman, Abigail was a teacher, political advisor, farm supervisor, and manager of the family money.

In 1825—six years after Abigail died—her oldest son was elected America's sixth president. John Quincy Adams followed in his father's footsteps, but he learned his life lessons at his mother's knee.

> I long to hear that you have declared an independency. And by the way, in the new code of laws... remember the ladies and be more generous and favorable to them than your ancestors. Do not put such unlimited power into the hands of husbands. Remember, all men would be tyrants if they could.
>
> —March 31, 1776

An **ambassador** is a person officially sent by one country as its representative to another country.

HISTORICAL IMAGE

Library of Congress

Abigail Adams is best known as the wife of President John Adams and for her extensive correspondence. She was also the mother of John Quincy Adams, who became the sixth president of the United States. The daughter of a minister, she was a devoted reader, studying the works of William Shakespeare and John Milton among others. Adams did not, however, attend school, which was common for girls at the time.

Abigail married John Adams in 1764. Busy first with his law practice and then as an active participant of the American Revolution, her husband spent a lot of time away from home. Abigail was also left to carry much of the burden at home, raising their children and caring for the family farm. The couple remained closed by corresponding with each other. It is believed that they exchanged more than 1,100 letters.

A strong advocate of women's rights, Abigail Adams expressed concern about how the new government would treat women. In one of her many letters to her husband, she requested that he "Remember the Ladies, and be more generous and favourable to them than your ancestors." Abigail Adams often expressed her thoughts on political matters with her husband. Throughout his career, Abigail had served an unofficial advisor to him. Their letters show him seeking her counsel on many issues, including his presidential aspirations. Adams remained a supportive spouse and confidante after her husband became the president in 1797. Some critics objected to Abigail's influence over her husband, calling her "Mrs. President."

Abigail Adams' Letter to John Adams
June 18, 1775

Boston, Sunday, 18 June 1775

Dearest Friend,

The day—perhaps the decisive day—is come, on which the fate of America depends. My bursting heart must find vent at my pen. I have just heard that our dear friend, Dr. Warren, is no more, but fell gloriously fighting for his country; saying, Better to die honorably in the field, than ignominiously hang upon the gallows. Great is our loss. He has distinguished himself in every engagement, by his courage and fortitude, by animating the soldiers and leading them on by his own example. A particular account of these dreadful, but I hope glorious days, will be transmitted to you, no doubt, in the exactest manner.

"The race is not to the swift, nor the battle to the strong; but the God of Israel is He that giveth strength and power unto his people. Trust in him at all times, ye people, pour out your hearts before him; God is a refuge for us." Charlestown is laid in ashes. The battle began upon our intrenchments upon Bunker's Hill, Saturday morning about three o'clock, and has not ceased yet, and it is now three o'clock Sabbath afternoon.

It is expected they will come out over the Neck tonight, and a dreadful battle must ensue. Almighty God, cover the heads of our countrymen, and be a shield to our dear friends! How many have fallen, we know not. The constant roar of the cannon is so distressing that we cannot eat, drink, or sleep. May we be supported and sustained in the dreadful conflict. I shall tarry here till it is thought unsafe by my friends, and then I have secured myself retreat at your brother's, who has kindly offered me a part of his house. I cannot compose myself to write any further response. I will add more as I hear further.

Tuesday afternoon
I have been so much agitated, that I have not been able to write since Sabbath day. When I say that ten thousand reports are passing, vague and uncertain as the wind, I believe I speak the truth. I am not able to give

you any authentic account of last Saturday, but you will not be destitute of intelligence. Colonel Palmer has just sent me word that he has an opportunity of conveyance. Incorrect as this scrawl will be, it shall go. I ardently pray that you may be supported through the arduous task you have before you. I wish I could contradict the report of the Dr's death; but it is a lamentable truth; those favorite lines of Collins continually sound in my ears: "How sleep the brave" etc.

I must close . . . I have not pretended to be particular with regard to what I have heard because I know you will collect better intelligence. The spirits of the people are very good; the loss of Charlestown affects them no more than a drop in the bucket.

I am, most sincerely, yours,

Portia

Note: As was the custom of the time, Abigail and John Adams adopted pen names in their correspondence: Abigail was Diana, after the Roman goddess of the moon, and John was Lysander, after the Spartan war hero. He often addressed his letters to his "Dear Adoreable" or "My dear Diana," but Abigail wrote to "My Dearest Friend." Later, Abigail replaced the pen name Diana with that of Portia, the patient wife of the great Roman politician Brutus.

An excerpt from
Abigail Adams' Letter to John Adams
March 31, 1776

I long to hear that you have declared an independancy—and by the way the new Code of Laws which I suppose it will be necessary for you to make I desire you would Remember the Ladies, and be more generous and favorable to them than your ancestors. Do not put such unlimited power into the hands of the Husbands. Remember all Men would be tyrants if they could. If particular care and attention is not paid to the Ladies we are determined to foment a Rebellion, and will not hold ourselves bound by any Laws in which we have no voice, or Representation.

That your Sex are Naturally Tyrannical is a Truth so thoroughly established as to admit of no dispute, but such of you as wish to be happy willingly give up the harsh title of Master for the more tender and endearing one of Friend. Why then, not put it out of the power of the vicious and the Lawless to use us with cruelty and indignity with impunity. Men of Sense in all Ages abhor those customs which treat us only as the vassals of your Sex. Regard us then as Beings placed by providence under your protection and in immitation of the Supreem Being make use of that power only for our happiness.

Elizabeth Burgin
"INDEFATIGABLE"

The air had the tang of salt, underlying the stench of unwashed bodies and sickness. As Elizabeth Burgin stepped out of her small boat and onto the ship, she shivered in the biting wind, trying to keep her balance as the choppy waves rocked the deck underfoot. She carried only a basket of food . . . but she also carried something that couldn't be seen: hope.

The Revolutionary War was raging between the British and the American patriots. British prison ships were anchored in New York harbor. On board were hundreds of American prisoners of war. The ships were crowded and filthy, there was very little food or water, and many men died from diseases like smallpox and yellow fever.

Elizabeth Burgin, who lived in New York, was one of the few American women allowed onto these ships to help the prisoners. Men were not permitted on board. Elizabeth visited the prisoners often. She brought them food and provided the only contact they had with the outside world. She could deliver messages to their families and tell them the news of the war.

From 1776 to 1783, the British forces occupying New York City used abandoned or decommissioned warships (above) anchored just offshore to hold those soldiers, sailors, and private citizens they had captured in battle or arrested on land or at sea.

One evening, as Elizabeth left the prison ships and returned to shore, she was stopped by an American officer named George Higday. He was part of George Washington's Culper spy ring in New York City. Higday had a plan to secretly free some of the American prisoners, but he needed help to alert them about the plan. He knew that Elizabeth had access to the ships. She would be able to tell the men to be ready for escape. Elizabeth agreed, and over the next few weeks, she helped to smuggle more than two hundred prisoners off the prison ships and to freedom. Because the British did not count the number of prisoners on their ships, they did not realize how many men were escaping until George Higday was arrested. Higday's wife told the British about Elizabeth Burgin, and the British offered a reward of two hundred pounds for her capture. This was equal to almost twenty years' pay for a British soldier. It made Elizabeth's capture very tempting. She was almost caught, but escaped to Long Island without her children or any of her possessions. "William Scudder came to Long Island in a Whale boat and I made my escape with him we were being chased by two boats half way to the Sound them got to New England and came to Philadelphia," she later wrote.

We know very little about Elizabeth Burgin and exactly how she helped save these men. She might have disappeared completely into history if not for what happened next. Once she reached Philadelphia, without any money or any belongings, Elizabeth wrote a letter to the Board of War, asking them to allow her to return to New York under a flag of truce so that she could get her children. She received an answer from board's secretary:

> Madam, Last evening took an opportunity of writing upon Mr. Mattock, informed him of your circumstances and particularly in the manner and for what you were obliged to leave New York. Also informed him that you intended making application for a flag [of truce]. From my representation of your character, your polite and humane conduct towards the American prisoners in general, and one in particular, he has promised to pay particular attention to your application and grant you anything in his possession were it possible. I shall wait upon you this evening and depend a stone shall not be left unturned by me to procure anything you may want. Madam, I am your Most Obedient Servant, Robert Campbell.

Elizabeth was permitted to return to New York to her children, but she was not allowed to bring

On prison ships like the HMS *Jersey*, the quarters were crowded and the prisoners were given little food or water. Diseases like smallpox and yellow fever spread easily.

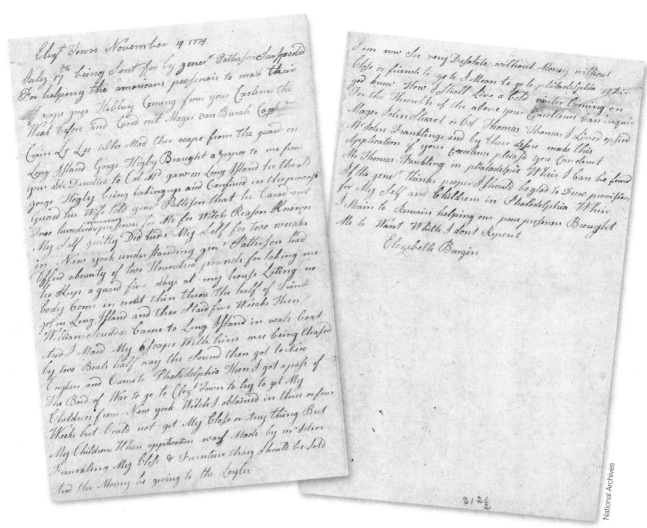

In this letter from Elizabeth Burgin to Reverend James Calville, written on November 19, 1779, Burgin asks for assistance. She was in New Jersey with her three children, forced to flee her home in New York and hide from the British for her role in helping American prisoners escape from prison ships in New York Harbor.

her furniture or any other belongings. As a result, Elizabeth found herself without any money or any place to go. Desperate, she wrote another letter, but this time to General George Washington himself:

> I am now sir very desolate without money without clothes or friends to go to. I mean to go Philadelphia where God knows how I shall live a cold winter coming on . . . If the General thinks proper I should be glad to draw provisions for myself and children in Philadelphia where I mean to remain.

Elizabeth ended her letter by saying, "Helping our poor prisoners brought me to want which I don't repent." Even though she found herself without money or a place to go because of her role in helping American prisoners, she never regretted her actions.

George Washington read her letter and then wrote to the Continental Congress, saying, "Regarding Elizabeth Burgin, recently an inhabitant of New York. From the testimony of our own (escaped) officers . . . it would appear that she has been indefatigable for the relief of the prisoners, and for the facilitation of their escape. For this conduct she incurred the suspicion of the British, and was forced to make her escape under disturbing circumstances."

In 1781, the Continental Congress awarded Elizabeth Burgin a pension in thanks for the part she played in helping the cause of the Revolution. Because of her letters, we at least have a small glimpse of an ordinary woman who did something extraordinarily brave for her country.

George Washington
AND SLAVERY

George Washington was well known as a patriot and our first president, but he was also a farmer. In this painting, Washington stands among African American field workers harvesting grain; Mount Vernon in background.

Many people wonder how George Washington, the father of liberty and freedom, could own slaves. By our modern social values and ethics, it is difficult to understand the world in which Washington lived—a world where slavery was common and people were not treated equally.

At the age of 11, Washington inherited ten slaves in his father's will. He was certainly accustomed to the institution of slavery. His father, brothers, and neighbors used slaves to work their land, keep their houses, and even help care for their children. Between 1743 and 1775, Washington purchased an additional 50 to 75 slaves, and Martha Custis brought 25 slaves into her marriage with Washington in 1759. By that time, Washington was working hard to establish a successful farming

By Nancy E. Hayward, *Footsteps*, © by Carus Publishing Company. Reproduced with permission.

operation at Mount Vernon, and to establish himself in Virginia society. The acquisition and management of land and property was a measure of one's social standing.

An Economic Dependency

Like his contemporaries, Washington was dependent upon a colonial plantation system that used slave labor. He and other large landowners had thousands of acres under cultivation. Since there were few **indentured servants** available to work the land, colonists had to look elsewhere for labor. By the late 1600s, slavery had become firmly rooted in the plantation economy. Slave labor offered a permanent labor force that was economically more advantageous than contracting with indentured servants or **itinerant** free men.

In the Chesapeake Bay region in the 1700s, most slave owners knew their slaves and often worked in the fields with them. At smaller properties and farms, slaves often shared their owners' homes. George Washington certainly knew most of the slaves at Mount Vernon. He was familiar with their names, their work skills, their families, and their personalities. Yet his relationship with them always remained formal. One possible exception was Billy Lee, who served Washington throughout the Revolutionary War, and was the only slave granted immediate freedom in Washington's will.

A Shift in Attitude

Although Washington probably viewed slavery as a normal aspect of his world when he was a young man, his attitude began to change as he grew older. Prior to the revolution, he promised not to sell any slave without his or her permission, because he did not wish to break up family units. (There is one recorded exception—he did order the sale of a slave who had been causing serious problems on the estate.) Washington's experience in the Revolutionary War probably had the greatest influence on his attitude toward slavery. He spent eight years leading the army—much of it in the North, where slavery was far less common than at home in Virginia—and saw firsthand an economic system that did not depend upon slavery. More important, the concepts and ideals for which he was fighting were directly opposite to the system that viewed human beings as property. Almost certainly, Washington saw the irony in this situation.

In 1794, he wrote to a friend, "Were it not then, that I am principled against selling Negroes, as you do cattle in the market, I would not, in

> **Indentured servants** agree to work for another person for a given length of time, as an apprentice to a master.
>
> **Itinerant** refers to people whose work or profession requires them to travel from place to place.

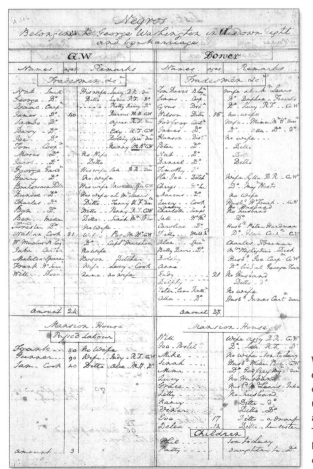

Courtesy of Mount Vernon Ladies' Association

Washington kept detailed records of his slaves and updated these accounts regularly. This page is from his 1799 Census of Slaves.

By Nancy E. Hayward, *Footsteps*, © by Carus Publishing Company. Reproduced with permission.

Abolitionists refer to people who worked to end slavery.

Dower slaves were slaves given to a widow when her husband died.

twelve months from this date, be possessed of one, as a slave...."

As president, Washington was approached by **abolitionists** who wanted his support. Although his personal attitude had changed, Washington considered the issue of slavery volatile enough to tear the struggling young nation apart. He felt the southern states would never agree, and refused to take a public stand. As early as 1786, however, he wrote to his friend John Francis Mercer:

> I never mean (unless some particular circumstances should compel me to it) to possess another slave by purchase; it being among my first wishes to see some plan adopted by the Legislature by which slavery in the Country may be abolished by slow, sure, and imperceptible degrees.

Washington also had an economic reason for wanting slavery abolished. He was an extremely practical man. Both his calculation of the economic return on slaves and his experience at Mount Vernon made him question the economic viability of the system. Washington was, in fact, responsible for feeding and clothing a community of more than 300 people, almost one half of whom were either too old or too young to work.

Granting Freedom

In 1793, he wrote to British agriculturist Arthur Young and proposed renting all but the Mansion House Farm to British tenant farmers. Part of this plan called for freeing his slaves, who would then be paid by the tenant farmers to work the land. The plan illustrates how deeply torn Washington had become over the issue of slavery. If successful, the plan would have provided them with a means of support. Washington feared that freeing slaves without proper training in a trade would set them adrift in the world. The plan, however, was never implemented. Instead, Washington chose to use his will as the means to free the 123 slaves at Mount Vernon who belonged to him. He also stipulated in his will that younger slaves be trained in a skill or trade before being freed, and that those too old or too ill to work be cared for by his estate. Washington's struggle with slavery, however, was only partly successful since, by law, he was unable to free the **dower slaves** (slaves owned by the estate of Martha Washington's first husband). As a result, family units were broken apart and separated. Thus, he understood better than most the cost slavery would eventually have on our nation.

In his will, Washington specified that children whose parents were unable or unwilling to care for them would be bound by the Court until reaching the age of 25. Under his specific direction, they were to be taught to read and write and to be taught a "useful occupation."

Image courtesy of John T. Frey, Clerk Fairfax Circuit Court

By Nancy E. Hayward, *Footsteps*, © by Carus Publishing Company. Reproduced with permission.

GENERAL OF THE CONTINENTAL ARMY:
June 15, 1775 to December 23, 1783

PRESIDENT OF THE UNITED STATES:
April 30, 1789 to March 4, 1797

BIRTH DATE:
1732 at Pope's Creek, Virginia

DEATH DATE:
1799 at Mount Vernon, Virginia (Age 67)

HEIGHT:
6' 2"

WIFE:
Martha Dandridge Custis Washington
(Married in 1759)

CHILDREN:
None

RELIGION:
Anglican/Episcopalian

POLITICAL AFFILIATION:
None

GEORGE WASHINGTON

DID YOU KNOW?

★ **George Washington did not attend college.**
When George's father died in 1743, George's formal education ended. Unlike his father and two older half-brothers, lack of money prevented the boy from studying in England, and unlike many of the Founding Fathers, Washington did not attend college. Always sensitive to this lack of formal education, Washington embarked upon a lifelong pursuit of self-education. Washington was an avid reader and was continually seeking the latest texts on a variety of subjects ranging from military arts to agriculture and political topics.

★ **Washington helped establish a number of charitable organizations, schools, and colleges.**
Despite not having a formal education, Washington was a strong supporter of education. Toward the end of the Revolution, he gave 50 guineas to Washington College in Chestertown, Maryland, which was used to purchase scientific equipment. In his will, Washington left money for the support of a free school for poor and orphaned children in Alexandria, Virginia, and for Liberty Hall Academy, which later became Washington & Lee University. Washington also left money for the establishment of a national university within the Federal City (Washington, DC), but this never came about.

MOUNT VERNON

★ **Washington was called the "foremost farmer" of America.**
An Englishman described Washington as the "foremost farmer" in America after visiting Mount Vernon. Washington, who believed that America should become a "granary to the world," was a pioneer in improving many aspects of farming. His advanced crop rotations, use of fertilizers, experimentation with crops, and innovative farm equipment made him one of the leading agricultural leaders in America.

★ **Washington did not have children of his own.**
Washington was fond of children, but he and Martha did not have any children of their own. Martha Washington had two children, John Parke Custis and Martha Parke Custis, from her previous marriage. There were always children in the Washington household throughout their marriage. Together they raised Mrs. Washington's two children, as well as two of her four grandchildren, and several nieces and nephews. A great-grandchild was born at Mount Vernon just two weeks before George Washington's death.

MARTHA WASHINGTON

★ **Washington lost more battles than he won, but his leadership helped secure American independence.**
Given Washington's ultimate success during the Revolution, it's important to consider that he lost more battles than he won throughout his military career. In many of the battles that Washington either directly led or played an important role in, his forces were defeated. Despite the long list of defeats, Washington brought many important characteristics to his military command. His ability to rally men under fire, his ability to sustain the Continental Army's morale, his administrative talents, and his grasp of the larger strategy all made Washington the great general that history remembers and celebrates.

★ **Washington was the first to sign the Constitution.**
As the President of the Constitutional Convention, George Washington was the first to sign this important document.

WASHINGTON CROSSING THE DELAWARE

★ **Washington was unanimously elected President of the United States, twice.**
At this early stage of the United States, presidents were selected only through the vote of the Electoral College, not by popular vote. The 69 votes that Washington received in 1789, and the 132 he received in 1792 represented all of the available Electoral College votes, thereby making Washington the only president in United States history to have been unanimously elected.

Oney Judge
Washington's Runaway Slave

She was born in 1773, an enslaved person in one of the most famous households of her time: Mount Vernon, the home of George Washington and his wife, Martha. By the time she died in New Hampshire 75 years later, she had become one of the best-known of Washington's slaves, because Oney Judge told her story to an abolitionist newspaper, the story of someone who actually escaped from the household of the United States' first president.

Oney's mother was an enslaved person named Betty, who worked as a seamstress at Mount Vernon. Oney's father, Andrew Judge, was an indentured servant who came from England. In exchange for his passage to America and his room and board, he agreed to work as a tailor for the Washingtons for four years. When Andrew Judge gained his freedom, however, Oney and her mother stayed behind, still slaves belonging to Washington's wife, Martha Custis. Oney grew up in the Washington manor house, a playmate and servant to Martha Washington's granddaughter, Nelly Custis. She also became an expert at sewing.

When the Washington household moved first to New York City in 1789, and then to Philadelphia in 1790, Oney was one of the seven slaves they brought with them. Soon Oney had become Mrs. Washington's personal attendant, helping her dress and powder her hair for official receptions, going with her to social events and visits, and running errands in the city. Oney also made friends with many of the free blacks living in Philadelphia at the time. They told her about liberty and freedom, ideas that Oney found appealing.

In 1796, Washington decided to spend his summer back at Mount Vernon. Oney knew that if she returned with the family to Virginia, her chance of seeking the freedom she had heard so much about would be very slim. Mrs. Washington had also told Oney that she intended to give her as a gift to her oldest granddaughter, Elizabeth Custis, who was going to be married. Oney refused to accept the idea that she would be given like a possession, no different from a piece of furniture. She decided to escape.

"Whilst they were packing up to go to Virginia, I was packing to go; I didn't know where, for I knew that if I went back to Virginia, I should never get my liberty. I had friends among the colored people of Philadelphia, had my things carried there before hand, and left while the Washingtons were eating dinner," Oney told a newspaper years later. Her friends hid her until they could find a passage on a ship that was heading north. Soon Oney found herself in Portsmouth, New Hampshire.

Meanwhile, Mrs. Washington was quite upset at the idea that her property was gone. She even suspected that someone had stolen Oney away, since she felt that Oney had been given a good life with the Washingtons and couldn't possibly have wanted to leave. She persuaded the president's steward to place an advertisement offering a reward for Oney's return:

> Absconded from the household of the President of the United States, ONEY JUDGE, a light mulatto girl, much freckled, with very black eyes and bushy black hair. She is of middle stature, slender, and delicately formed, about 20 years of age... Ten dollars will be paid to any person who will bring her home, if taken in the city, or on board any vessel in the harbor: and a reasonable additional sum if apprehended at, and brought from a greater distance, and in proportion to the distance.
>
> FREDERICK KITT, Steward
> May 23, 1796

Oney might have lived peacefully in Portsmouth if it hadn't been for a moment of very bad luck. As she was walking through the streets of the town one day, she passed Elizabeth Langdon, who was a friend of Martha Washington's granddaughter and had visited the Washington home in Philadelphia many times. Elizabeth recognized Oney and tried to talk to her, but Oney scurried away. But the damage was done. Elizabeth passed the word back to George Washington that she knew where his wife's escaped slave was. Washington himself had signed a Fugitive Slave Act in 1793 (probably putting his signature on it just a few feet from where Oney was working), which guaranteed the rights of slaveholders to regain their property when their slaves escaped. Washington knew that slavery was no longer a popular institution in the North, and he had even replaced many of his slaves with indentured servants. But that did not stop him from immediately writing to the customs officer in Portsmouth, Joseph Whipple. He asked Whipple for help in getting Oney back.

Whipple found Oney and talked with her. He did not want to force her to return to Virginia, because he was afraid it would cause a riot among the anti-slavery people in Portsmouth. Instead, he offered her a deal: he would persuade the Washingtons to promise to free her after their deaths, if she returned to them now on her own. Oney refused. Washington himself was not happy when he heard about the deal, and Oney's response:

> I regret that the attempt you made to restore the Girl (Oney Judge as she called herself while with us, and who, without the least provocation absconded from her Mistress) should have been attended with so little Success. To enter into such a compromise with her is totally inadmissible, for ... it would neither be politic or just to reward unfaithfulness ... and thereby discontent the minds of all her fellow-servants who by their steady attachments are far more deserving than herself of favor.

In 1797 Washington retired from the presidency. Oney was still living in Portsmouth, now married to a sailor named Jack Staines and the mother of a baby. Washington sent his nephew, Burnwell Bassett, to Portsmouth, to again try to bring Oney back to Virginia. This time the Langdon family helped Oney. When Bassett had dinner with them and told them of his mission, they sent word to Oney and she went into hiding with her family. After Washington died three months later, Oney recalled that "... they never troubled me any more after he was gone."

Oney lived the rest of her life as a free woman, although she was still technically a fugitive slave. She learned to read, and told her story to the antislavery newspaper *The Granite Freeman* in 1845. She died in Greenland, New Hampshire in 1848, remembered by the title of the article about her: "Washington's runaway slave."

Olaudah Equiano

Sailing from Slavery to Freedom

Being captured in Africa as a slave in the 1750s was not an unusual story. Many young men were abducted from their villages and forced to become slaves. Olaudah Equiano's story started the same way, when he was kidnapped from his village of Eboe in what is now Nigeria, along the Niger River. His father was a village leader and it was expected that Olaudah would also grow up to be a chief, judge, or elder of his people.

But all that changed when Olaudah was stolen. As a slave, he went from master to master in Africa until he found himself at the African coast and on a white man's slave ship heading for Barbados. Olaudah eventually ended up in the colony of Jamestown, where he was purchased by Michael Henry Pascal, a lieutenant in the Royal Navy. Here is where Olaudah's story becomes unusual. In the seven years that he was owned by Pascal (who gave him the name Gustavas Vassa), Olaudah not only traveled the world on the ships that Pascal commanded, but became educated, too. This would enable him, as an adult, to write his autobiography in 1789. His story would not only show his wonder at all the new things he was experiencing, but also his reaction to the often-terrible ways that Europeans treated slaves.

Olaudah had hopes that Pascal would be kind enough to free him, so he was shocked when Pascal abruptly sold him during a stop in England. He found himself passed between several more masters during the next few years. He continued to travel the world on slave ships, naval vessels, and trading ships. When he served in a ship belonging to one of his masters, Robert King, he was able to start his own side business of buying and selling goods. He saved enough money to buy his freedom in 1766. He returned to England where he was able to go to school as well as work as an assistant to a scientist, Dr. Charles Irving. Irving was an inventor who was working on a machine that would turn seawater into fresh water. In 1773, with Dr. Irving, he was part of an expedition trying to discover the legendary Northwest Passage, which would allow ships to sail to the Pacific Ocean by going through the Arctic. The ship became icebound and Olaudah nearly drowned.

Olaudah returned to England and became an active abolitionist, speaking and writing against the English slave trade and the cruelty of many slave owners. He also worked to help freed slaves find new homes. He married Susannah Cullen in 1792 and had two daughters. His 1789 autobiography, *The Interesting Narrative of the Life of Olaudah Equiano, or Gustavus Vassa, the African*, went through eight editions in England and one in America and was widely read.

Olaudah Equiano died in 1797. It wasn't until ten years after his death that slavery was officially abolished in England. But it is thanks to Olaudah's circumstances as a slave, and his education and travels, that we are able to understand through his words more about what it meant to be an enslaved person at that time.

PRIMARY SOURCE

Olaudah Equiano's Account

In his autobiography The Interesting Narrative of the Life of Olaudah Equiano, or Gustavus Vassa, the African, *Equiano recounts his kidnapping by Africans at the age of eleven.*

One day, when all our people were gone out to their work as usual, and only I and my dear sister were left to mind the house, two men and a woman got over our walls and in a moment seized us both, and, without giving us time to cry out, or make resistance, they stopped our mouths, and ran off with us into the nearest wood. Here they tied our hands, and continued to carry us as far as they could, till night came on, when we reached a small house where the robbers halted for refreshment, and spent the night.

We were then unbound, but were unable to take any food; and, being quite overpowered by fatigue and grief, our only relief was some sleep, which allayed our misfortune for a short time. The next morning we left the house, and continued travelling all the day. For a long time we had kept [to] the woods, but at last we came into a road which I believed I knew. I had now some hopes of being delivered; for we had advanced but a little way before I discovered some people at a distance, on which I began to cry out for their assistance: but my cries had no other effect than to make them tie me faster and stop my mouth, and then they put me into a large sack.

HISTORICAL IMAGE

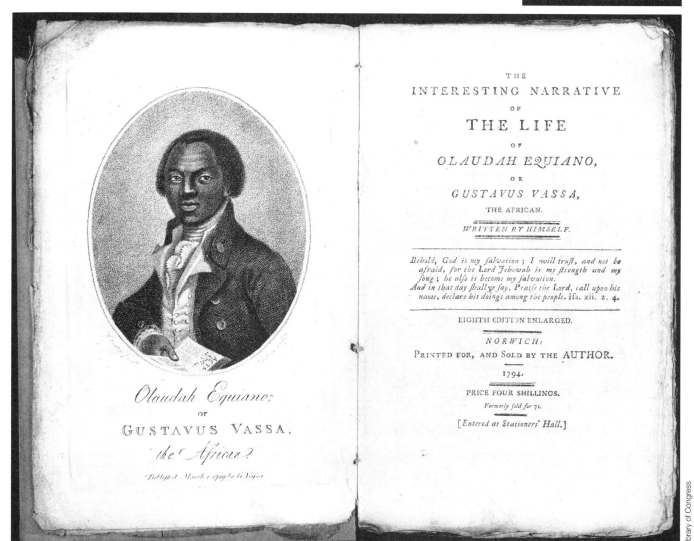

Olaudah Equiano was born in 1745 in what is now Nigeria. He wrote an autobiography about his life, which tells of being kidnapped from Africa as a child and sold into slavery. He bought his freedom and became part of the abolition movement. He died on March 3, 1797, in London.

HISTORICAL IMAGE

Olaudah Equiano would have traveled on his expedition in 1773 on a ship much like the ones shown here when he accompanied Dr. Charles Irving to the Arctic, searching for the Northwest Passage from Europe to Asia.

Petitioning for Freedom

The colonists challenging Great Britain for their liberty and independence did not have African Americans in mind when they engaged in their protests.

During the Revolutionary War, African Americans seized hold of the ideas of equality, freedom, and representation that circulated widely in the Colonies. They used these revolutionary doctrines to condemn slavery and their inferior place in American society and to demand rights that were reserved for white Americans.

Even before the Revolutionary War broke out, enslaved people in the Northern colonies formally requested their freedom from political authorities. A Boston slave named Felix submitted a "humble Petition" on behalf of "many slaves" living in Massachusetts. Felix may have been the first enslaved person to petition his colony's government, calling for an end to slavery. Slaves and their children, he charged in 1773, could not "enjoy any Thing, no, not even Life itself, but in a Manner as the Beasts that perish. We have no Property! . . . We have no City! No Country!" Shortly after, six slaves from Thompson, Massachusetts, boldly demanded "ample relief" from the legislature, for "as men, we have a natural right" to freedom, they said.

In 1779, two Connecticut slaves demanded "nothing, but what we are fully persuaded is ours to claim." Insisting that they, too, were "Creatures of . . . God," they were "Convinced of

The image (above) accompanied the 1837 publication of abolitionist John Greenleaf Whittier's antislavery poem *Our Countrymen in Chains*.

In June 1775, the Committee of Correspondence for Massachusetts' Worcester County published this notice (left) supporting the end of slavery.

Prince Hall submitted the bill above to a Colonel Craft of the Patriot forces for five leather drumheads he had made for the Boston Regiment of Artillery.

our Right . . . to be free . . . and can never be convinced that we were made to be Slaves."

Through their words, enslaved men and women made clear that they neither accepted the justness of their enslavement nor believed that revolutionary ideas belonged only to white colonists. Drawing upon political and religious principles, one group "held in a state of Slavery within a free and Christian Country" insisted that they had been unjustly enslaved "by the cruel hand of power" and "stolen" from Africa. This was wrong, they argued, for they held in "common with all other men, a naturel right to our freedoms."

In 1777, a former Boston slave, Prince Hall, and eight others reminded the Massachusetts legislature of the inconsistency of whites' denouncing their own supposed enslavement by

Antislavery Milestones

- The first colony to abolish slavery was Vermont in 1777. During or right after the American Revolution, many of the northern states began the process of eliminating slavery. Pennsylvania (1780), Massachusetts (1783), Connecticut and Rhode Island (1784), and New York (1799) adopted laws that allowed for the gradual freedom of the enslaved.

- The British government passed a law abolishing the importation of slaves in 1807.

- The United States passed a law that ends the importation of slaves in 1808.

- Great Britain voted into law the Slave Emancipation Act of 1833, ending slavery in the British Empire.

- The Civil War between the Union (the Northern states) and the Confederacy (Southern states that seceded from the Union) over slavery began in 1861 and ended in 1865.

- President Abraham Lincoln issued the Emancipation Proclamation on January 1, 1863, which abolished slavery in the Confederacy, but not in the border states or the southern states that were controlled by the North.

- The Thirteenth Amendment abolished slavery throughout the United States in 1865.

the British while they owned their own slaves. The men called upon the legislators to uphold "the Natural Rights of all men" by abolishing slavery.

While American and British troops fought one another in 1780, a group of seven "freemen" living in Dartmouth, Massachusetts, condemned American policies toward blacks, using the white colonists' arguments against taxation without representation. Describing themselves as "Chiefly of the African Extraction," the men objected to paying taxes to their community while being deprived of representation in government. By "reason of Long Bondag and hard Slavery," they bitterly wrote to the Massachusetts legislature in Boston, "we have been deprived of Injoying the Profits of our Labouer or the advantage of Inheriting Estates from our Parents as our Neighbouers the white people do" even though they were established taxpayers. Taxation without representation—a familiar complaint of white colonists—had reduced them to a state of poverty. They argued that this was particularly wrong at a time when "many of our Colour [as is well known] have cheerfully Entered the field of Battle in defense of the Common cause."

Paul Cuffe, who would one day become a wealthy shipbuilder and merchant, was one of the seven signers. Cuffe and his brother had refused to pay taxes for three years to protest their lack of political rights. They were jailed for nonpayment.

In most cases, these petitions did not immediately alter conditions for the slaves demanding freedom and greater rights. But the arguments were eventually heard. Some white Northerners grew increasingly uncomfortable with the apparent **hypocrisy** of seeking more rights for themselves while limiting the rights of Africans and African Americans. By the end of the 1700s, Northern states had passed laws calling for the gradual emancipation of slaves. Eventually, the institution of slavery came to an end in the North—but not in the South.

Although black Northerners continued to live and labor under greater restrictions than whites, they had effectively used the language and principles of the American Revolution to call their own slavery into question. In the decades that followed, black Americans would continue to draw upon the principle of equality to illustrate how the United States was not living up to its founding ideals and would press relentlessly for change.

Sixteen white officers sent this petition to Congress requesting that a free black named Salem Poor (see highlighted line above) be rewarded for his valor.

Hypocrisy is defined as saying or feeling one thing and doing another.

Mum Bett
"Her name ought to be preserved"

British writer Harriet Martineau said of Elizabeth Freeman (later known as Mum Bett), "A woman once lived in Massachusetts whose name ought to be preserved in all histories of the state." But who was Mum Bett, and why should we remember her?

Elizabeth Freeman was born around 1742. Her parents were enslaved, and she and her sister were sold to Colonel John Ashley of Sheffield, Massachusetts, when Elizabeth was only six months old. She worked for Ashley for 40 years, and was eventually known as Mum Bett. One day when Ashley's wife tried to hit Mum Bett's sister with a heated kitchen shovel, Bett blocked the blow with her arm. She would have scars from the shovel for the rest of her life. Bett was so furious with her mistress that she left the house and refused to return. Colonel Ashley went to court to force her to return, since she was his property.

But Mum Bett had been listening carefully for years, whenever the wealthy men she served talked about the Bill of Rights and Massachusetts' new state constitution. She decided that if those documents claimed that all people were born free and equal, then those laws must apply to her, too. So she sued Colonel Ashley for her freedom.

Bett's case, which soon included another of Ashley's slaves, a man named Brom, went to court. The jury decided in their favor, making Bett and Brom the first enslaved people to be freed under the Massachusetts Constitution. Ashley also had to pay them thirty shillings each and their court costs. Bett went to work for the lawyer who had helped her win her case.

Mum Bett died a free woman in 1829, in the free state of Massachusetts that she helped create. One of her great-grandchildren was W. E. B. Du Bois, author, historian, and civil rights advocate.

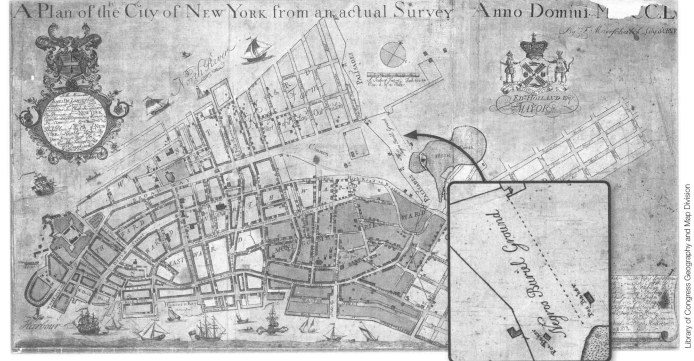

NEW YORK CITY'S
African Burial Ground

When it comes to studying the lives of Colonial America's enslaved people, their burial sites can become classrooms, answering questions found in few other places.

In many instances, native Africans lived near European immigrants during the early years of colonial settlement. When Africans and their descendants formed a small minority in these communities, the custom was to bury everyone in the same area. However, as the numbers of enslaved and free blacks increased, racial prejudice mandated that separate plots be set aside for blacks and whites.

A 1689 New York law prohibited blacks—free and enslaved—from being buried with whites. Perhaps it was this law that led to the development of what became known as the "Negros Buriel Ground." This area, originally located in the Dutch settlement of New York, is now in the heart of the New York City borough of Manhattan.

The location of the "Negros Buriel Ground" is clearly marked on this 1755 map of New York City.

A plot of land measuring five and one-half acres, the "Negros Buriel Ground" became the resting place for what scientists believe to be over 10,000 people of African descent. The first burials actually occurred in the 1600s; the last, in the 1800s. Gradually, as New York City expanded, new construction took over the site, with buildings being raised first around and then directly on top of the graves.

In 1991, construction workers uncovered the remains of people who had been buried there more than 200 years earlier. Howard University anthropologists first removed the more than 400 skeletons. They then focused on studying the remains to learn all they could about these early American residents.

By Dianne Swann-Wright, *Footsteps*, © by Carus Publishing Company. Reproduced with permission.

The African Burial Ground in New York City, a national monument, is the single-most important, historic urban archaeological project undertaken in the United States.

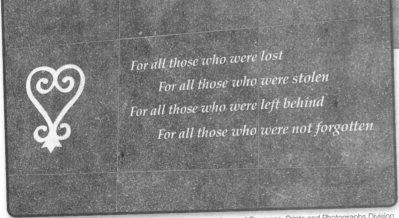

For all those who were lost
For all those who were stolen
For all those who were left behind
For all those who were not forgotten

Top and bottom: Carol M. Highsmith Archive, Library of Congress, Prints and Photographs Division

Analysis of the bones revealed important information about the lives and deaths of the buried men, women, and children. Many had suffered from poor nutrition. Others had died as the result of acts of violence, such as beatings or gunshot wounds. There were clues that suggested what beliefs people may have had and what they valued. Some of the men and women had had their teeth filed to points or into "hourglass" shapes, following distinct African traditions.

The graves also held items that had been buried along with those who died, such as beads, shells, and African symbols of faith and spirituality. One man may have been buried in his American Revolution uniform, as buttons from such a uniform were found in his coffin. A woman shared a coffin with her infant child. A broken arm bone appeared to have been the result of a person trying to ward off a fatal blow.

The "Negros Buriel Ground" has since been renamed the African Burial Ground. Community members and people throughout the United States and many countries in Africa have honored its existence and preservation. While research using the actual remains has ended, historians continue to use the anthropological findings as a basis to learn more about the people who lived during that time.

By Dianne Swann-Wright, *Footsteps*, © by Carus Publishing Company. Reproduced with permission.

A Closer Look at the Big Five

Among the largest tribes of the Southeast between the 1500s and 1700s were the Cherokees, Creeks, Choctaws, Chickasaws, and Seminoles. By the 1820s, they were referred to as the "Five Civilized Tribes" because they adopted governing systems and customs like those of the United States. Speech similarities were apparent also. The Cherokees spoke a language related to other Iroquoian languages, such as Seneca, while the Creeks, Choctaws, Chickasaws, and Seminoles belonged to the Muskogean language family.

In addition, each tribe had to deal with Europeans as they arrived in North America. The Cherokees, Creeks, and Choctaws developed a prosperous trade with these Europeans, which helped strengthen the Indians' economic position.

However, with the arrival of Spanish explorer Hernando de Soto in 1539, the life these large tribes were accustomed to began to change. The Indians lost a good deal of their populations to the diseases introduced by Europeans. In a smallpox epidemic in 1738, more than ten thousand Cherokees died.

The tribes lived on land that England, France, Spain—and later the United States—highly valued and sought. The Indians found themselves in the middle of the politics among these countries and suffered as a result. For example, the Cherokees and Creeks sided with England during the American Revolution. When England lost and withdrew from America, the Indians were treated as if they had lost the war themselves. But even those who allied themselves with the winning side in different conflicts found themselves on the losing side in the end.

Following is a look at the distinct identity of each tribe.

The Cherokees

The largest group of Iroquoian speakers in the Southeast, the Cherokees probably migrated from the Northeast more than two thousand years ago. In the Southeast, this tribe occupied the southwest Allegheny mountain region of Virginia, the Carolinas, parts of Tennessee, northern Georgia, and northern Alabama. They lived in small villages, each with a seven-sided council

The Cherokee Indians most often allied themselves with the British in colonial America. This delegation of Cherokee chiefs was invited to London in 1762.

Peter Newark American Pictures/Bridgeman Images

By Barbara Krasner-Khait, *Cobblestone*, © by Carus Publishing Company. Reproduced with permission.

Not all contact between the first European settlers and the Southeast Indians was friendly, but some groups did establish prosperous trading relationships.

house, representing the seven Cherokee clans. By 1800, they had organized themselves into a single Cherokee Nation. In 1835, there were about 16,500 Cherokees living in the Southeast.

Referring to themselves as the "Principal People," the Cherokee Nation was strong, and its members stood ready to defend its territory and rights. Of all the southeastern tribes, however, the Cherokees made the most serious efforts to adopt the ways of the Europeans and colonists around them. Sequoya invented a system that allowed his fellow Cherokee Indians to read and write their own language. Some Cherokees also adopted Christianity, set up schools, and published the *Cherokee Phoenix*, an English–Cherokee-language newspaper.

The Choctaws

The Choctaw Indians occupied present-day Alabama and southern Mississippi. Stories of how the Choctaws originated tell of two brothers, Chactas and Chicsa, who led their clans from the West. They traveled together but eventually separated due to bad weather. The clan of Chactas became the Choctaws, and the clan of Chicsa became the Chickasaws.

The Choctaws were known for their agricultural expertise. William Bartram, a **botanist** who explored the region in 1777, described the Choctaws as "most ingenious and industrious husbandmen, having large plantations, or country farms, where they employ much of their time in agricultural improvements, . . . by which means their territories are more generally cultivated, and better inhabited than any other Indian republic that we know of." The Choctaws believed that all members shared their territory, but each family was responsible for its own **subsistence**.

The Choctaws were at war constantly throughout the eighteenth century with the neighboring Chickasaws and Creeks. Prior to the Choctaws' removal by the U.S. government, there were nearly twenty-four thousand of their tribal members in the Southeast.

The Chickasaws

The smallest of the five tribes, the Chickasaws occupied areas in modern-day northern Mississippi, the northwestern tip of Alabama, and south Tennessee. They prided themselves on their military skill and gained wide respect for defending their homeland. The Chickasaws successfully fought off Spanish soldiers under Hernando de Soto in the 1540s. They also repelled French invasions several times and became enemies of the Choctaws, who were allies of the French. About four thousand Chickasaws existed in 1827.

The Creeks

A confederacy of related tribes known as the Creeks lived east of the Choctaws in Alabama and western Georgia.

A **botanist** is one who studies the science of plants.

Subsistence is the act of maintaining life.

These tribes included the Alabamas, Yuchis, Cowetas, Coosas, Tallapoosas, Tuskegees, and later the Natchez and Shawnees. In 1832, there were about twenty-three thousand Creek people. They called themselves Muscogulges.

The Creeks played one European nation against another and profited from the outcome. For example, in the early eighteenth century, the Creeks offered friendship to the British in the Carolinas to protect themselves against the Spanish in Florida and the French in Louisiana. This also helped them fight against tribes allied with the Spanish and the French. Their numbers grew as **refugees** from uprooted Indian communities joined them. The Creeks were neutral during the French and Indian Wars (1754–1763) but sided with the British during the American Revolution.

The War of 1812 proved to be the undoing of the Creeks. In 1813, the British helped a conservative group of Creeks known as the Red Sticks to fight the Americans. General Andrew Jackson, whose army included many Cherokee warriors, defeated the Red Sticks. As a result, the Creeks lost a great deal of their power and about one quarter of their population.

The Seminoles

The Seminoles of Florida consisted of several groups of Creeks who moved to that area in the eighteenth and early nineteenth centuries. Fiercely independent and freedom loving, the Seminoles lived in villages of about one hundred members. Their palmetto-thatched huts, called chickees, were built around an open square. They cultivated the land, and each family had its own garden. Everyone worked in communal plots to grow food for the needy and for guests.

> **Refugees** are people who flee in search of shelter or protection during times of war or oppression.

Solomon McCombs, a Creek artist, painted to preserve a record of the way of life of his people. Here, men and women play stickball (similar to lacrosse) in his *Creek Indian Social Ball Game*.

Solomon McCombs, *Creek Indian Social Ball Game*, c.1957, Watercolor on paper, Museum purchase, 1957.7, ©2014 Philbrook Museum of Art, Inc., Tulsa, Oklahoma

Fred Beaver, *Seminole Family at Work*, 1948, Watercolor on board, Museum purchase, 1948.18, ©2014 Philbrook Museum of Art. Inc., Tulsa, Oklahoma

***Seminole Family at Work**, offering a view of traditional Seminole daily life, was painted by Creek-Seminole artist Fred Beaver.*

The Seminoles were expert builders of watercrafts. This allowed them to venture great distances. They explored the Gulf of Mexico and even reached Cuba and the Bahamas. Seminole villages became a haven for runaway slaves up until the Indians' removal from Florida in 1835. After Spain sold Florida to the United States in 1819, slavecatchers seized full-blooded Seminole Indians and runaway slaves and sold them both in slave markets. By 1832, the Seminoles numbered about six thousand.

Between 1816 and 1821, the United States negotiated several treaties with four of these Indian nations. As a result, the Cherokees gave up small parcels of land in northern Alabama and Georgia, east Tennessee, and western North Carolina. The Creeks surrendered a large tract of land in central Georgia. The Chickasaws sold western Kentucky, western Tennessee, and part of northern Alabama. The Choctaws ceded large blocks of land in western Alabama.

These were not easy negotiations. The tribes did not agree to give up all that the federal government asked for, despite pressure to do so. And in the end, each of the five tribes was subject to the United States' decision to forcibly relocate them to the Oklahoma Territory under the Indian Removal Act of 1830.

A small group of Seminoles, most of whom had settled in Florida's Everglades, were able to resist the forced removal. Smaller groups of Choctaws, Cherokees, Chickasaws, and Creeks also remained in their homelands, and their descendants can be found there today.

By Barbara Krasner-Khait, *Cobblestone*, © by Carus Publishing Company. Reproduced with permission.

Delaware Tribe Speech

UNNAMED (DELAWARE AND TWELVE OTHER TRIBES)

The Council of 1793 tried to persuade the U.S. government to honor its own treaties and use the Ohio River as a boundary across which settlement by whites would be forbidden. The government, meanwhile, wanted to push all the tribes across the Mississippi. The Native Americans proposed another plan, which follows.

"Our only demand is the peaceable possession of a small part of our once great country" (1793)

Money to us is of no value, and to most of us unknown; and as no consideration whatever can induce us to sell the lands on which we get sustenance for our women and children, we hope we may be allowed to point out a mode by which your settlers may be easily removed, and peace thereby obtained.

We know that these settlers are poor, or they would never have ventured to live in a country which has been in continual trouble ever since they crossed the Ohio. Divide, therefore, this large sum of money which you have offered us among these people; give to each, also, a proportion of what you say you would give to us annually, over and above this very large sum of money, and we are persuaded they would most readily accept of it in lieu of the lands you sold them. If you add, also, the great sums you must expend in raising and paying armies with a view to force us to yield you our country, you will certainly have more than sufficient for the purpose of repaying these settlers for all their labor and their improvements.

You have talked to us about concessions. It appears strange that you should expect any from us, who have only been defending our just rights against your invasions. We want peace. Restore to us our country, and we shall be enemies no longer.

We desire you to consider, brothers, that our only demand is the peaceable possession of a small part of our once great country. Look back and review the lands from whence we have been driven to this spot. We can retreat no rather, because the country behind hardly affords food for its present inhabitants, and we have therefore resolved to leave our bones in this small spot to which we are now confined.

ROAD TO A CONSTITUTION

September 1774
First Continental Congress meets to consider action against British; adopts both **Declaration and Resolves** and **Articles of Association** in October.

> The **Declaration and Resolves** and the **Articles of Association** were two documents passed by the First Continental Congress in 1774 and presented to King George III. They outlined a number of the Patriots' grievances against British rule.

April 1775
Revolutionary War begins at battles of Lexington and Concord in Massachusetts.

July 1776
Congress adopts Declaration of Independence.

November 1777
Second Continental Congress adopts Articles of Confederation.

1781
In March, Articles of Confederation become law of the land after approval by last of the states. In October, Revolutionary War fighting ends with surrender of British at Yorktown.

Declaration of Independence

1783
Treaty of Paris, signed on September 3, establishes formal terms for ending Revolutionary War.

1785
Delegates from Virginia and Maryland meet to settle disputes over navigational rights to Potomac River; set date for Annapolis Convention.

September 1786
Only five states attend Annapolis Convention to discuss relations among states; date is set for convention of all states.

May–September 1787
Constitutional Convention held in Philadelphia; Constitution is written and sent to states; three states ratify it by mid-December.

State House, Philadelphia

1788
Eight more states ratify Constitution, giving more than two-thirds majority needed to become law.

1789
New York City becomes first capital of United States. George Washington becomes first president; first Congress meets, writes a bill of rights, and sends it to states for ratification.

1790
Philadelphia becomes temporary U.S. capital. Rhode Island is last state to ratify Constitution, making it unanimous.

1791
First ten amendments to Constitution, known as The Bill of Rights, are adopted.

George Washington

1800
Washington, D.C., becomes permanent U.S. capital.

By Mark Clemens, *Cobblestone*, © by Carus Publishing Company. Reproduced with permission.

THREE MEN THREE PLANS

The one thing the Constitutional Convention delegates found easy to agree on was George Washington's election to preside over the convention.

The men who came together at the Pennsylvania State House in 1787 were a diverse group. Some were farmers; others were lawyers. Some were well-educated; others were self-taught. They did not all know one another, and they represented states with different interests. A few had strong opinions about what had to be accomplished at the Constitutional Convention. Others were undecided about the future course of the country. Some thought they would simply be rewriting the weak Articles of Confederation, while others hoped to discuss a new framework for self-government. Despite their differences of background and opinion, they all came willing to work, listen, argue, and most important, compromise. And these qualities enabled them to achieve something remarkable.

FAST FACT ALTHOUGH 74 DELEGATES WERE APPOINTED TO THE CONVENTION, ONLY 55 ATTENDED SESSIONS.

The convention was supposed to open in mid-May, but not all the delegates had arrived in Philadelphia by then, so the date kept getting pushed back until there was a **quorum**. By May 25, the delegates were ready to begin work. The first order of business was easy—the unanimous election of George Washington as president of the convention. The many decisions that followed proved much more difficult to make.

While there was general agreement that the states should be united under a national government, feelings about how that government should be structured varied greatly. Some delegates continued to believe that the states should hold most of the power. Others were convinced that the country needed a strong central government to rescue it from its economic troubles and gain the respect of foreign powers.

VIRGINIA OFFERS THE FIRST PLAN

A few days before the convention opened, James Madison and Governor Edmund Randolph of Virginia met with Robert Morris and other representatives from Pennsylvania to prepare a plan to put in front of the delegates. Although Madison probably wrote it, the 34-year-old Randolph presented it.

As one of Washington's aides-de-camp during the Revolution and Virginia's former attorney general, Randolph had proven himself a popular leader and a gentleman. Those qualities were apparent on May 29 as he eloquently announced the 15 resolutions set forth in Madison's Virginia Plan. It called for a "supreme Legislative, Executive and Judiciary." The legislature would be bicameral (composed of two houses), with the lower house elected by the people and the upper house elected by members of the lower. The number of seats allotted each state in both houses would be determined by that state's population or wealth. An executive officer would be appointed by the legislature and the judiciary.

Delegates from the smaller states, however, did not like the idea of a legislature based on "proportional representation." Nearly half of the nation's population lived in Virginia, Pennsylvania, and Massachusetts. They argued that if seats were apportioned according to a state's population or wealth, the smaller states would not be represented fairly, and the larger states would rule the country.

Over the next two weeks, the delegates, who were sitting as a **committee of the whole**, debated the Virginia Plan. Latecomers from some of the smaller states lent their support to the opposition, but the larger states would not relent. Then the smaller states, under the leadership of 42-year-old William Paterson of New Jersey, decided to propose a plan of their own.

NEW JERSEY'S SECOND PLAN

The son of an Irish shopkeeper, Paterson had enrolled in the College of New Jersey (later called Princeton University) when he was just 14. After graduating with a master's degree in 1766, he worked as a small-town

Virginia's Edmund Randolph

A **quorum** is the minimum number of members of a group necessary to make the meeting's business official.

Working as a **committee of the whole** means that the votes taken were merely recommendations to be presented to the convention for a final vote at a later date.

FAST FACT NO MORE THAN 11 STATES EVER VOTED AT THE CONVENTION. RHODE ISLAND BOYCOTTED IT AND DID NOT SEND DELEGATES AT ALL, AND AFTER TWO OF NEW YORK'S THREE DELEGATES LEFT ON JULY 10, THE REMAINING NEW YORK DELEGATE DID NOT CAST HIS STATE'S VOTE. MEANWHILE, NEW HAMPSHIRE'S REPRESENTATIVES DID NOT ARRIVE UNTIL JULY 23.

New Jersey's William Paterson

lawyer. He was elected to the First Continental Congress and filled a vacancy left by the secretary. Later, he was named attorney general of New Jersey.

Paterson is probably best known for his New Jersey Plan, which he proposed to the convention on June 15. In it he called for a one-house legislature in which all states would be represented equally, as well as an executive board elected by the legislature and a federal Supreme Court. The larger states opposed Paterson's plan, and four days later, following an impassioned speech by Madison, the delegates voted 7 to 3 to reject it.

As the temperature rose inside the State House chamber, tempers grew shorter. On June 29, the convention appeared on the edge of collapse, as the debate over proportional representation deteriorated into angry mudslinging. Some of the smaller states threatened to leave if the larger states did not give in on this point.

Another vote on July 2 resulted in a tie—5 for the Virginia Plan, 5 against, and 1 undecided. The delegates seemed hopelessly deadlocked. In one final effort to resolve the problem, a committee composed of one delegate from each state was formed. Representing Connecticut was a self-made lawyer and jurist named Roger Sherman.

The men wore wool suits despite the high temperatures inside the State House in Philadelphia. Today it is known as Independence Hall.

By Karen H. Dusek, *Cobblestone*, © by Carus Publishing Company. Reproduced with permission.

CONNECTICUT CALLS FOR COMPROMISE

Connecticut's Roger Sherman

A fellow delegate wrote of Roger Sherman: "... no man has a better Heart or a cleaner Head ... it is remarked that he seldom fails." In fact, during the debates, while those around him were losing their tempers, the 60-year-old Yankee remained calm and never lost sight of the delegates' common goal: to create a strong and able government.

Unable to afford a college education when he was young, Sherman had studied on his own while supporting himself as a surveyor and shoemaker. He became skilled as a lawyer, mathematician, and judge and was to hold some form of political office for 50 years in a row. He also was the only person to sign all the documents on which our country was founded—the Declaration and Resolves, the Articles of Association, the Declaration of Independence, the Articles of Confederation, and the Constitution. His extensive political experience had taught him the value of compromise.

Sherman's idea to resolve the deadlock was simple: a two-house legislature, with seats in one house apportioned according to population, and in the other, equal representation. The convention quickly adopted Sherman's Connecticut Compromise, and the convention was back on track.

Although the delegates would face other issues in the coming weeks, they would seem minor compared with the controversy over representation. On September 17, 1787, after 4 months of exhausting work, 38 of the delegates present signed the Constitution they had struggled to create. Oddly enough, Randolph chose not to sign, although he later urged his state to support ratification.

SLAVERY

The Founding Fathers tried to tackle the issue of slavery, but they quickly realized that there was no easy solution. They decided to focus on the difficult task of creating a strong government for the new nation, and left to the next generation the tough decisions about how to eliminate an institution that kept people in bondage.

But the question of how to count enslaved people did become the focus of heated debate. Slaves were viewed as property; they were not considered individual people with rights. Still, southerners, who owned the most slaves, wanted them counted. Northern delegates, most of whom did not own slaves, feared that this would give the southern states unfair power. In the end, the delegates worked another compromise: They agreed to count each enslaved person as "three-fifths of a person" for the basis of determining state populations and political representation.

While there were some who strongly objected to the constitution specifically because of its compromises regarding slavery, most thought it was worth the cost. We can only wonder what the founders would have done if they had known that it would take nearly 100 years and a bloody four-year civil war to put an end to slavery. Perhaps they would have agreed that this was one compromise that came at too great a price.

A Product of Argument and Compromise

The men who wrote the U.S. Constitution had various goals, and they disagreed about many of them. They wanted a strong national leader, but not a king. They wanted laws made by representatives of the people, but not rule by a mob. And, they wanted courts of law that would act independently, using the guidelines set by the Constitution.

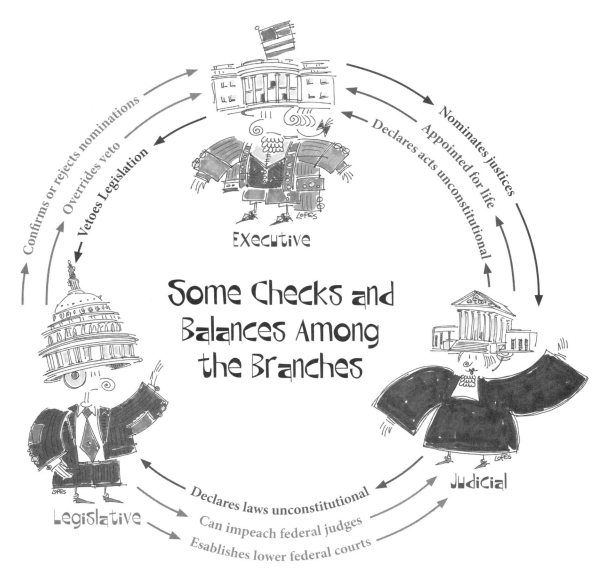

Some Checks and Balances Among the Branches

After weeks of argument and compromise, the Framers developed a plan that created a new kind of government. Beginning with: "We the people of the United States . . . ," the Constitution implies that it is the people who choose—and, if necessary, change—their government and its leaders.

The Framers were skeptical of a powerful government. They divided power among three branches: legislative, executive, and judicial. The Constitution spells out the specific duties of each branch, as well as what each one may not do. Finally, the Constitution gives each branch ways to limit the actions of the other two. This system is called "checks and balances." For instance, the president (executive branch) can veto, or turn down, laws passed by Congress. On the other hand, if Congress (legislative branch) can gather enough votes, it can override the president's veto.

More than two hundred years have passed since this great document was written. Since then, to keep up with changing times, Congress has passed other laws that expand and further interpret the Constitution's basic ideas.

The Capitol

A Look at the Legislative Branch

People often think of the executive branch—the president and others in his administration—as the center of government. The Constitution, though, places the legislative branch first. Article I sets up a two-house Congress—the Senate and the House of Representatives. Both make their own rules and choose their own leaders. To be a senator, one must be at least thirty years old; representatives must be twenty-five.

Today, the Senate has one hundred members—two from each of America's fifty states. Voters from each state elect their senators to six-year terms. (Originally, the writers of the Constitution did not trust the "common citizen" voters, so state legislatures chose senators. In 1913, that was changed by an amendment to the Constitution.)

The House of Representatives is supposed to reflect changing American public opinion. Its members are elected every two years. The number of representatives from each state depends on the state's population. If a state gains or loses population, the number of representatives it has may change. Every state is promised at least one representative, however. In 1910, Congress limited the total House membership to 435.

The Constitution spells out many Congressional powers. Important jobs include making national laws, imposing taxes, coining money, maintaining an army and navy, declaring war, and authorizing government spending. Congress has the power to pass any laws needed to carry out those duties.

The Constitution also defines things Congress cannot do. For example, it cannot tax goods exported by a state. Similarly, the Constitution lists tasks that individual states must not do. A state cannot issue its own money, for instance.

The White House

Exploring the Executive Branch

The Constitution names just two members of the executive branch—the president and the vice president. Unlike the specific tasks the Constitution lists for Congress, it describes the president's job in very general terms. Mainly, according to Article II of the document, the president must "take care that the laws be faithfully executed." The president also is commander in chief of the armed forces. In addition, he names **diplomats**, grants pardons, and makes other major appointments to his administration.

The Constitution says even less about the job of the vice president. And, there is no mention of the Cabinet, which consists of the men and women who head various governmental departments and advise the president. The Framers of the Constitution would be very surprised at the size of the executive branch today.

Many people do not realize that Americans do not vote directly for a president.

The Constitution sets up a complicated system called the Electoral College. Voters in each state actually choose electors, who are pledged to support a certain candidate (though legally they can change their vote). The electors then meet, cast their votes, and choose a president.

According to the Constitution, a president must be at least thirty-five years old and must have been born an American citizen. A candidate is elected to

> **Diplomats** are people who have been appointed to represent a government in its dealings with other governments.

a four-year term. Constitutional amendments have changed some aspects of electing and replacing the chief executive. For example, a 1951 amendment ruled that a person can be elected only twice to the presidency.

The Supreme Court

The Juice on the Judicial Branch

The job of the judicial branch, as described in Article III of the U.S. Constitution, is to interpret the laws made by Congress. The Constitution establishes a Supreme Court and gives Congress the power to establish lower federal courts. (Each state also has its own court system.) The president appoints all federal court judges, including the justices of the Supreme Court. The Senate must approve all these appointments.

The Supreme Court has original **jurisdiction** in a few types of cases, such as disputes between states or those involving diplomats. All other cases come to the Supreme Court on appeal; that is, they have been decided in a lower court, but the lawyers want another opinion. The Supreme Court is the final authority in such cases.

> **Jurisdiction** is the right and power to interpret and apply laws. "Original jurisdiction" means that a court is the first to hear a case.

One of the Supreme Court's best-known powers is the ability to declare a local, state, or federal law unconstitutional. This power to review laws to see if they disagree with the principles of the Constitution is not actually in the document. It was established in a landmark court decision of 1803, in the case of *Marbury v. Madison*. Chief Justice John Marshall declared, "It is emphatically . . . the duty of the judicial department to say what the law is." This decision made clear that, as Article VI states, the Constitution is "the supreme law of the land."

The U.S. Court System

There are state and federal courts in the U.S. system. State courts handle state law-related cases, while federal courts address criminal and civil suits related to federal law. To appeal a case means to request the right to try the case again in front of a higher court.

Federal Courts:
U.S. Supreme Court
U.S. Court of Appeals
U.S. District Court
Tariff Court
Tax Court

State Courts:
State Supreme Court
Court of Appeals
General Trial Courts
Municipal Courts

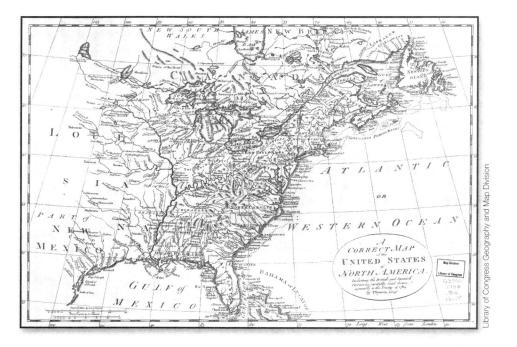

The Facts of Federalism

To fully understand the workings of America's central government, it is important to understand what federal means. According to the American Heritage Dictionary, federal is defined as "a form of government in which a union of states recognizes the **sovereignty** of a central authority while also keeping some powers of government on a local level."

What does that mean for us in the twenty-first century? In a simplified way, it means that certain powers are divided between the federal, or central, government and the fifty state governments. The federal government in Washington, D.C., is responsible for things or events that affect America's citizens as a nation. This ranges from a national taxing system to the kinds of relationships the United States has with other countries in the world. The state governments, meanwhile, provide localized control of issues that pertain more specifically to each of the states. These include such topics as maintaining roads and structures, determining education issues, and establishing individual state taxing systems.

Our Founding Fathers—with their suspicion of a strong central government and support of states' rights—might be surprised today to see how the federal government has evolved. Laws passed by Congress and interpreted by the Supreme Court more often have supported the establishment of a strong national government at the expense of the states.

A map of the United States (above), including the British and Spanish territories, published after the treaty of 1784.

Sovereignty means supremacy or power.

A Quiet Room

Jefferson showed his first draft of the Declaration of Independence to John Adams and Benjamin Franklin.

"When in the Course of human events, it becomes necessary for one people to dissolve the political bands which have connected them with another, and to assume among the powers of the earth, the separate and equal station to which the Laws of Nature and of Nature's God entitle them, a decent respect to the opinions of mankind requires that they should declare the causes which impel them to the separation."

Thomas Jefferson needed a place to stay. After spending the winter months at home in Virginia, he was ready to resume his duties as a member of the Second Continental Congress meeting in Philadelphia in May 1776. Jefferson settled on a quiet, pleasant apartment on the outskirts of the city. It was on the second floor of a brick house on the corner of Market and Seventh streets.

Jefferson found everyone in the Congress talking about independence. On June 7, Richard Henry Lee, another Virginia delegate, presented a resolution that began "Resolved, That these United Colonies are, and of right ought to be, free and independent States, that they are absolved from all allegiance to the British Crown, and that all political connection between them and the State of Great Britain is, and ought to be, totally dissolved." John Adams of Massachusetts quickly seconded the motion. The resolution caused an uproar because some of the colonies were not ready to declare independence.

After several days of debate, the Congress decided to postpone the vote on Lee's resolution until July 2. Meanwhile, in anticipation of a favorable vote at that time, a committee was appointed to prepare a document explaining to the world why the Colonies were separating from Britain. Jefferson and Adams were appointed to this committee, along with Benjamin Franklin, Roger Sherman, and Robert R. Livingston.

Thirty-three-year-old Jefferson was the second-youngest member of the

The Second Continental Congress met in a room (above) at the Pennsylvania State House, today known as Independence Hall (below).

Continental Congress. Quiet and shy, he was chosen to write the declaration because he had displayed a talent for putting things into words. For instance, in 1774, he had written a set of instructions for the Virginia delegation to the First Continental Congress. It eventually was published under the title "A Summary View of the Rights of British America."

Using a portable writing desk that he had designed himself, Jefferson worked quietly in his rented rooms. He had no books or pamphlets to refer to. For many years, he had been reading, thinking, and writing about British liberties and discussing these subjects with friends. He knew what he wanted to say.

Jefferson wrote carefully, making changes as he went along. He began by declaring that the Colonies were now a single, independent nation. No longer bound to England, their people wanted to explain the reasons for the separation. Jefferson then stated that "We hold these truths to be self-evident, that all men are created equal, that they are endowed by their Creator with certain unalienable Rights, that among these are Life, Liberty, and the pursuit of Happiness."

Jefferson explained that to secure their rights, people form governments. These governments, in turn, get their power from the consent of the people. He said that when a government does not protect its people, "it is the right of the people to alter or abolish it." Jefferson listed the many ways in which the king of England had failed to protect the colonists' rights, causing the people much suffering and misery.

When Jefferson completed his draft, he showed it to Adams and Franklin. They made a few changes. On June 28, the document was submitted to the Congress. On July 2, the delegates voted in favor of Lee's resolution. They then turned to a discussion of Jefferson's declaration.

The Congress deleted about one quarter of the original text and made some additional changes in wording. Adams defended his friend's work, but Jefferson himself remained silent. He did

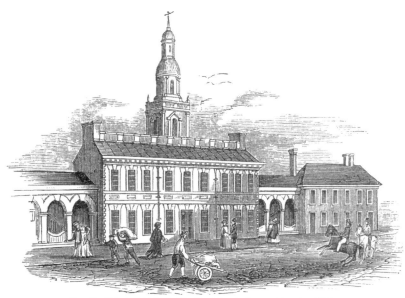

From *The Pictorial Field-Book of the Revolution*, by Benson J. Lossing, 1860.

By Virginia Calkins, *Cobblestone*, © by Carus Publishing Company. Reproduced with permission.

not think it proper for him to speak. He was particularly upset, however, when the Congress cut out the section condemning the slave trade. The delegates understood that some colonies might refuse to sign the declaration if King George was accused of masterminding the slave trade.

The Congress reworded the second-to-last paragraph to include the words of Lee's resolution. On July 4, 12 of the 13 colonies approved Jefferson's declaration. On July 9, the one remaining colony, New York, adopted a resolution supporting the declaration. On July 15, it was laid before Congress to become "The Unanimous Declaration of the Thirteen United States of America." **Broadside** copies were sent to officials of each colony to be read aloud in public places and to the commanding officers of the Continental troops. In New York, General George Washington had the Declaration of Independence read to his troops in a special ceremony. The American people celebrated with parades, the ringing of bells, and the lighting of bonfires. It was August 2 before the declaration was written on parchment and officially signed by the members of the Congress.

The Declaration of Independence ends with the words "[a]nd for the support of this Declaration, with a firm reliance on the protection of divine Providence, we mutually pledge to each other our Lives, our Fortunes and our sacred Honor." The members of Congress took great risks when they signed the Declaration of Independence. The British considered them traitors who deserved to be hanged. The delegates' names were not published until several months after the signing, but they suffered in many ways for their courage. Some had their homes looted and farms and businesses destroyed by the British. Others were forced into hiding or imprisoned. Despite the dangers, few things gave Jefferson greater satisfaction than his role in writing this important American document.

"That whenever any Form of Government becomes destructive of these ends, it is the Right of the People to alter or to abolish it, and to institute new Government, laying its foundation on such principles and organizing its powers in such form, as to them shall seem most likely to effect their Safety and Happiness."

This draft of the Declaration of Independence in Jefferson's hand is in the collection of the Library of Congress.

A **broadside** is a large sheet of paper with print on one side.

The Declaration was signed by 56 brave members of the Continental Congress. The original document is on display in the Rotunda of the National Archives.

FAST FACT THE FINAL DRAFT OF THE DECLARATION OF INDEPENDENCE USES "UNALIENABLE," BUT TODAY "INALIENABLE" IS MORE COMMONLY USED.

A Bitter Debate

Members of the Second Continental Congress disagreed on many important issues. The debate on whether and when to declare American independence, for instance, was long and bitter. The argument over what should be included in the written declaration also was harsh. One of the biggest battles surrounding the draft of the Declaration of Independence involved a section on slavery.

From most delegates' viewpoints, the Declaration simply needed to state that the Colonies had decided they were independent of England, and why. But Jefferson wanted the document to include a description of the kind of nation he felt Americans should have. In the Declaration's second paragraph, Jefferson spoke of human equality, stating that the purpose of government was to "secure" every human's right to "life, liberty and the pursuit of happiness."

Jefferson also wrote a passage condemning slavery and placed it on a list of grievances against the king. Jefferson arranged these complaints in order of significance, with the antislavery section as the last and most important. It began with this statement: "[The king] has waged cruel war against human nature itself, violating its most sacred

Despite being a slave owner himself, Thomas Jefferson included strong words about the evils of slavery in his draft of the Declaration. When Southern colonies refused to consider the document with those passages included, they were removed.

ships that transported the slaves from Africa to America. Even delegates who disapproved of the slave trade hesitated to blame the king, especially since the responsibility for slavery was on the Americans. So, that entire section was stricken from the Declaration.

Even if the antislavery passage had been kept in the Declaration of Independence, it would not have freed the slaves. It might have forced Americans to face the problem of **abolition** sooner, however, rather than in the next century. But the members of the Continental Congress decided that independence—and a hazardous war against Great Britain—required their complete and united support. The problem of slavery would have to wait for another generation of Americans to tackle.

rights of life & liberty in the persons of a distant people who never offended him, captivating & carrying them into slavery." Jefferson wrote another 160 words, blaming the slave trade almost entirely on King George III.

Jefferson knew this section would be controversial. Americans already were divided on the subject of slavery. Adams, Franklin, and religious groups such as the **Quakers** wanted an end to it. But one third of the Congress either owned or had once owned slaves. Jefferson himself had 200.

The delegates most opposed to an antislavery statement in the Declaration were from Southern colonies. Some Northerners agreed with them. After all, New England provided most of the

> **Quakers** are members of a religious group, also known as the Society of Friends, who tolerate other cultures and oppose war.
>
> **Abolition** means ending or stopping a practice or system, in this case, slavery.

"A Republic, If You Can Keep It"

Benjamin Franklin had had a full life prior to the Constitutional Convention of 1787. He died just three years later in 1790.

The title of this article is the answer Benjamin Franklin gave outside the 1787 Constitutional Convention when he was asked what form the new American government would take. His reply does not seem to hold much optimism or confidence, does it? Franklin and the other Founding Fathers knew that what they had introduced—the Constitution of the United States—was a radical experiment in self-government. They realized that many different pressures (both internal and external) on America could cause their plan to fail.

The Convention

Eighty-one-year-old Franklin was the oldest member of that convention. But he shared certain attitudes and experiences with others who were younger. The fifty-five attendees formed a cross section of America's governing class at that time. Almost all the men had extensive political experience as lawmakers, governors, or state officials. Twenty-nine (including George Washington) had served in the Revolutionary War. Thirty-five were lawyers or judges. Thirteen were businessmen or merchants, and twelve owned plantations operated by slave labor. A few were wealthy, but most were not. A number of them had been born into America's leading families; others, like Franklin and Alexander Hamilton, were self-made. More than half had been college-educated or privately tutored. In general, as one historian noted, this **elite** group was "well-bred, well-fed, well-wed, and well-read."

> **Elite** means a group with superior intellectual, social, or economic status.

Aware that the protection of individual liberties was of the utmost importance to some Americans, the delegates agreed to include a Bill of Rights (left) with the Constitution.

The convention attendees (below) represented vastly different states. But constant debate and discussion—both formal and informal—allowed them to come to some agreement.

The Nature of Power

As a group, America's Founding Fathers understood the uses and the nature of power. They knew that the new government needed some amount of power in order to survive. Realistically, it would be necessary for the government to be able to tax, regulate commerce, declare war, and manage foreign affairs. At the same time, these Framers of the Constitution also feared power.

They knew from history that too much power in any one location or vested in any one person was dangerous. They believed, in the words of British historian John Dalberg, Lord Acton, that "Power tends to corrupt, and **absolute** power tends to corrupt absolutely."

In addition, during the 1770s and 1780s, many Americans felt a good deal of loyalty toward their individual

> **Absolute**, in this case, means complete and unlimited.

James Madison helped frame the Constitution and worked hard to get it accepted by the delegates.

> A **judiciary** is the system of courts of law that administer justice.
>
> **Aristocrats** are members of a ruling class or nobility.
>
> **Virtuous** means showing moral righteousness.
>
> **Liberal** means not limited to traditional views or attitudes.

states. The concept of one united country was, in many ways, just a hopeful idea. With the Articles of Confederation in 1781, the Founding Fathers attempted to create a loose union of the thirteen original colonies, but that was unraveling by the second half of the decade. The Articles had not given enough power to the national government. Each individual state was stronger than the nation as a whole.

As a result, the 1787 Framers used the Constitution to give the new government enough power to perform its duties. Yet, they also split up the national government into branches that had a system of checks and balances.

Most of all, many of the Framers feared the power of an elected majority. They knew that the earliest attempts at a representative government—democracy in Athens and the Roman Republic—had not lasted long. So while the Founding Fathers agreed that a stronger national government was needed, they were not willing to give anyone or any group—not a king, not a president, not an aristocracy, not a Congress, not a **judiciary**, not the people—too much power.

Human Nature

In general, the Framers feared power because they had a realistic, yet almost unfavorable, view of human nature. Some were Puritans, who believed that "The Word of God... informs us that the heart is deceitful above all things and desperately wicked." Others were gentle **aristocrats**, like James Madison, who wrote, "If men were angels, no government would be necessary." Some, like Hamilton, felt that people were mainly motivated by greed, so he wanted a strong economy, with thriving banks, businesses, and cities. Thomas Jefferson came to the opposite conclusion. He thought that only small farmers—removed from economic temptations of commerce and big cities—could be relatively **virtuous**, **liberal**, and free.

Interestingly, although the Founding Fathers created a government of, by, and for the people, they did not want everyone to vote. Only white men who owned property qualified as citizens under their republican form of government. The Framers expected this elite group to act as built-in "screens" for men who were unfit to govern.

The Framers were tough and practical. They would not let anything get in the way of what they believed would work. Most of the Founding Fathers knew that the Constitution was better than the Articles of Confederation. They also realized that some founding patriots, like Samuel Adams and Patrick Henry, would refuse to

Unlike Madison, Patrick Henry strongly opposed the Constitution because he believed it threatened states' rights.

The U.S. government's strength and flexibility today is a testament to the commitment of the men who attended the 1787 convention.

Tyranny is a government in which a single ruler has absolute power.

support the new Constitution. These leaders would say that it allowed the national government to become too powerful—a certain path to **tyranny**. Adams' and Henry's main concern was protecting individual liberties. Probably half of all Americans at the time thought the same way. After all, England's control of the Colonies still was fresh in their minds.

But the Framers fought to have the new Constitution accepted, state by state. And they compromised. For example, although they believed a Bill of Rights to be unnecessary, the promise was made to add one. This concession enabled the Constitution to be voted in as the law of the land. Ultimately, the Bill of Rights addressed concerns shared by Adams and Henry. It specifically guaranteed many individual liberties such as the freedoms of speech, religion, and the press, and the right to publicly assemble.

The crafting of the Constitution was masterful. It was strong enough to provide the foundation on which our present-day government is built. But it also was flexible, allowing for interpretation as times change. Things that we accept readily today—political parties, equal rights for women and minorities, an income tax—are not mentioned anywhere in the Constitution. Some have evolved as important pieces of the political process. Others are official changes in the form of amendments to the Constitution. The Founding Fathers were successful in providing a law for the United States that could evolve, change, and adjust, and still remain strong.

By Malcolm C. Jensen, *Cobblestone*, © by Carus Publishing Company. Reproduced with permission.

Congress shall make no law respecting an establishment of religion, or prohibiting the free exercise thereof; or abridging the freedom of speech, or of the press; or the right of the people peaceably to assemble, and to petition the government for a redress of grievances.

THE FIVE FREEDOMS

The opening words of the First Amendment Bill of Rights are often called the Five Freedoms: freedom of religion, freedom of speech, freedom of the press, freedom to assemble peacefully and join together for a cause, and freedom to petition the government to right a wrong or correct a problem.

Between 1630 and 1640, 20,000 Puritans sailed for New England. They came to America to find religious freedom—but only for themselves. They had little tolerance or respect for the Native Americans who had made their home in the area for thousands of years.

Freedom of religion, which means being able to worship according to any religion that you want, was extremely important in America, where many people came from other parts of the world where they were persecuted for practicing their own religions. This portion of the First Amendment also prevents the government from establishing an official religion, as well as the freedom to practice—or not practice—whatever religion we want.

In a speech made to the Virginia Convention in 1775, Patrick Henry declared, "Give me liberty or give me death!"

Freedom of speech gives Americans the right to speak out and express their opinions without government interference or the fear of being punished for speaking freely. This is one of America's most cherished freedoms, compared to many other places in the world where people can be punished for speaking out.

Freedom of the press is related to freedom of speech because it gives the press—newspaper, magazines, websites, books, et cetera—the right to publish news, information, and opinions without interference from or censorship by the government. It also guarantees the rights of regular people to publish their own newspapers, magazines, newsletters, and more.

Workers created newspapers in this 18th century printing workshop, an industry that expanded significantly with the popularity of print during this time.

Freedom to assemble peacefully and join together in groups for a cause is another very important freedom. Throughout American history, individuals and groups have gathered together in public places to support their causes, everything from civil rights to suffrage to unions, and even including unpopular groups like the Ku Klux Klan. This freedom guarantees that people have the right to gather in public to march, protest, demonstrate, carry signs, and otherwise express their views in a nonviolent way. It also means that they can freely join any groups and organizations that they want to.

Colonists held many meetings to protest British treatment before the American Revolution.

Finally, **freedom of petition** protects the ways that Americans have for letting their government know what they like and don't like, or what they want to change. It gives them the right to appeal to their government in favor of or against policies that affect them or that they feel very strongly about. It also gives Americans the right to gather signatures on petitions, and to lobby their government representatives for or against pieces of legislation.

During the women's suffrage movement in New York City in the early 1900s, society leaders gathered signatures on petitions for women's right to vote.

Many people feel that these freedoms represent the best of America's commitment to create a society that is both free and responsible. Even today, Americans continue to exercise these freedoms every day, whether they are worshipping at the church of their choice, speaking their opinions during a public meeting, printing editorial comments in a newspaper, protesting against policies they think are unfair, or demanding change from the government.

A CHAT WITH THOMAS JEFFERSON
(ALSO KNOWN AS ... WILLIAM BARKER)

Writer Barbara Hall chatted with Thomas Jefferson recently. Or did she? Read on to find out whom she really spoke to and what they talked about . . .

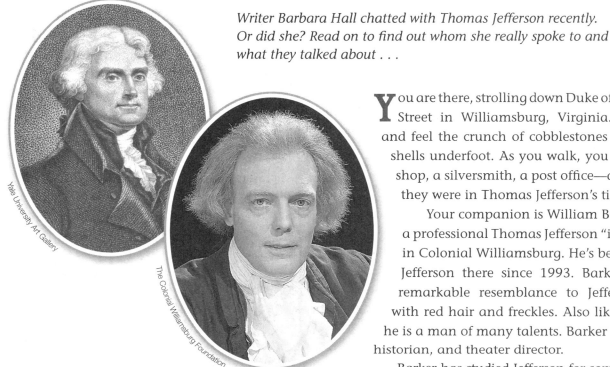

You are there, strolling down Duke of Gloucester Street in Williamsburg, Virginia. You hear and feel the crunch of cobblestones and oyster shells underfoot. As you walk, you pass a wig shop, a silversmith, a post office—all much as they were in Thomas Jefferson's time.

Your companion is William Barker. He is a professional Thomas Jefferson "interpreter" in Colonial Williamsburg. He's been playing Jefferson there since 1993. Barker bears a remarkable resemblance to Jefferson—tall, with red hair and freckles. Also like Jefferson, he is a man of many talents. Barker is an actor, historian, and theater director.

Barker has studied Jefferson for some 20 years. He even created a one-man show about our nation's third president. He has interpreted Jefferson everywhere from schools and corporations to the White House and the Palace of Versailles in France.

As you walk along, Barker might be singing to himself. After all, Thomas Jefferson loved music. He often sang aloud as he walked or rode his horse. He was a gifted violinist, historians tell us. They also say that Mr. Jefferson was a quiet—even shy—man. He experienced hardship in his life, including deaths in his family and money problems in his old age. But he never lost his spirit, finding enjoyment in everything from a pet mockingbird to great art collections in Paris.

It was probably this spirit that helped him as he contributed to the early days of our country's freedom. He wrote the Declaration of Independence and served as the nation's third president. As William Barker reminds us, Thomas Jefferson played an important role in some of the most significant events of early America.

As Barker notes, Thomas Jefferson was in Philadelphia in the spring of 1776, when an important meeting took place. For several years, Americans had become increasingly fed up with British rule. Trouble

Thomas Jefferson (above, left) was a scholar, the governor of Virginia, a writer of the Declaration of Independence, and considered one of the Founding Fathers. William Barker (above, right), a professional interpreter, has been playing Jefferson for years.

By Barbara Hall, *Appleseeds*, © by Carus Publishing Company. Reproduced with permission.

had been brewing in the Colonies. The members of the Second Continental Congress decided it was time to tell Britain that the thirteen American Colonies would no longer submit to British authority. It was time to declare independence from Britain. They would write a document stating this fact.

The members knew that Thomas Jefferson, the quiet Virginian, was a fine writer. So they asked him to write the document. At the time, no one knew the incredible significance the Declaration of Independence would come to have. It was not considered a huge responsibility to write this document. But we know today that they chose the right man for the job. Jefferson's words still ring out today: "We hold these truths to be self-evident, that all men are created equal."

The American Revolution followed, when colonists fought Britain for their independence. By the time the Revolution was over, the colonists had won. In 1789, Thomas Jefferson became secretary of state for America's first president, George Washington. When our second president, John Adams, was elected in 1797, Jefferson was chosen vice president. Then, in 1801, Thomas Jefferson was elected the third president of the United States.

Many people wondered what kind of president Jefferson would be. After all, a man who kept a mockingbird as a pet wasn't a typical head of state. In the end though, the American people weren't disappointed.

Thomas Jefferson was responsible for purchasing the Louisiana Territory—800,000 square miles of land west of the Mississippi River. Today, it is seen as one of the "crowning jewels" of Jefferson's presidency. By buying this enormous area of land from France, Jefferson doubled the size of our young nation.

Once the Louisiana Purchase was underway, President Jefferson was ready for another adventure: sending Meriwether Lewis and William Clark on a journey of exploration. Jefferson had been dreaming of this trip for 20 years. The men left in May 1804 with

Colonial Williamsburg is a restored town, re-created to look like Williamsburg did in the 1700s. Visitors can experience life in colonial America.

A BIT OF JEFFERSONIAN ADVICE:

"DON'T MISTRUST YOUR VISION. AND THINK FOR YOURSELF."

a group called the Corps of Discovery. They traveled for more than two years, all the way to the Pacific Ocean and back. During their 8,000-mile journey, they filled notebooks with descriptions and drawings of the land, the animals, the plants, and the people they encountered. William Barker believes that without Jefferson's genius, none of this would have been possible.

Barker—whose own ancestors settled in Virginia long ago—calls Williamsburg the "most incredible stage set in the world to do Jefferson." Williamsburg gives Barker the opportunity to become Thomas Jefferson in a way no other setting does. As he walks the streets, he chats with visitors, answering their questions as only someone who really understands Jefferson could.

Thomas Jefferson, he says, "was a man who knew how far the word can go. He explained things in clear and simple terms, easily and clearly." Jefferson treasured the world around him. "Every blade of grass was of interest to him. He was a kind and compassionate man." Barker continues, "He particularly loved animals." He had an aviary—a large group of caged birds—at his home, and many other pets.

Thomas Jefferson loved children and understood them well, Barker says. Jefferson had a great deal of curiosity. He liked to have young people around him at his Monticello home and enjoyed sharing his interests and delights with them. Finally, William Barker passes on a bit of Jeffersonian advice to kids: "Don't mistrust your vision. And think for yourself."

Thomas Jefferson would have agreed with that.

By Barbara Hall, *Appleseeds*, © by Carus Publishing Company. Reproduced with permission.

The Bill of Rights

James Madison proposed several amendments to the First Congress in 1789, in response to concerns that the Constitution did not include specified guarantees of liberties and rights. Within two years, ten amendments which provided the protection of fundamental liberties in the United States, called the Bill of Rights, were approved.

AMENDMENT I
Congress shall make no law respecting an establishment of religion, or prohibiting the free exercise thereof; or abridging the freedom of speech, or of the press; or the right of the people to peaceably assemble, and to petition the Government for a redress of grievances.

AMENDENT II
A well-regulated Militia, being necessary to the security of a free State, the right of the people to keep and bear Arms shall not be infringed.

AMENDMENT III
No soldier shall, in time of peace, be quartered in any house, without the consent of the Owner, nor in time of war, but in a manner prescribed by law.

AMENDMENT IV
The right of the people to be secure in their persons, houses, papers, and effects against unreasonable searches and seizures, shall not be violated, and no Warrants shall issue, but upon probable cause, supported by Oath or affirmation, and particularly describing the place to be searched, and the persons or things to be seized.

AMENDMENT V
No person shall be held to answer for a capital, or otherwise infamous crime, unless on a presentment or indictment of a Grand Jury, except in cases arising in the land or naval forces, or in the Militia, when in actual service in time of War or public danger; nor shall any person be subject for the same offence to be twice put in jeopardy of life or limb; nor shall be compelled in any criminal case to be a witness against himself, nor be deprived of life, liberty, or property without due process of law; nor shall private property be taken for public use, without just compensation.

AMENDMENT VI

In all criminal prosecutions, the accused shall enjoy the right to a speedy and public trial, by an impartial jury of the State and district wherein the crime shall have been committed, which district shall have been previously ascertained by law, and to be informed of the nature and cause of the accusation; to be confronted with the witnesses against him; to have compulsory process for obtaining witnesses in his favor, and to have the Assistance of Counsel for his defence.

AMENDMENT VII

In suits at common law, where the value in controversy shall exceed twenty dollars, the right of trial by jury shall be preserved, and no fact tried by a jury, shall be otherwise reexamined in any Court of the United States, than according to the rules of the common law.

AMENDMENT VIII

Excessive bail shall not be required, nor excessive fines imposed, nor cruel and unusual punishments inflicted.

AMENDMENT IX

The enumeration in the Constitution, of certain rights, shall not be construed to deny or disparage others retained by the people.

AMENDMENT X

The powers not delegated to the United States by the Constitution, nor prohibited by it to the States, are reserved to the States respectively, or to the people.

HISTORICAL IMAGE

This is one of the most famous representations of the signing of the Declaration of Independence. It portrays the presentation of the first draft of the Declaration to the Second Continental Congress on June 28, 1776, a week before it was officially adopted. It was painted by John Trumbull in 1817 and hangs in the Rotunda of the U.S. Capitol in Washington, D.C.

HISTORICAL IMAGE

This print is a reproduction of a painting by J.L.G. Ferris, entitled Writing the Declaration of Independence, 1776. *It was part of a series called* The Pageant of a Nation. *The scene shows Benjamin Franklin, John Adams, and Thomas Jefferson meeting in Jefferson's rooms in Philadelphia as they review a draft of the Declaration of Independence.*

This lithograph portrait of Thomas Jefferson, third president of the United States, was created by Henry R. Robinson and published sometime between 1840 and 1851.

Benjamin Banneker's Letter to Thomas Jefferson

Benjamin Banneker was a free African American scientist, surveyor, almanac author, and farmer. Born in Maryland to a free African American woman and a former slave, Banneker had little formal education and was largely self-taught. He is known for being part of a group led by Major Andrew Ellicott that surveyed the borders of the original District of Columbia, the federal capital district of the United States.

Banneker's knowledge of astronomy helped him author a series of almanacs. He corresponded with Thomas Jefferson, drafter of the United States Declaration of Independence, on the topics of slavery and racial equality. Abolitionists and advocates of racial equality promoted and praised his works.

On the evening of August 19, 1791, Banneker lit a candle and sat down to write an important letter to Secretary of State Thomas Jefferson. The letter began:

Maryland, Baltimore County,
Near Ellicot's Lower Mills August 19th. 1791.
Thomas Jefferson Secretary of State

Sir, I am fully sensible of the greatness of that freedom which I take with you on the present occasion; a liberty which Seemed to me Scarcely allowable, when I reflected on the distinguished, and dignifyed station in which you Stand; and the almost general prejudice and prepossession which is so previlent in the world against those of my complexion.

Sir how pitiable is it to reflect, that altho you were so fully convinced of the benevolence of the Father of mankind, and of his equal and impartial distribution of those rights and privileges which he had conferred upon them, that you should at the Same time counteract his mercies, in detaining by fraud and violence so numerous a part of my brethren under groaning captivity and cruel oppression, that you should at the Same time be found guilty of that most criminal act, which you professedly detested in others, with respect to yourselves.

Jefferson's reply:

Philadelphia, Aug. 30. 1791.

Sir, I Thank you sincerely for your letter of the 19th instant and for the Almanac it contained. No body wishes more than I do to see such proofs as you exhibit, that nature has given to our black brethren, talents equal to those of the other colors of men, and that the appearance of a want of them is owing merely to the degraded condition of their existence . . .

   I can add with truth, that no body wishes more ardently to see a good system commenced for raising the condition both of their body & mind to what it ought to be, as fast as the imbecility of their present existence, and other circumstances which cannot be neglected, will admit.

Founding Father

In 1754, 22 years before the British colonies became the United States, a cartoon appeared in a Pennsylvania newspaper. It was a picture of a snake cut into pieces. The pieces were labeled with the initials of the 13 colonies. (N.E. stood for the New England colonies.) Beneath the snake were the words "Join, or Die." The newspaper was Ben Franklin's *Pennsylvania Gazette*, and the cartoon was probably drawn by Ben Franklin himself.

The meaning of the cartoon was clear to Franklin's readers. Superstition said that if a snake is cut into pieces, it will survive if its parts are put back together before sunset. The pieces of Franklin's snake were the colonies. The cartoon was warning that unless the colonies joined together, they would die, just like a snake.

For a long time, Franklin had felt that the colonies were too disconnected. He noted that six Iroquois Indian nations had managed to unite. Why couldn't British colonists do the same thing?

Later in 1754, colonists and Indians met in Albany, New York. There Franklin proposed a "Plan of Union" to unite the colonies. Though

The painting of Franklin in his famous fur cap (above) was made a year after independence was declared. Franklin's cartoon (below) urged the colonies to join together years before they united in the Declaration of Independence.

the plan was approved, nothing came of it. Neither the colonists nor the British were ready for Franklin's dream of a united America.

In the years that followed, Franklin continued in public service. He traveled to England as a representative of the colonies. But by March 1775, it was clear that England and the colonies would soon be at war. Franklin quickly went home.

The day after he arrived in Philadelphia, Franklin was asked to join a meeting of the Continental Congress. For the second time, this group of representatives from all 13 colonies gathered in Philadelphia. For the second time, they talked about how to deal with their growing problems with England.

While the Continental Congress was in session, Franklin wrote a letter to a newspaper. In it, he suggested that the rattlesnake would be a good symbol for the colonies. The rattlesnake had many good qualities, Franklin explained. It was reluctant to strike and always gave its enemy fair warning. But when forced to fight, it was deadly. Franklin felt that the rattlesnake was a brave but dangerous animal. A picture he had seen of a rattlesnake had 13 rattles on its tail—the exact number of colonies!

As a member of the Continental Congress, Franklin helped form the ideas that became the Declaration of Independence. This document, written by Thomas Jefferson, contained words that must have touched Franklin's heart: "We, . . . the Representatives of the United States of America . . ." The United States! Had the pieces of Franklin's snake finally come together?

At the Continental Congress, Franklin was an important adviser to the committee on the Declaration of Independence.

Later, in Paris, Franklin represented the newly independent states. Walking with his grandsons, the Americans attracted a crowd.

During the Revolution, Franklin worked hard to win support for the new nation in its war with Great Britain. Here, Franklin is received by the king and queen of France (seated on the right).

Franklin is well known for his witty sayings.

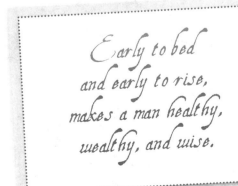

Early to bed and early to rise, makes a man healthy, wealthy, and wise.

Franklin didn't have time to wonder. He was soon on his way to France to ask for help in the war against England. He stayed in France through the rest of the war. While there, Franklin helped work out a peace treaty between the United States and England. When he returned to Philadelphia in 1785, Ben Franklin was 79 years old. But his country needed his services.

The 13 newly United States had written a set of rules for governing the country called the Articles of Confederation. But people weren't happy with the articles. In fact, after a few short years, it began to seem that the United States weren't really united at all. Franklin's snake was still in pieces.

A meeting was held in Philadelphia to fix the articles. Sick and weak, 81-year-old Franklin was by far the oldest man at that important meeting. The members, or delegates, decided to write a whole new set of rules. The rules they came up with became the United States Constitution.

When the Constitution was ready to be signed, many people were unhappy with the details. In fact, it looked like the Constitution might "die." Ben Franklin was worried. He wrote a speech in which he admitted having doubts about the Constitution. But, he wrote, he had often been wrong during his long life. He was willing to give the Constitution a chance. He asked the others to do the same.

Franklin was too sick to give the speech himself. His friend and fellow Pennsylvanian, James Wilson, read it for him. It was a powerful speech, and it did the trick: The other delegates approved the Constitution almost unanimously. Thank you, Ben Franklin!

It is said that Franklin wept as he signed the document. Perhaps he was thinking of the cartoon drawn 33 years before. When Franklin died three years after signing the Constitution, he knew that the parts of his snake had joined together at last.

A slip of the foot you may soon recover; but a slip of the tongue you may never get over.

A penny saved is a penny earned.

When it was time to sign the Constitution, Franklin urged all to sign it, "for the sake of our posterity"—the generations to come.

MAKING CHANGES

The Founding Fathers clearly did not want their government to be so easy to change that it would be rewritten completely by future generations. But the delegates did establish a procedure for amending the Constitution when that need would arise.

Article V of the Constitution spells out two ways to change the Constitution. One method calls for a constitutional convention, assembled at the request of two-thirds of the states. Delegates from every state would attend the convention for the purpose of proposing amendments. This method has never been used.

The second method has been used for all 27 amendments added to the Constitution since 1787. Here's how it works: A proposal for an amendment is approved by a two-thirds majority of both the Senate and the House of Representatives. Then the proposal is submitted to the states, where it is voted on either by each state legislature or at special state conventions. Three-fourths of the states must approve the amendment for it to become a law. Since 1918, most proposed amendments have had a seven-year time limit during which the states may pass the amendment.

Amendments have been adopted to abolish slavery and to protect the rights of newly freed people and other Americans (Thirteenth, Fourteenth, and Fifteenth Amendments); to give women the right to vote (Nineteenth Amendment); and to lower the voting age from 21 to 18 (Twenty-sixth Amendment).

Other amendments provide rules for the election of our government officials. One amendment limits the number of terms a president may serve (Twenty-second Amendment). Another calls for senators to be elected by the public (Seventeenth Amendment); before this amendment, senators were elected by their state legislatures. The Twenty-third Amendment gives citizens who live in the District of Columbia representation in the Electoral College and therefore a voice in who will become president. Two amendments cancel each other out: The Eighteenth Amendment barred the sale of alcohol, while the Twenty-first Amendment repealed this law and leaves it up to the states to decide how to regulate alcoholic beverages.

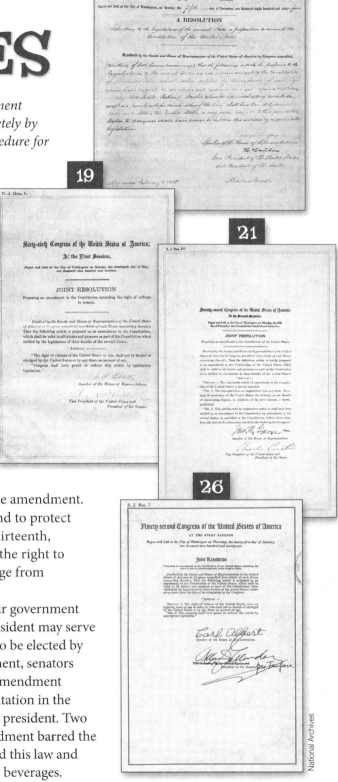

FAST FACT THE TWENTY-SEVENTH AMENDMENT REGULATING CONGRESSIONAL SALARIES ORIGINALLY WAS PROPOSED IN 1789 WITHOUT A TIME LIMIT AND WAS DECLARED RATIFIED 203 YEARS LATER.

Celebrating Citizenship!

September 17 is Citizenship Day in the United States. Citizens are official members of a nation. Citizens enjoy special rights, and they have special duties, too. See why citizenship is special every day.

> A constitution is a set of rules and laws that tell how a government is organized and run.

Special Rights

The **Constitution** of the United States protects everyone in America. It allows freedom of speech and freedom of religion. It protects people from unlawful actions. The Constitution safeguards other rights, too.

Yet only citizens enjoy certain rights. Citizens of age 18 and older can vote. Voting lets citizens decide who will run the government. In some states, citizens can vote to make or change laws, too. Only citizens can hold political office.

"United States citizens have so much power," says 22-year-old Yelena Havryliuk. Before coming to America, she lived in Russia and the Ukraine. When Americans speak out and vote, says Yelena, "it feels like the government cares and your voice is heard."

Citizenship lets adults sit on juries. Juries decide issues of fact in court cases. Citizens also can get a United States passport. They get protection and any necessary help while traveling to other countries.

Certain jobs go only to citizens. Born in Great Britain, Sophie Cayless became a U.S. citizen at age 23. Only then was she able to join the U.S. National Park Service. "I felt proud to be a park ranger in some of the most beautiful areas on Earth!" says Sophie. "My citizenship gave me the opportunity to have that connection with the land and to inspire others to love and care for it, too."

America's founders signed the Constitution on **September 17, 1787.**

Duties of Citizenship

Along with rights, citizenship also brings responsibilities. Citizens owe allegiance, or loyalty, to the United States. That's a promise you make whenever you say the Pledge of Allegiance.

Citizens must support and defend the Constitution of the United States and obey laws. They must respect other people's rights. Citizens must defend America, too. Sometimes this means that they must serve in the military.

Becoming a Citizen

Most Americans become citizens automatically. They are born in the United States. *Jus soli*, or right-of-birthplace citizenship, also goes to people who are born in Puerto Rico, Guam, and the U.S. Virgin Islands.

Certain people born **abroad** enjoy *jus sanguinis*, or right-of-blood citizenship. Generally, at least one parent must be a citizen who has lived in America.

Other people come to America as **immigrants**. Many become naturalized citizens. "America has many good things to offer," notes Nelly Vileikis. Nelly came from Columbia in South America. Abbas Lamouri, her husband, came here from Algeria in Africa.

Yelena Havryliuk explains why she became a citizen. "This country gave me so many opportunities," says Yelena. "I want to give something back. I would be proud to be a United States citizen."

Applicants for citizenship must live in the United States for a set time—usually five years. Applicants must read, write, and speak basic English. They must also understand U.S. history and government.

Applicants must show "good moral character." Fingerprinting and an FBI background check are part of the process. The U.S. Immigration and Naturalization Service (INS) interviews people, too.

Coming to America more than 100 years ago

abroad: in a foreign country

immigrant: a person who settles somewhere after coming from another country

Most important, applicants must accept the Constitution. Plus, notes Yelena, "You have to like this country and like living and serving people here."

New naturalized citizens take an oath of allegiance. Sophie, Abbas, and Nelly all felt "very proud" at that moment.

Be Proud

No matter how anyone becomes a citizen, all citizens are equal. All are important. "With the rainbow of nationalities in the United States, we can appreciate everyone's culture," explains Ernestine Fobbs at the INS. "That's what we are about."

"Always take advantage of opportunities that we have as United States citizens," urges Ernestine. "Never take it for granted."

"Love your country," adds Nelly. "Be proud to be an American."

Hundreds of thousands of people become naturalized citizens each year.

Applying for citizenship

Taking the oath of citizenship

Land of Opportunity and Obstacles

Meet Sofiya, *a professional actress from New York. She looks American, speaks perfect English, and recently earned her Master's degree from New York University, so one might be surprised to learn that she lived in Uzbekistan until 1990. She shared the story of her family's immigration and their hopes for starting a new life in the United States in a recent interview.*

In what city were you born? How old were you when you first arrived in the United States?

I was born in the city of Samarkand, in what is now the country of Uzbekistan. But when I was born there in 1983, Uzbekistan was not a country but a territory of the former Soviet Union. So my first language was Russian. My family left Samarkand when I was six years old, in the fall of 1989, right as the Soviet Union was collapsing. We arrived to New York on February 7, 1990.

Describe your homeland. What language do you speak there? How did your community differ from where you live today?

Samarkand is located in Central Asia. I remember it as being very dry and sandy and rocky. It is one if the oldest cities in the world, dating back to 700 BC, so its architecture is significantly older than anything you'll find in America. It has also been influenced by various civilizations. Samarkand was once a key trading location along the Silk Road and a crossroads for a lot of cultural exchange. This region was conquered over and over by dominant empires of the time, and ultimately by the Russians. There are many very old mosques and other religious structures.

Sofiya's father and half-sister in Samarkand in the late 1970s.

The languages of this region are primarily Persian-based dialects and Russian. My parents speak a dialect called Bukhori, which is based in Persian and Hebrew. They also speak Russian, and I grew up only speaking Russian.

Our community in Samarkand was called the Bukharian community, a Sephardic Jewish group that lived in this part of the world for over 3,000 years. After the collapse of the Soviet Union, this community migrated to the U.S. and Israel. It no longer exists in Uzbekistan.

Ours was a very **insular** community in Uzbekistan. Family life was central. Most married quite young and had large families. Trade and small business were popular professions for men. Women mostly stayed home and acted as **matriarchs**.

The Bukharian community has retained a good deal of its insular culture here in the United States. It's still a very tightly connected community. Family and religious traditions are still considered central tenets, but wealth acquisition is becoming a top priority. Most of these changes are the result of modernization. It was a much more agricultural existence in Uzbekistan, and here, of course, we live in an urban landscape. Also, Bukharin women are now significantly more educated, independent, and self-sufficient. Unlike many Bukharin parents, my father encouraged my sister and me to pursue our education and careers.

What do you miss about your homeland?

I miss the relationship to food that we had in Uzbekistan. Everything was hard-earned and never taken for granted. We never lacked food but there certainly wasn't an abundance of it the way there is here in America. I miss that intimate relationship to food. We always knew where it came from and how much work went into preparing it. There's something special about that, and it sets a different rhythm to daily life and daily interactions.

What I miss the most about Samarkand are my grandmother's chickens and the juicy Samarkand tomatoes and melons, which are unlike any other.

Why did you and your family leave your native country? Describe your trip to the United States.

We left the Soviet Union because it was becoming incredibly unstable politically, which was very dangerous for Jewish communities. The rights of Jews in the Soviet Union were always very limited and we were never granted citizenship even though we lived there for generations. My Soviet passport categorized my nationality as "Jew." In Samarkand, my parents lacked the opportunity to get an education or professional training because they were Jewish.

Once the collapse began, it was even worse because **anti-Semitism** could no longer be kept in check. Many private Jewish organizations in America and around the world began helping Jews escape from the Soviet Union at this time. When we escaped in 1989, there was no direct way to get to the U.S. We traveled from Uzbekistan to Moscow, then to

> **insular:** separated from other people or cultures, not knowing or interested in new or different ideas
>
> **matriarch:** a woman who is the head of a family
>
> **anti-Semitism:** hostility toward or discrimination against Jews

On Sofiya's birth certificate, her parents' nationality is listed as "Jew." Jews were not granted full citzenship in the Soviet Union, even after living there for several generations.

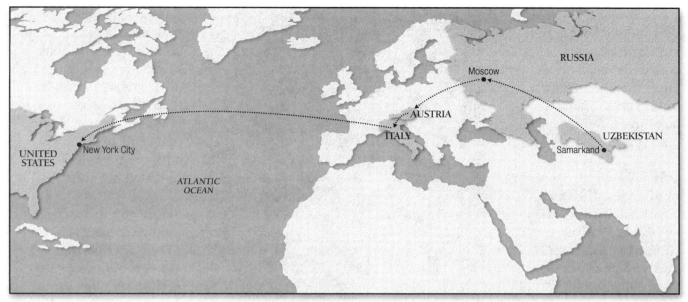

Sofiya and her family made the long journey from their homeland to the United States in 1989, a time of political instability in the Soviet Union.

Austria, then to Italy, and then finally to New York. This took about five months. Despite the language barriers and financial hardships and the absolute unknowns of whether we'd ever make it to America, our trip is still the most wonderful and magical memory of my childhood.

Before you came, what did you think life in the United States would be like? How did you think your life would be different in the United States as compared to in your homeland?
At six years old, when we left Uzbekistan, I imagined America would be a place with unlimited bicycles and the happiest of times. I thought we were going to the best place in the world. My parents believed America was a land of no discrimination and a truly organized and functional society where capitalism kept everything running smoothly. I think they expected very little corruption here.

Once you arrived in the United States, what did you experience? Was it different from what you expected?
Yes, very different. I believe my mother's first words upon landing in JFK airport were, "Oh, it's so dirty." Life in America was very rough for the first decade or so for my parents. There were endless bureaucratic hassles, and they faced a lot of discrimination and animosity as immigrants. Fortunately, my father was given support and advice by local agencies and members of our community. He returned to school to get an education as an X-ray technician, an occupation that would support our family. My mother was also able to find work as a beautician in beauty salons and supported our family while my dad went to school for four years. This is actually a career that many Bukharian immigrants (both women and men) went into to support their families upon arriving in America. While there were many challenges as immigrants in a new land, such as learning the language and earning a living that would support our family, my parents also had greater opportunity than they had in Uzbekistan.

As for me and my younger sister (we were seven and five years old, respectively), things were confusing and difficult at first, but we learned English pretty quickly and were fluent within four months or so.

I think the biggest disillusion was the dream of profound success that is possible in America. My parents worked grueling hours and succeeded in their own right, but they also struggled significantly. I watched them shoulder the immense challenge of having to learn a new culture and identity that their children absorbed faster than them. Overall, immigration entailed significant unforeseen challenges.

What kinds of challenges did you experience adjusting to life and culture in the United States? Did you change the way you related to your family and friends?
The first years brought obvious challenges like learning the language, the history, the holidays, the sports, the food, the entertainment, the culture, and so on. But the deeper challenges have been ever-evolving. They began as basic identity issues, like trying to dress and sound American, but every step toward self-discovery and self-exploration was accompanied by a sense of being other or not truly American, and this has stayed with me into my adulthood. It certainly affected my choice of friends and social spheres, and probably every choice in my educational career. I'm also sure it was the greatest factor in my finding a true home in theatrical arts, where worlds and identities were more fluid and dynamic than what most people of a singular cultural upbringing perceive and experience.

Have you experienced any discrimination in the United States? What advice would you give to recent immigrants from your country about this problem?
I've actually never experienced discrimination in the U.S. as an immigrant because I don't look or sound foreign, but my parents have because

Sofiya, with her father, mother, and sister in 1988, a year before they began their journey to America.

they speak English with accents. I've also seen other immigrants experience prejudice. My advice to any immigrant would be to make sure you have a community that can help you deal with prejudice and discrimination.

What do you believe it means to "be an American"? Do you believe a person can be "an American" and still retain his or her culture?
I don't think I know what it means to be an American. I remember when our family got citizenship here in 1996. We had been here for six years. My parents were summoned to take a citizenship test and we all studied for months. We studied the names and histories of all the states and state capitals, the presidents, and some other very basic bits of historical information. My parents passed, making all four of us American citizens. Maybe I felt American that day.

I think that America affords each and every immigrant the freedom to choose to retain as much or as little of his or her culture as they want.

What laws do you think the United States should have toward immigration and immigrants?
I think any person who wants entry into this country for the purpose of bettering his or her life should be allowed to be here. And I think any undocumented person in this country should be granted a path to citizenship and full rights.

PRIMARY SOURCE

Excerpt from the Civics (History and Government) Questions for the Naturalization Test

There are 100 civics (history and government) questions and answers for the naturalization test to become a citizen. The civics test is an oral test and the United States Citizenship and Immigration Services (USCIS) Officer will ask the applicant up to ten of the 100 civics questions. An applicant must answer six out of ten questions correctly to pass the civics portion of the naturalization test. A sampling of questions and then the answers follow. Would you pass the test?

AMERICAN GOVERNMENT

A: Principles of American Democracy

    5. What do we call the first ten amendments to the Constitution?

    6. How many amendments does the Constitution have?

B: System of Government

    16. Who makes federal laws?

    21. The House of Representatives has how many voting members?

C: Rights and Responsibilities

    49. What is one responsibility that is only for United States citizens?

    51. What are two rights of everyone living in the United States?

AMERICAN HISTORY

A: Colonial Period of Independence

    62. Who wrote the Declaration of Independence?

    68. What is one thing Benjamin Franklin is famous for?

B: 1800s

    71. What territory did the United States buy from France in 1803?

    76. What did the Emancipation Proclamation do?

C: Recent American History and Other Important Historical Information

79. Who was the President during World War I?

81. Who did the United States fight in World War II?

INTEGRATED CIVICS

A: Geography

88. Name one of the two longest rivers in the United States.

91. Name one U.S. Territory.

B: Symbols

96. Why does the flag have 13 stripes?

98. What is the name of the national anthem?

C: Holidays

99. When do we celebrate Independence Day?

100. Name two national U.S. holidays.

ANSWERS

AMERICAN GOVERNMENT

5. The Bill of Rights
6. Twenty-seven (27)
16. Congress (Senate and House of Representatives)
21. Four hundred thirty-five (435)
49. serve on a jury; vote in a federal election
51. freedom of expression; freedom of speech; freedom of assembly; freedom to petition the government; freedom of worship; the right to bear arms

AMERICAN HISTORY

62. Thomas Jefferson
68. U.S. Diplomat; oldest member of the Constitutional Convention; first Postmaster General of the United States; writer of "Poor Richard's Almanac"; started the first free libraries
71. The Louisiana Territory
76. Freed slaves in the Confederate states (most Southern states)
79. Woodrow Wilson
81. Japan, Germany, and Italy

INTEGRATED CIVICS

88. Missouri River; Mississippi River
91. Puerto Rico; U.S. Virgin Islands; American Samoa; Northern Mariana Islands; Guam
96. The stripes represent the 13 original colonies.
98. The Star-Spangled Banner
99. July 4
100. New Year's Day; Martin Luther King, Jr. Day; Presidents' Day; Memorial Day; Independence Day; Labor Day; Columbus Day; Veterans Day; Thanksgiving; Christmas

Who Has the Right to Vote?

Many Americans take for granted their right to vote. Today, seven out of every ten Americans are allowed to vote. (Most of the rest are not yet old enough.) But it hasn't always been this way.

Check out this timeline—it shows important changes in the history of American voting.

1787 The Constitution of the United States creates the federal (national) government. The Constitution leaves all decisions about voting to the individual states. Most states decide to allow only white, property-owning men over the age of 21 to vote. Many people believe that property owners have a stronger interest in government. Women, African Americans, and poor people are not allowed to vote.

1821 New York State drops the property-owning requirement for white males only. Soon, other states do the same.

1870 The Constitution is amended, or changed, to give African American men the right to vote. This is called the 15th Amendment.

1920 Again, the Constitution is amended, this time to give women the right to vote. This is the 19th Amendment.

1965 Congress passes the Voting Rights Act of 1965. This law says that the unfair voting practices in many states, which make it difficult or impossible for African Americans to vote, are illegal and have to stop. For the first time, African Americans are able to vote without being harassed or beaten.

1971 The 26th Amendment to the Constitution lowers the voting age from 21 to 18. This is because young American soldiers are dying in a war in Vietnam, and many people believe it is unfair that young men under 21 can be sent to fight and die in a war but are not allowed to vote.

By Mike Weinstein, *Appleseeds*, © by Carus Publishing Company. Reproduced with permission.

What's next?

"A good president needs to be a person who keeps their promises and tells only the truth and does not start wars."
—Hannah

Some people would like to drop the voting age from 18 to 16—or maybe even lower. Find out more at: www.freechild.org/SNAYR/suffrage.htm.

Today, with few exceptions, every American citizen 18 years old or older is allowed to vote. The exceptions vary from state to state. For example, some states do not allow people to vote who have committed serious crimes or are mentally incompetent.

If you were allowed to vote, would you take the time to learn about the important issues? Would you learn about where each candidate stands on these issues? Then, would you make the effort to go to the polls and vote?

America's Boldest Experiment

"Congress shall make no law respecting an establishment of religion, or prohibiting the free exercise thereof. . . ."
—First Amendment, U.S. Constitution

These first sixteen words of the First Amendment are responsible for the boldest and most successful experiment in freedom of religion the world has ever seen. More than two hundred years have passed since the Bill of Rights was added to the U.S. Constitution. America is now a nation made up of millions of people who practice many different religions openly and freely. The strength and diversity of religion in the United States are due almost entirely to the full protection of religious freedom guaranteed by the First Amendment.

The founders of our nation believed that religious freedom is an inalienable right of all human beings; that is, we are born with this right and it cannot be taken away. Thomas Jefferson, James Madison, and other supporters of religious freedom in early America knew that governments throughout history had denied people that inalienable right. These men were aware that much blood had been shed through the centuries for the sake of religious freedom. They envisioned a new kind of nation in America. The United States had to be a land where people of many faiths could live together peacefully as citizens. These citizens also must be allowed to debate their religious differences without the threat of violence.

As the primary author of the First Amendment, Madison knew that true religious freedom would mean that the government must not be allowed to either impose or oppose religion. He also realized that laws were needed to ensure that every citizen had the right to practice or not practice any religion. Both of those principles

By Charles C. Haynes, illustrated by Tim Foley, *Cobblestone*, © by Carus Publishing Company. Reproduced with permission.

now are embodied in two parts, or clauses, of the U.S. Constitution's First Amendment.

The first part—"Congress shall make no law respecting an establishment of religion, . . ."—is called the Establishment clause. According to U.S. Supreme Court rulings, this means that the government may not declare an official national religion. It also means that the government may not prefer one religion over another or prefer religion over no religion. Where religion is concerned, the government always must remain neutral.

The Establishment clause prevents both political control over religion and religious control over government. In other words, it separates church from state. But the clause does not separate religion from public life. Throughout American history, religious groups and individuals have been deeply involved in moral and social issues that affect the lives of all citizens. The Civil Rights Movement of the 1950s and 1960s, for example, was started and supported by African American churches.

The second part of the First Amendment—"Congress shall make no law . . . prohibiting the free exercise [of religion] . . . ."—is called the Free Exercise clause. It protects the right of all citizens to practice whatever religion they choose. It also protects the right to not practice any religion at all.

By Charles C. Haynes, illustrated by Tim Foley, *Cobblestone*, © by Carus Publishing Company. Reproduced with permission.

The freedom to practice religion is not an unlimited right, however. Under the Free Exercise clause, we are free to believe whatever we wish. But the Supreme Court has ruled that in rare cases the government may limit or even forbid certain religious conduct. For example, if a religion believes in human sacrifice, the government will not permit that practice. The courts call it a "compelling state interest" when something endangers the health, safety, or general well-being of society at large.

Taken together, these two clauses of the First Amendment truly safeguard freedom of religion. The government is kept separate from religion, and each citizen's right to freely choose his or her faith is protected. Under this arrangement, Americans are able to live with their deepest differences and to build one nation out of many peoples and faiths. In a world still torn apart by religious and ethnic conflict, religious freedom in America is a beacon of hope for all humankind.

No Governmental Interference... at Any Level

When the First Amendment became part of the U.S. Constitution in 1791, it applied only to the federal government. But in the next century, after the Civil War, the Fourteenth Amendment was added to the Constitution. It prohibits the states from depriving any person of liberty: "... No State shall make or enforce any law which shall abridge the privileges or immunities of citizens of the United States; nor shall any State deprive any person of life, liberty, or property, without due process of law...."

In this century, the Supreme Court ruled that the liberties protected under the Fourteenth Amendment include those listed in the First Amendment. As a result, the First Amendment now applies to all levels of government, including state and local governments.

Freedom of the Press
How Far Does It Go?

When the Bill of Rights was adopted in 1791, the printed word was the only means of communication. That is why the First Amendment reads in part, "Congress shall make no law . . . **abridging** the freedom . . . of the press." Today, television, radio, movies, and computer technology such as the Internet also are protected by the First Amendment and freedom of the press. All these methods convey ideas and information.

The First Amendment does not list any specific exceptions, but it does not protect all types of speech. For example, the U.S. government can limit freedom of the press when it comes to the use of **obscenity**. And advertising can be regulated to prevent false, misleading, or unfair ads. The First Amendment also does not prevent private citizens from suing publishers for **libel**. There are issues of national security, too. Printing secrets about U.S. troop strengths or stories that encourage U.S. soldiers to join the opposition during wartime are not always protected by the First Amendment.

> **Abridging** means limiting or restricting.
>
> **Obscenity** means indecency or offensiveness in words or pictures.
>
> **Libel** is a false story that damages someone's reputation.

By Mike Wilson, illustrated by Tim Foley, *Cobblestone*, © by Carus Publishing Company. Reproduced with permission.

On the other hand, the First Amendment strongly protects the publication of other types of speech. Political speech—written or otherwise—concerning the government is protected. But what about speech that may be found treasonous (disloyal) to the U.S. government? Fortunately, it is considered desirable in the United States to debate government policy openly. Prohibiting newspapers from publishing stories that criticize, for instance, our government's decision to declare war against another country would violate the First Amendment. In 1971, Supreme Court justice Hugo Black reminded Americans that "the press was protected by the First Amendment so that it could bare the secrets of government and inform the people."

As a matter of fact, during the 1960s, many newspapers and magazines printed stories opposing U.S. involvement in the Vietnam War. The articles frequently were not popular with many U.S. citizens. But the First Amendment defended the press's right to publish unpopular opinions.

Public discussion of issues is very important in the United States. This makes it difficult for the government to **censor** stories before they are published. The government can try to prevent a story from being reported or printed at all. Or it can try to enforce a "prior restraint." This places a restriction on further publication or distribution of something considered offensive.

The Supreme Court ruled that prior restraint is permitted only if the publication of a story would cause a "clear and present danger." This was established in the 1931 case of *Near v. Minnesota*. The Court maintained that the stories in question were harmful but did not pose a danger. Some news stories, however, do create a "clear and present danger." In 1979, a federal district court ruled in *United States v. Progressive, Inc.* that a magazine could be prevented from publishing instructions on the making of a hydrogen bomb.

As Justice Oliver Wendell Holmes once said, defending freedom of thought requires us to protect not just those who agree with us, but also those who express "thought(s) we hate." The First Amendment protects our right to communicate and discuss unpopular opinions.

> To **censor** means to examine material and remove what is considered objectionable.

Brown v. Board of Education

A group of parents in Topeka, Kansas, decided to take a stand in 1951. For more than 50 years, a policy of "separate but equal"—in practice, separate but unequal—had kept black and white people segregated on many levels in the United States. The Topeka families wanted their children to be admitted to the white grade schools in their neighborhoods instead of being sent across town to attend all-black schools. When their children were denied admittance to the white schools, the parents sued the Topeka Board of Education.

The case, known as *Brown v. Board of Education of Topeka, Kansas*, went all the way to the Supreme Court. The question the justices had to consider was, "Does segregation of children in public schools . . . on the basis of race, even though the physical facilities and other 'tangible' factors may be equal, deprive the children of the minority group of equal educational opportunities?"

The Topeka Board of Education and other segregated school systems argued that the schools they ran for black students were just as good as their schools for white children. Because the schools were equally good, though separate, the school boards insisted that they were complying with the law that had been established by the Supreme Court in an 1896 case called *Plessy v. Ferguson*. That case related to street cars, but had been used to defend "separate but equal" segregation in many other aspects of life.

On May 17, 1954, after three years of hearing arguments, the Supreme Court came to a unanimous and momentous decision. Overturning that 1896 case, Chief Justice Earl Warren wrote, "In the field of public education the doctrine of 'separate but equal' has no place. Separate educational facilities are inherently unequal."

The Court agreed that sometimes (though certainly not always) the teachers, buildings, books, and course of study in black schools were just as good as those in white schools. Still, black children were being deprived of equal protection under the law. The Court's opinion read: "To separate [black students] from others of similar age and qualifications solely because of their race generates a feeling of inferiority as to their status in the community that may affect their hearts and minds in a way unlikely ever to be undone." No matter how fine the black schools might be, it still was unfair to prevent black students from studying alongside white students. Racial discrimination no longer had a place in America's public schools. Despite the Court's ruling, it took many years before the law was fully obeyed. The Civil Rights Act of 1964 speeded up the process.

Brown v. Board of Education of Topeka, Kansas, made the American school system more democratic and fair for all citizens. As a landmark Supreme Court decision, it became a catalyst for other civil rights gains in public accommodations, housing, voting, recreation, and employment opportunities.

And Let's Not Forget... CIVIL RIGHTS ACT OF 1964

Many Southern states had spent decades trying to get around the 13th, 14th and 15th Amendments and refused to enforce equality. So, during the civil rights movement of the 1960s, African Americans looked to the federal government in Washington, D.C., for help. On July 2, 1964, President Lyndon B. Johnson signed one of the most sweeping civil rights laws in U.S. history. Giving the U.S. Justice Department the responsibility of enforcing it, the Civil Rights Act of 1964 made segregation illegal. It also prevented discrimination in the workplace, as well as in education, housing, and public places. And it protected the right to vote as a civil right. Unlike the first civil rights laws in the mid-1800s, the 1964 act prevented discrimination based on religion, sex, or national origin, not just on race or color.

Tinker v. Des Moines:
Defending the Right to Protest

Mary Beth Tinker and her brother, John, display two black armbands. The students from North High School were suspended from classes along with three other students for wearing the bands to quietly protest the Vietnam War.

It seemed like just a small act of protest. On December 16, 1965, three students came to two Des Moines, Iowa schools wearing black armbands. John and Mary Beth Tinker and Christopher Eckhardt were protesting the war in Vietnam, especially the loss of American lives there and their belief that a cease-fire was necessary. They didn't shout slogans or attempt to tell other students about this protest. They simply decided to wear the armbands as a kind of peaceful protest known as civil disobedience, which is refusing to obey a law or rule in order to protest a government action. In this case they were breaking a school district rule that prohibited anything that might cause a disturbing situation in the school.

Christopher Eckhardt was fifteen years old on that morning. He attended Roosevelt High School. Many years later, he remembered what it was like to walk into school wearing the armband:

> We walked quietly through the doors on the northeast side of the building, and up the stairs to my corner locker. . . . I took off my overcoat, and there for all the world to see, was my scarlet letter. Well, really it was just a two inch wide piece of black cloth pinned to my jacket.

Christopher was suspended from school. At the Harding Middle School in Des Moines, Mary Beth Tinker, who was 13, was also suspended. John Tinker, who was also 15, did not wear his armband until the next day, when like his sister and his friend he was also sent home on suspension.

In most schools, an incident like this, which was carried out by students who didn't show any aggression or even protest verbally, would be handled quickly and soon forgotten. But there was a larger issue underlying the December 16 protests. It had to do with students' right to free speech. The incident began to attract attention beyond the school. The Eckhardt and Tinker families contacted the Iowa Civil Liberties Union (ICLU) and asked them if it was legal for the school district to prevent students from wearing armbands. The ICLU asked the Des Moines school board to review the actions of the school administrators and to protect the students' right to free speech. But the school board argued that they felt the protest, even if it was peaceful, could be disruptive and even cause violence in the schools. The arguments over this incident would blossom into a debate over whether students' rights to free speech and free expression under the United States Constitution stopped at the door of the school. The case would go to court many times over the next three years, until it reached the highest court in the land: the United States Supreme Court. *Tinker v. Des Moines* would become a landmark in judicial history.

Christopher Eckhardt commented again, years later, that he was surprised that the case would reach the Supreme Court.

> I knew at the time that the U.S. Supreme Court consisted of nine dudes in black robes who made decisions that affected the rest of the country. But never in my wildest dreams did I ever think we would end up in front of the Supreme Court.

But it was not a quick trip into U.S. legal history. The ICLU sued the school district on behalf of the three students, which went to trial in the U.S. District Court. The case was automatically tried in a federal court because it had to do with the U.S. Constitution or its amendments. The judge ended up ruling against the Tinkers and Christopher Eckhardt, saying that while the students did have the right to free speech, the school administrators acted properly in restricting a situation that they thought might be disruptive or dangerous.

However, the students and their families were not done. They appealed the decision and the case went to the next level: the Eighth Circuit U.S. Court of Appeals. Cases are only tried when there is a possibility that a lower court committed an error. The hearing was set for April of 1967, and the decision of the court was split 4–4 between the eight sitting judges on the case. This automatically meant that the lower court's decision was upheld, and the school district's ban on armbands was still in effect. The families were disappointed, but their lawyer, Dan Johnston, realized that the Appeals Court's ruling was in conflict with two Fifth Circuit Court of Appeals rulings on two different incidents in other places, which also dealt with students and their freedom of speech in school. Because of this, he felt that the *Tinker v. Des Moines* case had a chance of being heard by the U.S. Supreme Court, the highest court in the country. Johnston filed a writ of certiorari, which was a petition asking for the Supreme Court to review the case. On March 4, 1968, the Supreme Court decided to hear the case.

On November 12, 1968, the Tinker and Eckhardt families were in the courtroom of the Supreme Court building in Washington, D.C., to hear the arguments in

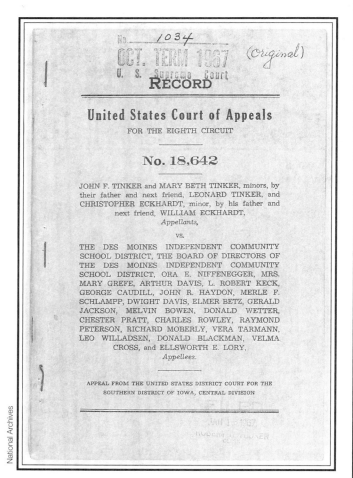

Cover page of the court record of John Tinker's testimony

their case. Each lawyer had only 30 minutes to argue for his side of the case. The justices asked questions of the lawyers, often interrupting their arguments. Some justices were clearly sympathetic to the students, while others sided with the school board and were sometimes hostile in their questions. Justice Thurgood Marshall, who seemed sympathetic to the case, questioned Allan Herrick, the attorney for the school district:

> **Q (Marshall):** How many [students] were wearing arm bands?
>
> **A (Herrick):** There were five suspended for wearing arm bands.
>
> **Q:** Any wearing arm bands that were not suspended?
>
> **A:** Yes, sir, I think there were two.
>
> **Q:** That makes seven . . . seven out of 18,000? And the School Board was advised that seven students wearing armbands were disrupting 18,000? Am I correct?

Christopher Eckhardt remembered hearing this exchange and Justice Marshall's disbelief, and feeling confident that they would win the case. And on February 24, 1969, he found out that he was right: the Court had voted 7–2 in favor of the Tinkers and Eckhardt. They ruled that students have First Amendment protection at school, provided that their expression of that right does not cause a disruption. It had taken three and a half years, but these three students were finally cleared of any blame from their 1965 act of protest.

Tinker v. Des Moines still stands as a legal precedent for students' rights to free speech. In the almost fifty years since the case, however, there have been Supreme Court rulings that have seemed to erode those student rights. Because *Tinker v. Des Moines* had a narrow focus on a specific situation—students were protected by the First Amendment only in specific circumstances—it might not apply to future cases with different circumstances. But it still stands as one of the most important court cases in U.S. history. In the words of Justice Abe Fortas, who wrote the court's official opinion:

> Any word spoken, in class, in the lunchroom, or on the campus, that deviates from the views of another person may start an argument or cause a disturbance. But our Constitution says we must take this risk; and our history says that it is this sort of hazardous freedom—this kind of openness—that is the basis of our national strength and of the independence and vigor of Americans who grow up and live in this relatively permissive, often disputatious, society.

Other Supreme Court Cases . . . That Affect You!

Since Tinker v. Des Moines *in 1969, there have been other Supreme Court cases that affect teens in particular. These are usually cases whether Supreme Court has to find a balance between the rights of students and the need of school officials to protect all students as a group. Many students do not realize that what they are and are not allowed to do in school may be directly related to a Supreme Court case.*

Ingraham v. Wright, 1977

Is it hard to imagine being paddled or spanked at school? In 1977, a 14-year-old boy named James Ingraham was sent to the principal's office in his middle school. His teacher said he was being "rowdy" in the school auditorium. Because James' school district allowed corporal punishment (physical punishment such as spanking or hitting), the principal decide to give James five swats with a paddle. James refused, claiming he hadn't done anything wrong, but he was held down and given 20 swats instead. He suffered bruises and had to stay out of school for ten days. He and his mother sued the principal and other school officials, claiming that James' punishment violated the 8th Amendment because it was "cruel and unusual punishment."

Verdict: The Supreme Court ruled against James, saying that the 8th Amendment was meant to protect criminals from being punished excessively by the government. The Court claimed that it did not apply to school children who did not behave. However, the Court did say that schools should be careful about when they decided to use corporal punishment, depending on the student's attitude, history, and physical condition.

Impact: This verdict leaves the decision of whether or not to even allow corporal punishment up to the individual state and local school districts. Currently about half the states allow it.

Hazelwood School District v. Kuhlmeier, 1988

Does freedom of speech also apply to school newspapers? This was the question that the Supreme Court had to address in 1988. Students enrolled in a journalism class in Hazelwood, Missouri, were responsible for writing and editing their school newspaper, *The Spectrum*. Two of the articles included in the final issue of the school year dealt with divorce and teen pregnancy. The names of the girls in the pregnancy article were changed, but in the divorce article, a student blamed her father for her parents' divorce, using her real name. The father was not given the opportunity to learn about the article or comment on it. The school principal was worried about privacy and whether the articles were appropriate for the school paper, and he prevented them from being published. The student journalists sued, saying that their right to freedom of speech had been violated.

Verdict: The Supreme Court ruled against the journalists, saying that the newspaper was school sponsored and it was not a public forum where everyone could share their views. Instead, the newspaper was a requirement of a journalism class and a supervised learning experience, and the school had the right to edit articles if it felt it was appropriate. The Court noted that educators do not offend First Amendment rights by controlling the style and content of student writing in a school-sponsored activity, as long as their reasons for editing the content is related to a serious educational concern.

Impact: This ruling makes it acceptable for schools to censor any form of student expression, such as yearbooks, theatrical productions, speeches, and creative writing. However, it does encourage schools to take a careful look at why they are censoring student expression, to balance the good of the school with the students' right to free expression.

West Side Community Schools v. Mergens, 1990

How many clubs are there at your school? Chances are there are many, for all kinds of interests and groups. In 1990, a senior at Westside High School in Omaha, Nebraska, asked the school's principal if she could start an after-school religious club. The principal refused to give permission, saying that a religious club would be illegal in a public school. The year before, Congress had passed the Equal Access Act, which required schools to allow political and religious student clubs if they allowed other kinds of student-interest clubs. This case would be the first test of this act.

Verdict: The Supreme Court ruled in favor of the student, saying that allowing students to meet and talk about religion after school did not mean that the school was sponsoring that religion. The Court said, "We think that secondary school students are mature enough and are likely to understand that a school does not endorse or support student speech" just because it allows it to take place.

Impact: If a school only allow clubs that are tied to its curriculum, like foreign languages or journalism clubs, then it doesn't have to allow clubs that aren't related to the curriculum. But as soon as it lets students form clubs according to their interests, such as an environmental club or a dancing club, which aren't part of the school's curriculum, then it also has to allow religious, political, and other types of clubs, too.